CULTURAL
MEMORY

AND THE

CONSTRUCTION
OF IDENTITY

EDITED BY
DAN BEN-AMOS AND
LILIANE WEISSBERG

WAYNE STATE UNIVERSITY PRESS • DETROIT

Library of Congress Cataloging-in-Publication Data

Cultural memory and the construction of identity / edited by
    Dan Ben-Amos and Liliane Weissberg.
        p. cm.
    Includes bibliographical references and index.
    ISBN 0-8143-2753-2 (pbk. : alk. paper)
    1. History—Philosophy. 2. Memory (Philosophy)
I. Ben-Amos, Dan. II. Weissberg, Liliane.
D16.9.C83 1999
901—dc21   98-24234

Earlier versions of chapters 1, 2, 4, 5 and 9 were previously
published. Peter Stallybrass's "Worn Worlds: Clothes,
Mourning, and the Life of Things" appeared in *Yale Review*
81.1 (1993): 35–50; Liliane Weissberg's "Memory Confined"
appeared in *documents* 4/5 (1994): 81–98; Tamar Katriel's
"Sites of Memory: Discourses of the Past in Israeli Pioneering
Settlement Museums" appeared in *Quarterly Journal of
Speech* 80.1 (1994): 1–20; Barbie Zelizer's "The Liberation of
Buchenwald: Images and the Shape of Memory" appeared in
*Remembering to Forget: Holocaust Memory through the
Camera's Eye*, © The University of Chicago; and Houston
Baker, Jr.'s "Critical Memory and the Black Public Sphere"
appeared in *Public Culture* 7.1 (1994): 3–33. Copyright 1994.
Reprinted by permission of Duke University Press. The poem
by A. D. Hope on page 211, "Meditation on a Bone," is reprinted
by permission of Curtis Brown (Aust) Pty Ltd., Sydney.

Designer: Mary Primeau

CONTENTS

INTRODUCTION

Liliane Weissberg

Learning Culture

On Whitmonday, May 26, 1828, the citizens of Nuremberg encountered a young stranger of about sixteen years of age standing awkwardly on one of their main town gathering places, the Unschlittplatz. He appeared both scared and lost, and was hardly able to talk. He carried a letter addressed to a cavalry captain named von Wessenig. The young man's first and only statement, barely understandable to anybody, perhaps least of all himself, was expressed in the dialect of the region. He said that he wanted to become a horseman, as his father had been.

But who was his father? Nobody in Nuremberg knew, and certainly the young man did not know, either; once he had learned how to speak, if only clumsily, he expressed no memory of any parents. Indeed, he seemed able to recall only an isolated life in a cave or cage. There were no major events in his life that he could recall, no narrative of his past he could offer. Shortly before his release from confinement, he encountered a person who taught him a prayer—the Catholic *Our Father*—and the words that would express his wish, namely to become what his father once had been. Devoid of parents and any sense of childhood—a notion on which late-eighteenth-century educational philosophy had just begun to obsess—this son from nowhere was henceforth viewed as "Europe's child."[1] But Europe proved unable to replace a caring father. A few years after his first public appearance, the young man became the victim in a murder case that was never solved, and the mystery of his death seemed to resonate oddly with the mystery that surrounded his life. He turned into a studied and mythologized object of cultural reference, and into the subject of literature and film.[2] He became Kaspar Hauser.

There is a rich literature that relates to Hauser's appearance, life, and death, and there has been much theoretical reflection not only on his late socialization, but also on

7

the anxieties that it provoked, and perhaps still provokes. Here was a person without a sense of personhood, who matured in the absence of any Oedipal constellation—one who questioned, moreover, the distinction between object and subject that German transcendental philosophy had just carefully put into place. Was Hauser deprived, his soul injured and abused, as his temporary caretaker, the lawyer Anselm von Feuerbach, suggested?[3] Or did he exchange paradise for the Nuremberg Unschlittplatz, only to experience new depths of pain?[4]

Whatever the answer would be, it could not be a straightforward one. Kaspar Hauser's case put not only his identity into question (Was he an impostor?[5]), but also his sense of self (Did he ever view himself as a distinct person? Did he really know who he was? And what would self-knowledge mean here?). Even in later years, Hauser would only respond to people if he was addressed in the third person, and by his proper name.[6] Similarly, his memory seemed both erratic and fluid, never trained to settle on social and linguistic reference points. Despite his several attempts at writing his autobiography, there was little that he could really tell.[7] It is precisely this lack of story, this ironic distance to our own (Western) tradition, that turned him into a reference point for our present cultural frame. Perhaps he would have never become what his father was. Perhaps he had already become just that.

Traditions, as Eric Hobsbawm reminds us, are made; they are invented and constructed.[8] This may seem obvious in regard to Christmas celebrations or the design and wearing of Scottish kilts. But what about our conception of the "individual" and this individual's "soul" or psyche, which relies so much on the father-mother-child constellation of the nuclear family, as Sigmund Freud urged us to believe? Can the Nuremberg citizens' (and our own) understanding of the individual be taken for granted? Would such a concept change in the future as well? And which "tradition" is at stake here?

The reflections on Hauser's belated integration into early-nineteenth-century society reveal the importance of class for an understanding of the role of fatherhood. Hauser, who was dependent on public donations in Nuremberg, and on much personal goodwill, had perhaps fallen from a high social position, one that he was, however, never able to assume. If Feuerbach's suspicions are correct, Hauser was the rightful successor to the throne of Baden. Purportedly, he was exchanged shortly after birth with a sickly child to grant his stepmother's oldest son a place in the succession.[9] While fatherhood was important for aristocratic families to secure the line of inheritance, political power, and title, aristocratic parents often kept a certain distance from their children, although perhaps rarely as much distance as in Hauser's case. A prince or king, moreover, would view all his subjects as his "children." Fatherhood was different for bourgeois society, which rose to power and recognition in the second half of the eighteenth century. A male citizen of early-nineteenth-century Nuremberg would have recognized the ruling sovereign as his *Landesvater* but still insisted on his own ruling power at home. It is indeed the rise of the bourgeoisie, the increasingly urban economy, as well as the emergence of the nuclear family structure that promoted the concept of the individual. Speechless and unsocialized, Kaspar Hauser at once questioned and confirmed this concept.

The Emergence of the Individual

The idea of the "individual" is a paradoxical offspring of both Enlightenment and romantic thought. Still a subject of the absolutist Prussian king Frederick II, Immanuel Kant declared that each person was free to express himself and decide on his actions—within limits, of course.[10] Romantic authors thereafter explored the limits of these decisions as part of a person's inner life. But to understand who and what each person was, he or she had to extend his or her being in time, reflect on his or her past as an imagined continuity of self. Thus, autobiographical writings flourished in the late eighteenth and nineteenth centuries, and most of them were no longer accounts of famous deeds and illustrious family bonds. Jean-Jacques Rousseau saw the importance of his *Confessions* in its declaration of personal independence; he viewed himself neither as famous nor important, but simply as different from any other man.[11]

In his *Present Past: Modernity and the Memory Crisis*, Richard Terdiman associates this insistence on the individual with another genre of prose writing, the novel. In nineteenth-

9

century novels—perhaps most obviously the tomes of Balzac, Dickens, Dostoevsky, and Tolstoy—the story of individuals was constructed within a larger historical setting and driven by the memory of past events. Thus, memory became a crucial tool and agent for insisting on the hero's (or author's) identity and his (or her) place in the world. It explained who a person was by reference to his or her history, often within a larger context. Memory's relationship to any notion of "truth" or factual evidence has become a complex one, however. Unlike historical documentation, memory seemed to rely on the individual's recollection. The genre of the novel could advertise memory's fictional nature more ardently than any autobiography could. Indeed, memory had traveled far from its conception as a rhetorical device during medieval times[12] or the visualized theater of the Renaissance period.[13] Object and process at once, it still seemed bound to language, however, and was itself an act of performance.

Memory was needed not simply to understand the past; it had to relate to who one was in the present. But the more a person felt the need to insist on memory and to construct his or her past, the more memory seemed to be in danger. Indeed, Kaspar Hauser–like problems, in slightly different form and shape, seemed to haunt the entire nineteenth century. The wish to tell one's story was met by the anxiety of being unable to do so, even though there was still the belief that there was a story to tell. Memory was celebrated but in constant crisis, a crisis that finally led to narratives that put continuity into question, such as the fragmented discourse of modernism with its steadily interrupted stream of consciousness.

But the crisis of memory was not reflected only in narrative devices. Memory loss turned into a serious personality disorder, a fractured sense of self to be countered and possibly cured by hypnosis, psychoanalysis, or, more recently, pharmaceuticals. Objects (or language turned into objects) became the means of regaining a cognizance of the past and promised a means to hold on to it. They demanded their own narrative. Museums, exhibitions, and collections enjoyed increasing popularity, and the language of these objects entered the vocabulary of realist prose. Monuments were erected in increasing numbers to safeguard against forgetting not just other persons and diverse events, but also oneself. This forgetting was inscribed in each object (turning them into peculiar fetishes of sorts) and also codified in the economic system itself. Like the objects it relied on, reified memory could be traded, and became part of the capitalistic system.

Marcel Proust's hero, for example, would be dependent on madeleines, or rather, on their subtle taste and smell, to recall the events of his past. Memory was both a fragile tool and the ultimate goal. It promised to be regained, but could evaporate quickly. It was marked by longing and celebrated as souvenir. While memory was not necessarily viewed as consciously constructed, it could be found in objects that were made for its purpose alone: *livres d'amité*, gilded baby slippers, hair jewelry, framed photographs. To appreciate them, the owner or viewer had to imagine him- or herself elsewhere, without the person or event these objects stood for, and he or she had to travel in time. Such travel could never be fully successful, and melancholy and a sense of loss were inscribed in all of these objects and their narratives. Memory was desired, but could never fully recover what had been lost. A person's longing for a harmonious reunification with his or her former self was always doomed to remain unfulfilled.

The philosopher Georg Wilhelm Friedrich Hegel, writing at the time of Kaspar Hauser's mysterious appearance and before Karl Marx's reformulation of economic theory, dreamed of such memory as a form of positive recollection both for each individual and for the Spirit. At the end of his *Phenomenology*, the utopia of this recollection appears as a harmony between self and world, past and present, subject and object. It also appears as the end of history. This end of history was perhaps briefly lived by Hauser, but not experienced by other philosophers or writers of the nineteenth century. Indeed, the nineteenth century was ardently "historical," insisting on history as a means to counter as well as to save memory. Written documents and recorded facts promised to aid a personal and often oral memory in crisis. History seemed to claim Truth and to vouch for an "objective" reality that would correct memory's seemingly subjective, unreliable stance in a world of objects. History was written and seemed thus verifiable. It was public. Memory would be banished to the private realm; like a naughty child, it was, moreover, in need of guardianship and guidance, and often censorship as well. History in turn developed into a respectable discipline, to be taught and studied at universities, although there was early on already a sense that history, too, could be constructed rather than discovered—that it, too, would follow its own historically varied agendas.

While memory's history intertwined with the history of history, it has only recently captured the interests of historians again. Books and journals (such as *History and Memory*) have tried to explore the relationship between both and to reflect on the new scholarly interest in memory. Jan Assmann sees three reasons for this shift. First, he stresses the increased importance of electronic media and artificial memory storage, which forces us to reconceptualize memory once again. Second, he points at the now oft-mentioned sentiment that we have entered a period of "post-histoire," a belatedness with regard to history that demands that we comment and work through the past rather than submit to experience—thus making Hegel's statement about the impending end of history a prediction for today. Finally, however, Assmann postulates that recent events like the Holocaust may defy any historical explanation, that they were witnessed by a generation that has begun to die out, and leave us with the question of what to remember, and how.[14] Much of the recent work on memory and its representation has, indeed, been concerned with the establishment of Holocaust and war memorials. But definitions of "history" also have changed. With recent interrogations into the constructedness of the historical discourse by scholars as diverse as Michel Foucault and Stephen Greenblatt, and the newfound interest in oral history, the study of memory has become crucial for historians as well.

Framing the Collective

But memory's stock has not only had a low and a high. Memory's own history, our understanding of what it is and how it functions, has radically changed in recent years. The computer is not the sole challenge to our notion of a personalized, individually owned memory.

Since the late eighteenth century, the political demands on memory have been particularly strong. The invention of nation-states called for a common past as well as a common future. Monuments urged the individual to remember, but to remember and define each individual as a member of a larger group. Museums were constructed as national museums and opened to the public as institutions representative of a shared past.[15] A person was to be defined not only as an individual, but within the bounds of a national identity as well, one that was constructed by symbolic acts like festivals or commemorations.[16] For this process of socialization, memory became an increasingly important tool.

Thus, Freud could both write about the individual psyche in the old Enlightenment/romantic tradition and insist on the notion of a collective culture.[17] The turn-of-the-century philosopher Henri Bergson was still preoccupied with the notion of a personal memory and its relationship to time. Bergson conceived of a flow of inner life (in contrast to outer experience), a *durée* that would counter the distinction between a past and a present self. He developed this idea in his *Essai sur les donées immédiates de la conscience* (Time and Free Will: An Essay on the Immediate Data of Consciousness [1889]) and, especially in relationship to the functions of memory, in *Matière et mémoire: Essai sur la relation du corps à esprit* (Matter and Memory [1896]).[18] His former student Maurice Halbwachs, however, showed less of an interest in subjective individuality and defined instead a very different concept of memory that he described as "mémoire collective."

Halbwachs worked with Emil Durkheim and was influenced by his sociological framework. For Halbwachs, memory was no accidental recall, no idiosyncratic venture. In his *Les Cadres sociaux de la mémoire* (The Social Frameworks of Memory [1925]),[19] his work on the legendary topography of the gospels in the Holy Land (1941),[20] as well as his posthumously published sketches and essays on collective memory,[21] Halbwachs insists on the social constructedness of any memory. People acquire or construct memory not as isolated individuals but as members of a society, and they recall their memories in society. For Halbwachs, there are no biological secrets of the brain, and perhaps no psychoanalytical secrets, either, as he appeals to his readers' own memories and asks them to recall their process of remembering:

> If we enumerate the number of recollections during one day that we have evoked upon the occasion of our direct and indirect relations with other people, we will see that, most frequently, we appeal to our memory only in order to answer questions

13

which others have asked us, or that we suppose they could have asked us. We note, moreover, that in order to answer them, we place ourselves in their perspective and we consider ourselves as being part of the same group or groups as they.[22]

Memory seems to answer expectations and is already framed by the answers it seeks. Language is an important factor in this equation. Words that are formed by social life, and that appear intelligible, offer themselves as both recollections and the language in which we recall. Language itself is already a system of social conventions that makes the reconstruction of "our own" past possible.

In the preface to *Les Cadres sociaux de la mémoire*, Halbwachs narrates his own tale of a wild child, a young girl:

> Recently thumbing through an old volume of the *Magasin Pittoresque*, I came across an extraordinary story. It was the story of a young girl nine or ten years old who was found in the woods near Châlons in 1731. There was no way of finding out where she had been born or where she came from. She had kept no recollection of her childhood. In piecing together the details she provided concerning the various periods of her life, one came to suppose that she was born in the north of Europe, probably among the Eskimos, and that she had been transported first to the Antilles and then to France. She said that she had twice crossed large distances by sea, and she appeared moved when shown pictures of huts or boats from Eskimo country, seals, or sugar cane and other products of the Americas. She thought that she could recall rather clearly that she had belonged as a slave to a mistress who liked her very much, but that the master, who could not stand her, had her sent away.

Halbwachs adds: "I reproduce this tale, which I do not know to be authentic, and which I have learned only at second hand, because it allows us to understand in what sense one may say that memory depends on the social environment" (37). In presenting this anecdote, Halbwachs is little concerned with the integrity of the self (or the authenticity of the story). Hauser may have suffered immobility due to the restrictions of forced enclosure. This nameless girl grows up traveling between continents and cultures, traversing the French colonial universe. Too little and too much mobility may add up to the same experience, however. To Halbwachs, the girl seems rootless and is unable to recollect the story of her past.

In interpreting the tale, Halbwachs focuses on the girl's loss of family. For Halbwachs, a family offers the possibility of social interaction; it is an institution in which the individual has to consider him- or herself in relation to others. And the family relates, in turn, to other institutions. Memories are shaped within these frameworks and may seem immune to the passage of time—that is, they can be reproduced without change. But reflection is also able to rearrange recollections for specific purposes. For Halbwachs, forgetting is not necessarily an individual failure, but rather a deformation of recollections: "Depending on its circumstances and point in time, society represents the past to itself in different ways: it modifies its conventions" (172–73). Events can be recalled only if they (or their mode of narrative) fit within a framework of contemporary interests. Society, in turn, modifies recollections according to its present needs. Social beliefs are collective recollections, and they relate to a knowledge of the present. Collective memory adjusts to, and shapes, a system of present-day beliefs (188).

Halbwachs is very concerned with a distinction between history and memory. He describes a collective memory, which hardly relies on writing, in contrast to history, which sets in when the collective memory disappears.[23] Memory, moreover, strives to recognize similarities, while history stresses discontinuities and difference. Tradition is finally nothing but deformed memory, more organized perhaps, and seemingly more "objective."[24] Halbwachs offers a rather general and grand sketch, but his concept of a collective memory may certainly illuminate some recent events, such as the ongoing rewriting of Eastern European history or President Bill Clinton's apology to African Americans for the legacy of slavery in the United States.

While Halbwachs's writings were hardly recognized until the 1970s, they have gained tremendous popularity, especially in the last decade. His insistence on language rather than event, on the constructedness of any recollection, indeed strikes a chord with the concepts of discourse developed by Foucault and recent formulations of cultural studies that take their cue from poststructuralist thought. But although Halbwachs described memory as a "collective" undertaking, it soon metamorphosed into a "cultural" one, following a shift in stress from the social group to its modes of production.

15

Aby Warburg, a prominent German representative of early *Kulturwissenschaften* (science of culture), speculated about the possibilities of a *kollektives Gedächtnis*, or collective memory; he seemed to be familiar with Halbwachs's work, although it is unclear whether it influenced his own writings.[25] German scholarship today still appears to be concerned with a "collective memory," and these discussions often resonate with another discussion about the recent past, that of a German *Kollektivschuld*, or collective guilt.[26] But even Warburg's understanding of *Kultur* would have differed from that of the supporters of "cultural memory," as it gained currency in British and American literary and social studies.[27] *Kultur* still implies dominant cultural forms, but the culture that cultural studies has in mind relates to "low culture" as well—to popular media and everyday conventions. And a third notion has emerged in recent years—that of "public memory." This term stresses the transgressive force with which memory, far from being private, displays itself in the marketplace and the political domain. If Halbwachs conceived of "collective memory" as describing social thought, terms like "cultural" and "public memory" comment further on the changes within this social thought and its discourse on memory.

Cultural Memory

Bergson placed time at the center of his contemplation of memory as a subjective experience. For Halbwachs, time no longer takes center stage. In his social world, memory depends on space and a notion of location. It is this idea that is crucial to the work of Pierre Nora.

Nora positions himself not at the "end of history," but perhaps at the end of memory, writing at a time "when there is so little of it left."[28] In contrast to the work of Halbwachs, who would implicate even his reader in an empirical case study of present-day behavior, Nora's writings look more strongly to the past. Like the souvenir of old, memory implies a sense of mourning. Walter Benjamin once declared the death of narrative because of our loss of experience, putting an end to the idea of a novel for our time.[29] Nora writes not about the loss of experience, but about the loss of the environment in which experience and its recollection can take place. The *milieux de mémoire* have disappeared. Not surprisingly, perhaps, Nora traces them back to seemingly simpler cultures, such as that of peasant life, and to a time before the advent of mass movements and a world economy. Nora even declares the absence of larger narratives that would unite us in a "nation-state," for example. Thus, we no longer have a living memory but deal only with its odd residue. The real environments of memory are gone, but the *lieux de mémoire* remain; present-day memory "crystallizes and secretes itself" (7) in such particular sites. Implicitly, Nora offers a history of the relationship between the "collective" and its "culture."

For Nora, memory is, first of all, not something to be recalled at will, but something societies are imbued with:

> If we were able to live within memory, we would not have needed to consecrate *lieux de mémoire* in its name. Each gesture, down to the most everyday, would be experienced as the ritual repetition of a timeless practice in a primordial identification of act and meaning. With the appearance of the trace, of mediation, of distance, we are not in the realm of true memory but of history. (8)

"Unviolated memory," as it still existed in more archaic societies, not only demanded closeness to everyday life, but also posited an unalienated bond between history and memory that was subsequently broken. With the passing of time, memory's call to presence became lost, and history could claim victory. Thus, while Halbwachs was eager to keep memory and history apart, Nora exposes their changing relationship to each other.

In an interesting rewriting of Bergson's philosophy of life, Nora now assigns "life" to memory. It exists only in living societies, and has meaning only in the present. History, in turn, represents and reflects the past. Memory, however, is "a perpetually actual phenomenon" (8) that can capture the present eternally. It is absolute, while history is relative; it claims objects, images, and space for itself, while history insists on the passing of time. As a democratic notion, it wants to belong to everyone, and negotiates between each individual and the collective. Despite its general decline, however, memory can still be traced in specific sites as it adheres to spaces, objects, gestures, and images. This modern memory—one that so beautifully meets the demands of nineteenth-century museums and collections—is largely an archival one. It can no longer demand any continuity, it relies on distance, it has become historical, and it lies at the center of present-day historical thought.

Nora's main project has been to write a history of French culture through a recovery of sites of memory. This took shape as a multiauthored, multivolume venture that reflects on French architecture, monuments, and public festivals. Nora and his colleagues offer an archeological and a geographical survey at once, mapping past time on present space. Perhaps no other recent work has been as influential for our present-day understanding of collective or cultural memory. Interestingly, however, it also links back to an *ars memoria* in which buildings, objects, and places have turned into theaters that help us both to recall and to construct our own historical identity in the process. For Nora, memory moves into the core of historical understanding.

Cultural Memory and the Question of Identity

The chapters in the present volume take the works of Maurice Halbwachs and Pierre Nora as their implicit or explicit frameworks as they explore the relationship between individual and collective, between past and present, in search of both lost *milieux* and present sites, testing the construction of individual as well as collective "identity." In this sense, they provide a reading that follows Nora's lead and offer case studies of cultural memories. As they explore each case, however, these chapters qualify Nora's theses as well.

Peter Stallybrass's "Worn Worlds: Clothes, Mourning, and the Life of Things" concentrates on clothing as a "site" of memory. Stallybrass does not view clothes primarily as objects of technological or artistic production, but considers first of all their use, how they are worn, and how they relate to the human body they encase. A piece of clothing can stand for the human body metonymically or produce its fetishistic ersatz, but it can also become a residue or ruin of sorts, a site of mourning. It does so not just by being there, or by being looked at, but by being worn again, and by thus making

18

recollection possible. Stallybrass's site needs to be more than merely visited or looked at; it needs to be inhabited again. In describing what it means to wear a jacket once worn by another person, Stallybrass writes about memory, but also about preserving its loss. In modern society, we may trade clothing or use it as a defining ornament, but we may be reluctant to see it as an object that itself bears meaning. Stallybrass argues that clothes can haunt the living, but they can haunt late capitalist society as well. The social formation of late capitalism, far from valuing such materializations, is embarrassed by the fetishization of objects, and prefers to deal with them as commodities.

My essay, "Memory Confined," speaks in the first-person singular as well, and offers a resolutely personal perspective. Whereas Stallybrass writes about the loss of a friend and about the significance of remembering him through an object of clothing, lost people and present objects seem to multiply in the United States Holocaust Memorial Museum in Washington, D.C., which opened in 1993. Here, hundreds of shoes are not displayed for wear, but rather collected and represented behind safety glass. "Memory Confined" is an essay about mourning, but also about recapturing the individual—via identity papers, via identification—among the statistical figures of war crimes. The establishment of a Holocaust museum, moreover, poses the question of how to present events that may defy representation, of how to exhibit objects without following an aesthetics designed for works of art. Pleasure is, indeed, something that collecting should produce, but that this particular collection and presentation should defy.

Museums belong to the nineteenth-century creations that certainly qualify as sites of memory, although they are artificially constructed for the purpose of recollection. Rituals, on the other hand, are part of Nora's vanished *milieux*. Dorothy Noyes and Roger D. Abrahams's chapter shows, however, that these rituals are still alive and well, even in industrialized Europe. Their essay, "From Calendar Custom to National Memory: European Commonplaces," focuses on a specific example. Calendar customs as invented traditions link local communities to state authority. Noyes and Abrahams develop a model of four stages. In the first stage, the collective repetition of practices produces a shared memory. At the second stage, community members enforce the continuity of customs,

19

largely for reasons of social control. At the third stage, provincial elites act as mediators between the local community and the urban political center; it is here that the "calendar customs" described become a mediation zone. Finally, at the fourth stage, the political elites try to convince the populace that their national project is valid by claiming that it is a broader view of local customary practices. This model integrates collective memory as communal memory into a larger political framework, one that is operative in the present, not only the past. Far from denying any "environments of memory" for contemporary life, Noyes and Abrahams show the kind of significance they may bear today.

Tamar Katriel's chapter, "Sites of Memory: Discourses of the Past in Israeli Pioneering Settlement Museums," reflects again on museum culture. Katriel, however, is less concerned with the possibility of representation than with the invention of a past for a current political agenda. The museum in question is a "heritage museum" that promotes a discourse that constructs a national Israeli identity but ignores Palestinian history. Katriel is concerned with the past that is portrayed through the choice and display of objects, as well as by the museum's guides and their narratives. These narratives provide a lesson about the distinction between "history" and "memory," and Katriel calls for a more nuanced view of the relationship between both as dialectically defined orientations of the past. Katriel describes the strategies involved in the museum's interpretation and the reading of the objects displayed, and she attempts to explore the culturally focal "sites of memory" as part of a critically oriented autoethnography.

Barbie Zelizer's essay, "The Liberation of Buchenwald: Images and the Shape of Memory," like my chapter, relates to the Holocaust and the possibility of its representation. But Zelizer is not concerned with a museum; instead, she concentrates on the photographic image. When the concentration camps were liberated at the end of World War II, journalists joined the Allied forces. Their photographs documented what the soldiers saw, but also shaped our views of these events—whether we experienced the war or not. Zelizer's essay describes the pictures taken at the time of the camps' liberation and attempts to trace how they became "generic" views. While these pictures have contributed to our present understanding

20

of the Holocaust, they have also influenced the discipline of photojournalism.

Roberta Pearson is concerned with visual images as well: not with still photographs, but with moving images. In her chapter, "Custer Loses Again: The Contestation over Commodified Public Memory," she considers television documentaries that depict events not witnessed by the camera operators or producers. The five examples, all shown in 1992 and 1993, claim to be visual and narrative reconstructions of events that date from the previous century, but they are presented as part of America's national memory. Like Katriel, Pearson explores the relationship between history and memory; unlike Katriel, however, Pearson does not explore the erasure of (Palestinian) history, but asks how erased (Native American) history can be reinserted into a more general discourse—and why and within which framework this move would be of interest to the public today. In the course of her argument, Pearson shows how television and the cinema have become important means to reprogram popular memory, and how they are much more effective today than popular reading material.

Reading material is the focus of Daniel Traister's argument in his essay " 'You Must Remember This . . .'; or, Libraries as a Locus of Cultural Memories." Traister is not so much concerned with the mass distribution of books, however, as with the collection and preservation of books and manuscripts in libraries. Like museums, libraries are sites in which a cultural memory is constructed and articulated. But while there has been much public awareness recently about the collection of artifacts in museums and exhibitions,[30] the collection of books has largely been taken for granted. Indeed, even scholars who use libraries regularly for research purposes, and who deplore the lack of certain items in a general collection, rarely reflect on acquisition and preservation decisions and their implicit agendas. At a time when discussions about electronic media and the Internet intensify, and just when the ownership of electronically transmitted intellectual property has become a highly debated issue, traditional libraries may emerge as specific sites as well as endangered repositories of collective memory.

Zelizer, Pearson, and Traister are concerned with the notion of the "documentary" and its relationship to cultural

21

memory. Robert Blair St. George in turn offers us a "documentary" as he retraces his visit to Thomas Jefferson's Monticello. "Placing Race at Jefferson's Monticello" is an act of looking and an act of reading. As St. George follows the traces of Monticello's slaves or "servants," he searches for what seems nearly erased and, at the same time, central to our cultural memory. In the course of his search, he shows the complexity of notions such as "black" or "mulatto," which seem to depend as much on gender and questions of class and ownership as on any definition of "race." Acting as detective and psychoanalytic critic, St. George uncovers material and psychological evidence. He tries to demonstrate how race and race relations have marked American architecture and our understanding of place, and how they have been made invisible for the modern tourist experience.

The issue of race and ethnicity connects several chapters. The United States Holocaust Memorial Museum and the "revisionist" television programs about General Custer presuppose ethnic minorities who were eliminated or whose existence has been threatened. In these cases, cultural memory becomes a form of mourning and a paradoxical sign of loss. The Israeli settlement museums construct a national agenda and symbolically deny the existence of particular ethnic groups. Television series and the tourist industry adapt images of specific population groups for public consumption—or erase their traces. Nostalgia could be at work in any of these cases, or at least the fantasy of undoing any form of discrimination and giving a voice to those already silenced.

Houston Baker, Jr.'s essay, "Critical Memory and the Black Public Sphere," deals with nostalgia in a slightly different way. It takes on a consciously African-American perspective that tries to reassign agency to memory and lend it the power of critique. Baker takes his cue from Jürgen Habermas's *The Transformation of the Public Sphere,* a study that focused largely on eighteenth-century Germany and Europe and the emergence of the bourgeois class. Baker asks whether one could argue for a black "public sphere" placed within the context of contemporary American society. Baker claims that an expressively black public sphere could suggest nostalgia, a purely aestheticized fascination with the past. Memory here is not needed to mourn, recreate, or discover; rather, it should counteract nostalgic fascination. To this end he explores the example of Martin Luther King, Jr.'s life and work and the popular perceptions surrounding it. Critical memory would stand in the tradition of public recollection and counter a collective enterprise. Much like Noyes and Abrahams—and at the same time, under very different terms—Baker reintroduces and claims memory for our daily life and experience.

This book on cultural memory has its origin as a collective endeavor. Faculty seminars have a long tradition at the University of Pennsylvania, and during the academic year 1993–94, a group of Penn faculty and doctoral candidates, as well as visitors from other institutions, met regularly to discuss issues in cultural studies and, more specifically, the notions of collective and cultural memory. Earlier versions of many of the chapters published in this book were originally presented in this seminar.

Dan Ben-Amos and I served as seminar organizers, and we would like to thank all the participants for their strong engagement in our enterprise. In addition to the authors of the present volume, we are particularly grateful to Margreta DeGrazia (English), Holly Pittmann (history of art and ancient history), Gary Tomlinson (music), Yosefa Loshitzky (film and communication), Charles Rosenberg (history and sociology of science), and Yael Zerubavel (Near Eastern studies) for their contributions and commitment. The constellation of the group proves that true interdisciplinary work is possible, and that issues concerning cultural memory are relevant to many areas and disciplines. Cultural studies, we have learned, thrives at the crossroads of the humanities and social sciences.

The faculty seminar in cultural studies was made possible through a generous grant from the Humanities Council of the University of Pennsylvania. We would like to thank our graduate groups in the Folklore and Folklife and Comparative Literature and Literary Theory departments, and in particular their administrative assistants, Marco A. Manzo and JoAnne Dubil, for their cheerful support. Amy Cohen and the staff of the Humanities Council tended the membership list and photocopied and distributed papers for each meeting. We would also like to thank the editors of *Yale Review, documents, Quarterly Review of Speech,* and *Public Culture* for their permission to reprint several previously published chapters. Avner Ben-Amos provided helpful bibliographic suggestions.

The idea of turning our discussions into a book emerged early on, but it was Arthur Evans, the director of Wayne State University Press, who greeted our project with much enthusiasm and helped turn it into reality. Stephen Hock aided with the final preparation of the book manuscript. We are grateful to him, as well as to the staff of Wayne State University Press, for helping us to transform it into a book that will be, hopefully, read as well as (re)collected.

Notes

1. See Jochen Hörisch, "Die Sprachlosigkeit des Kaspar Hauser," in *Ich möchte ein solcher werden wie . . . : Materialien zur Sprachlosigkeit des Kaspar Hauser*, ed. Jochen Hörisch (Frankfurt am Main: Suhrkamp Verlag, 1979), 271.
2. See Ulrich Struve, ed., *Der Findling: Kaspar Hauser in der Literatur* (Stuttgart: J.B. Metzler, 1992), and *Der imaginierte Findling: Studien zur Kaspar-Hauser-Rezeption* (Heidelberg: C. Winter, 1995).
3. See Anselm Ritter von Feuerbach, "Kaspar Hauser—Verbrechen am Seelenleben des Menschen (1832)," in *Ich möchte ein solcher werden wie*, 119–93.
4. Compare Kasper Hauser's autobiographical writings, *Ich möchte ein solcher werden wie*, 87–115.
5. See Struve, "Einleitung," in *Der Findling*, 3–5.
6. See Hörisch, "Die Sprachlosigkeit des Kaspar Hauser," 286.
7. Just a few months after his appearance, Kaspar Hauser was encouraged to pen his autobiography. His first sketch was completed in October 1829 and submitted to the Nuremberg police. In the following months, Hauser wrote several variants of this brief text.
8. Eric Hobsbawm, "Introduction: Inventing Traditions," in *The Invention of Tradition,* ed. Eric Hobsbawm and Terence Ranger (Cambridge: Cambridge University Press, 1983), 1–14.
9. Feuerbach published his "Mémoire—Wer möchte wohl Kaspar Hauser sein? Der Königin Caroline von Bayern übersandt" in 1832 (*Ich möchte ein solcher werden wie*, 194–203), and died shortly thereafter under mysterious circumstances. Feuerbach's death lent further credibility to his thesis.
10. Immanuel Kant, "Beantwortung der Frage: Was ist Aufklärung? (1783)." An English translation is included in *Foundations of the Metaphysics of Morals; and, What Is Enlightenment?*

2d ed., rev., trans. and intro. Lewis Beck White (New York: MacMillan, 1990).

11. Jean-Jacques Rousseau, *Confessions*, in *Oeuvres complètes* I (Paris: Gallimard, 1959), 3.

12. In medieval times, *memoria* was viewed as part of the rhetorical system, together with *inventio* (discovery of the subject), *dispositio* (organization of the subject), *elocutio* (use of figures), and *actio* (performance).

13. See Frances A. Yates, *The Art of Memory* (London: Routledge and K. Paul, 1966).

14. Jan Assmann, *Das kulturelle Gedächtnis: Schrift, Erinnerung und politische Identität in frühen Hochkulturen*, 2d ed. (Munich: Beck, 1997), 11.

15. Gwendolyn Wright, ed., *The Formation of National Collections of Art and Archeology* (Washington, D.C.: National Gallery of Art, and Hanover, N.H.: University Press of New England, 1996).

16. See John R. Gillis, ed., *Commemorations: The Politics of National Identity* (Princeton, N.J.: Princeton University Press, 1994).

17. See Sigmund Freud's general studies on *Totem and Taboo* (1913), mass psychology, and so forth, and the discussion of his notion of culture in Louis Rose, *A Freudian Calling* (Detroit: Wayne State University Press, 1998). Freud conceived of several models to describe the function of memory, perhaps most strikingly that of the "Magic Writing Pad."

18. *Essai sur les donées immédiates de la conscience* (Paris: Félix Alcans, 1889); *Matière et mémoire: Essay sur le relation du corps à esprit* (Paris: Félix Alcans, 1896). The latter book appeared in English translation as *Matter and Memory*, trans. Margaret Paul and W. Scott Palmer (London: S. Sonnenschein, 1911).

19. Maurice Halbwachs, *Les Cadres sociaux de la mémoire* (Paris, F. Alcan, 1925). Subsequent page citations appear parenthetically in the text.

20. Halbwachs, *La Topographie legendaire des Evangiles en Terre Sainte: Etude de mémoire collective* (Paris: Presses universitaires de France, 1941).

21. Halbwachs, *La Mémoire collective. Ouvrage posthume publie par Jeanne Alexandre* (Paris: Presses universitaires de France, 1950).

22. Halbwachs, *On Collective Memory*, ed. and trans. Lewis A. Coser (Chicago: University of Chicago Press, 1992), 38.

23. This distinction between writing and oral recollection is also stressed by Jacques Le Goff, whose exposition on memory

relies heavily on the work of André Leroi-Gourhan, including *La Mémoire et les rhythmes,* the second volume of *Le Geste et la parole* (Paris: A. Michel, 1964–65). See Le Goff, *History and Memory,* trans. Steven Rendall and Elizabeth Claman (New York: Columbia University Press, 1992), 58.

24. For a critique of Halbwachs's terminology and concepts, see, for example, Assmann, *Das kulturelle Gedächtnis,* 42–48.

25. See Jan Assmann, "Kollektives Gedächtnis und kulturelle Identität," in *Kultur und Gedächtnis,* ed. Jan Assmann and Tonio Hölscher (Frankfurt am Main: Suhrkamp, 1988), 9, 12.

26. Peter Reichel, *Politik mit der Erinnerung: Gedächtnisorte im Streit um die nationalsozialistische Vergangenheit* (Munich: Hanser, 1995).

27. Compare Liliane Weissberg, "Die Ausstellung des Fremden: Zur Literaturtheorie als *cultural studies,*" in *Literaturtheorie nach 1945,* ed. Lutz Danneberg and Friedrich Vollhardt (Stuttgart: J.B. Metzler Verlag, 1995), 499–531.

28. Pierre Nora, "Between Memory and History: *Les Lieux de Mémoire,*" trans. Marc Roudebush, *representations* 26 (Spring 1989): 7. Subsequent citations appear parenthetically in the text.

29. See Walter Benjamin, "Der Erzähler," published in English as "The Storyteller: Reflections on the Works of Nikolai Leskov," trans. Harry Zohn, in Benjamin, *Illuminations: Essays and Reflections,* ed. Hannah Arendt (New York: Schocken Books, 1969), 83–109.

30. See, for example, Peter Vergo, ed., *The New Museology* (London: Reaktion Books, 1991); Ivan Karp and Steven D. Lavine, eds., *Exhibiting Cultures: The Poetics and Politics of Museum Display* (Washington, D.C.: Smithsonian Institution Press, 1991); Ivan Karp, Christine Mullen Kreamer, and Steven D. Lavine, eds., *Museums and Communities: The Politics of Public Culture* (Washington, D.C.: Smithsonian Institution Press, 1992); Susan M. Pearce, *Museums, Objects, and Collections: A Cultural Study* (Washington, D.C.: Smithsonian Institution Press, 1992); Eilean Hooper-Greenhill, *Museums and the Shaping of Knowledge* (London: Routledge, 1992); Daniel J. Sherman and Irit Rogoff, eds., *Museum Culture: Histories Discourses Spectacles* (Minnesota: University of Minnesota Press, 1994); and Tony Bennett, *The Birth of the Museum: History, Theory, Politics* (London: Routledge, 1995).

1

WORN WORLDS: CLOTHES, MOURNING, AND THE LIFE OF THINGS

Peter Stallybrass

I have been writing about clothes since 1990. At first, I did so without even knowing that I was doing it. I had no inkling that I was writing about clothes other than as a by-product of my interest in sexuality, colonialism, and the history of the nation-state. Then, something happened that changed my sense of what I was doing. I was giving a paper on the concept of the individual when I was quite literally overcome. I could not read, and an embarrassing silence ensued.

When, later, I tried to understand what had happened, I realized that for the first time since his death, Allon White had returned to me. Allon and I were friends; we had shared a house; we had cowritten a book. After his death of leukemia in 1986, his widow, Jen, and I had both, in our different ways, tried to invoke Allon, but with remarkably little success. For others, there were active memories, active griefs. For me, there was simply a hole, an absence, and something like anger at my own inability to grieve. What memories I had seemed sentimental and unreal—quite incommensurable with the strident, loving articulateness that was Allon's. The one thing that had seemed real to me were long conversations with Jen about what to do with Allon's remains: with the hat that still stood on the bookshelf in his study, a hat that he had bought to conceal the baldness that had arrived long before the physical humiliations of chemotherapy; with his glasses that had been beside the bed and still looked at you. For Jen,

27

the question was of whether and how to reorder the house, what to do with Allon's books, with all the ways in which he had occupied space. Perhaps, she thought, the only way to resolve this problem was to move, leaving the house once and for all. But in the meantime, she gave away some of his books and some of his clothes.

Allon and I had always exchanged clothes, having shared a house together for two years in which we were communal in just about everything except our filth—that alone seemed irremediably individual, the object of the other's disgust. When Allon died, Jen gave me his American baseball jackets, which seemed appropriate enough, since I had by that time moved permanently to the United States. But she also gave me the jacket of Allon's which I had most coveted. He had picked it up in a secondhand shop down from Brighton station, and its mystery was, and is, simple enough to describe. It is made of a rather shiny black cotton and polyester weave, and on the outside it's still in good nick. But inside, much of the lining has been cut out, and the rest is in tatters, as if several angry cats had been at work with their claws. Inside, the only remnant of former glory is the label: "Made Expressly for Turndorf's by Di Rossi, Hand Sewn." I've often wondered if it was the "Di Rossi" that attracted Allon, as he adored the Italian look from his childhood, but most likely it was just the fit of the jacket.

Anyway, this was the jacket I was wearing when I read my paper on the individual, a paper that was in many ways an attempt to invoke Allon. But at no time in the writing of it did I feel any answering response. Like the paper, Allon was dead. And then, as I began to read, I was inhabited by his presence, taken over. If I wore the jacket, Allon wore me. He was there in the wrinkles of the elbows, wrinkles that in the technical jargon of sewing are called "memory"; he was there in the stains at the very bottom of the jacket; he was there in the smell of the armpits. Above all he was there in the smell.

So I began to think about clothes. I read about clothes, I talked to friends about clothes. The magic of cloth, I came to believe, is that it receives us: receives our smells, our sweat, our shape even. And when our parents, our friends, our lovers die, the clothes in their closets still hang there, holding their gestures, both reassuring and terrifying, touching the living with the dead—but for me, more reassuring than terrifying, although I have felt both emotions. For I have always wanted to be touched by the dead; I have wanted them to haunt me; I have even hoped that they will rise up and inhabit me. And they do literally inhabit us through the "habits" they bequeath. I put on Allon's jacket. However worn, it has outlived its wearers and, I hope, will outlive me. In thinking of clothes as passing fashions, we repeat less than a half-truth. Bodies come and go; the clothes that have received those bodies survive. They circulate through secondhand shops, through rummage sales, through the Salvation Army; or they are transmitted from parent to child, from sister to sister, from brother to brother, from sister to brother, from lover to lover, from friend to friend.

Clothes receive the human imprint. Jewelry lasts longer, and can also move us. But, even though it has a history, it resists the history of our bodies. Enduring, it rebukes our mortality, which it imitates only in the occasional scratch. On the other hand, food, which, like jewelry, is a gift that joins us to each other, rapidly *becomes* us and disappears.[1] Like food, cloth can be shaped by our touch; like jewelry, it endures beyond the immediate moment of consumption. It endures, but it is mortal. As Lear says disgustedly of his own hand, "it smels of mortalitie."[2] It is a smell that I love.

It is the smell that attaches a child to its comforter. A piece of cloth, a teddy bear, whatever. Cloth that can be put in the mouth, chewed upon, anything but washed. Cloth that bears the teeth marks, the grime, the bodily presence of the child. Cloth that decays: the teddy bear's arm falls off, the edge of the cloth frays. Cloth that endures and comforts. Cloth that, as any child knows, is *specific*. Once, looking after a friend's child, I couldn't find her comforter and attempted to "replace" it with a piece of cloth that looked exactly like it. She, of course, knew immediately that it was a fraudulent imitation, and I still remember her look of distrust and disgust at my betrayal. The comforter, however much it stands in for absences and loss, remains irrevocably its material self even as it is transformed by touch and lips and teeth.

As I thought about cloth, I rethought my own work on early modern England. To think about cloth, about clothes, was to think about memory, but also about power and possession. I began to see the extent to which Renaissance England was a cloth society. By this I mean not only that its industrial base was cloth, and in particular the manufacture of wool, but

29

also that cloth was the staple currency, far more so than gold or money. To be a member of an aristocratic household, to be a member of a guild, was to wear livery. It was to be paid, above all, in cloth. And when a guild member was set free, he or she was said to be "clothed."[3]

Let me clarify what I mean by a cloth society. In its most extreme form, it is a society in which values and exchange alike take the form of cloth. When the Inkas incorporated new areas into their kingdom, the new citizens "were granted 'clothes to wear . . . which among them is highly valued.'" But the gift was not, of course, disinterested. This "gift" of textile was, as John Murra puts it, "a coercive and yet symbolic reiteration of the peasant's obligations to the state, of his or her conquered status." In exchange for this supposed "gift," peasants were obliged by law "to weave cloth for crown and church needs." To the surprise of European invaders, while some state warehouses contained food, weapons, and tools, there were "a large number holding wool and cotton, cloth and garments."[4] Similarly, in the court of Emperor Akbar, there was "a special department for receiving the shawls and dresses (*khelats*) given as tributes or pledges by different notables and regions." As Bernard Cohn has argued, "The gift of dress was the essential act of homage and rule within the Mughal system of kingship, effecting the incorporation of the subject into the ruler's body."[5]

In a cloth society, then, cloth is both a currency and a means of incorporation. As it exchanges hands, it binds people in networks of obligation. The particular power of cloth to effect these networks is closely associated with two almost contradictory aspects of its materiality: its ability to be permeated and transformed by maker and wearer alike; its ability to endure over time. Cloth thus tends to be powerfully associated with memory. Or, to put it more strongly, cloth *is* a kind of memory. When a person is absent or dies, cloth can absorb their absent presence. The poet and textile artist Nina Payne writes of sorting through her husband's clothes after his death:

> Everything to be saved was stored in an upstairs closet, jackets and trousers that Eric or Adam might eventually use, sweaters, ties, three shirts made of soft-checkered cotton, blue-grey, brick red and yellow ochre. I saw that the grey one had been worn

once after ironing, then replaced on its hanger to be worn again. If I pressed my head into the clothes, I could smell him.[6]

"I could smell him." Dead, he still hangs there in the closet, in the shape of his body impressed upon the cloth, in a frayed cuff, in a smell.

What is most astonishing to me about insights like Nina Payne's is that, in societies like ours, that is to say, in modern economies, they are so rare. I think this is because, for all our talk of the "materialism" of modern life, attention to material is precisely what is absent. We are surrounded by an extraordinary abundance of materials, but their value is to be endlessly devalued and replaced. Marx, for all his brilliant insight into the workings of capitalism, was mistaken in appropriating the concept of "fetishism" from nineteenth-century anthropology and applying it to commodities. He was, I believe, right in insisting that the commodity is a "magical" (that is, mystified) form, in which the labor processes that give it its value have been effaced. But in applying the term "fetish" to the commodity, he in turn erased the true magic by which other tribes than our own (and, who knows, perhaps even we ourselves) inhabit and are inhabited by what they touch and love. To put it another way, for us, to love *things* is something of an embarrassment. Things are, after all, *mere* things. And to accumulate things is not to give them life. It is because things are *not* fetishized that they remain lifeless.[7]

In a cloth economy, though, things take on a life of their own. That is to say, one is paid not in the "neutral" currency of money but in material that is richly absorbent of symbolic meaning, and in which memories and social relations are literally embodied. In a capitalist economy, an economy of new cloth, new clothes, the life of textiles takes on a ghostly existence, emerging to prominence, or even to consciousness, only at moments of crisis. Yet such moments of crisis recur again and again as the trace elements of material life. Vladimir Nabokov, for instance, in his last novel, *Look at the Harlequins!,* describes how Vadim, after the death of his wife Iris, feels the need to banish those objects of hers that would overpower him:

A curious form of self-preservation moves us to get rid, instantly, irrevocably, of all that belonged to the loved one we

31

lost. Otherwise, the things she touched every day and kept in their proper context by the act of handling them start to become bloated with an awful mad life of their own. Her dresses now wear their own selves, her books leaf through their own pages. We suffocate in the tightening circle of those monsters that are misplaced and misshapen because she is not there to tend them. And even the bravest among us cannot meet the gaze of her mirror.

How to get rid of them is another problem. I could not drown them like kittens; in fact, I could not drown a kitten, let alone her brush or bag. Nor could I watch a stranger collect them, take them away, come back for more. Therefore, I simply abandoned the flat, telling the maid to dispose in any manner she chose of all those unwanted things. Unwanted! At the moment of parting they appeared quite normal and harmless; I would even say they looked taken aback.[8]

Nabokov captures the *terror* of the material trace. For Vadim, the life of these objects is bloated, monstrous, as if they themselves have usurped the place of their wearer. The dresses "now wear their own selves." But even as Vadim exterminates the monsters, they take on a new life: not just "normal and harmless," but "taken aback"—taken aback, perhaps, at his inability to take them back.

At such moments of crisis, these trivial matters, the matter of matter, seem to loom disproportionately large. What are we to do with the clothes of the dead? This question is addressed by Philip Roth in his autobiography, *Patrimony*. There, he describes how, after his mother died, his father "disappeared into the bedroom and started emptying her bureau drawers and sorting through the clothes in her closet. I was still at the door with my brother, welcoming the mourners who'd followed us back from the cemetery." Roth, disturbed by his father's refusal to perform the usual social functions, pursues his father into the bedroom:

The bed was already strewn with dresses, coats, skirts, and blouses pulled from the closet, and [my father] was now busily chucking things from a corner of [my mother's] lowest bureau drawer into a plastic garbage bag. . . . "What good is this stuff anymore? It's no good to me hanging here. This stuff can go to Jewish relief—it's in mint condition."

Like Vadim, Roth's father wants to erase the trace because

the trace seems empty, a reminder of all that has been lost. The clothes are only, and merely, themselves, with a specific material value. For Roth, there is something almost heroic in this repudiation: His father, he writes, "was now an old man living alone and . . . symbolic relics were no substitute for the real companion of fifty-five years. It seemed to me that it was not out of fear of her things and their ghostlike power that he wanted to rid the apartment of them without delay—to bury *them* now, too—but because he refused to sidestep the most brutal of all facts."[9]

Similarly, Laurence Lerner writes in a poem called "Residue" of his father getting rid of his mother's clothes after her death:

> My mother dying left a wardrobeful,
> A world half-worn, half-new:
> Old-fashioned underclothes; a row of shoes,
> Soles upward, staring; tangles of rings,
> Impatient opals, bargain bangles, pearls;
> And, flowered or jazzy, rayon, cotton, tulle,
> A hundred dresses, waiting.
>
> Left with that ragged past,
> My poor truncated father sold the lot.
> What could he do? The dealer shrugged, and said
> "Take it or leave it—up to you." He took
> And lost the fiver at the races.
> The empty wardrobe stared at him for years.[10]

There is an important sense in which the clothes *are* the pain the father feels. The dresses hang there, "waiting," they endure, but only as a residue that, in Donne's words, recreates "absence, darknesse, death; things which are not."[11] Yet even when they are gone, turned into instantly disposable cash, the wardrobe recreates the ghostly presence of the dresses that are no longer there. There is, indeed, a close connection between the magic of lost clothes and the fact that ghosts often step out of closets and wardrobes to appall us, haunt us, perhaps even console us.

Yet there is nothing *given* about this radical separation, this discarding of cloth, this relegation of it to the *merely* symbolic. And I want to try to attend to the different ways in which clothing figures in, and figures, the ruptures of our lives. Let me return again to the three shirts that Nina Payne preserved after her husband's death, which she stored away for future use. "The checkered shirts," she writes, "reappeared two years later":

> Jessie and Emily started putting them on over turtlenecks, tucking in the shirttails, rolling up the bottom of the sleeve, the way a woman will wear a man's garment and expand, playfully, upon the shape of their difference. My daughters made outfits out of a scattered assortment of clothing in which their father's shirts became an emblem and a sign. Eric was working nights at a restaurant that year following his graduation from high school. His schedule made it possible for him to avoid everyone in the family most of the time but we generally ate supper together on Sunday evenings. Once, when we were sitting round the table, he told the girls how ridiculous it was for them to be wearing shirts that were much too big for them. He said that he himself planned to wear the shirts and he didn't want them all worn out before he could fit into them. His sisters responded indignantly. The argument gathered undertow. I heard anger, accusation, and an exasperation bordering on despair. Under ordinary circumstances, I might have been called upon to give an opinion but no one dared ask for one. The phone rang. Adam got up to clear his plate and we all scattered for cover.
>
> The shirts continued to be worn. When he left home, Eric took the grey one with him. The next time I saw it, I recognized the fatal pink of red dye that had seeped into a load of wash. For a moment, I felt as though everything would lose its original color, bleach out, disintegrate. But Eric smiled at my stricken look. "The same thing happened to my underwear in sixth grade, do you remember?" and he opened the door to the cellar to bring up more wood.[12]

The title of Roth's autobiography is, we may recall, *Patrimony*, and that title takes on a peculiar and powerful resonance in Payne's writing.

In Roth's account, the mother's clothes are given away, but the father's legacy remains to be inherited (and dislocated) by the son. But Nina Payne preserves the clothes that become the site of grief and of struggle between her sons and daughters. Or rather, between the eldest son, Eric, who wants to put on the father's patrimony for himself, and the daughters, Jessie and Emily, with the younger son, Adam, as uncomfortable witness (he "got up to clear his plate"). Yet Eric, it seems, fails in his attempt to take the grief and the power of loss and of persistence for himself. "The shirts continued to be worn." And when he leaves, taking only one of them with him, the wornness by which presence is transmitted will be transformed into the wornness of the worn-out. Eric, who didn't want the shirts "all worn out before he could fit into them," discolors the gray shirt he takes with "the fatal pink of red dye." "For a moment, I felt as though everything would lose its original color, bleach out, disintegrate," Payne writes. Eric's response is to reiterate the persistence of loss: His father's shirt is transformed as his own underpants had been earlier. The shirt persists, joining parent to child, yet changing as it is reshaped by its new wearer.

The gendering of cloth, and of attitudes toward it, has itself been materially inscribed by the social relations through which, outside the capitalist marketplace where the male weaver and the male tailor became increasingly the norm, women have been both materially and ideologically associated with the making, repairing, and cleaning of clothes. It is diffi-cult fully to recapture the density and complex transformation of this relation between women of different classes and cloth. But throughout most of early modern Europe and the Ameri-cas, the social life of women was profoundly connected to the social life of cloth. In fifteenth-century Florence, for instance, young girls were taken on as servants for five to ten years, and their contracts stipulated that they would be given clothes and food, and, at the termination of their contract, a marriage dowry. The dowry was usually paid not in money but in clothes and bed linen.[13]

Men, of course, were also paid in livery, but they were rarely so consistently involved from early childhood in the production of cloth. As late as the nineteenth century in the United States, most young women were expected to have made twelve quilts for their dower chests before they were ready to marry, and the thirteenth was called the "Bridal Quilt." But if stitching was, for women, compulsory labor, it was also, as Elaine Showalter has argued, a means of produc-ing countermemories.[14] A New England mill worker, herself professionally engaged in the production of cloth, recorded her own life in the quilt she made. She writes in *The Lowell Offering* in 1845:

35

[H]ow many passages of my life seem to be epitomized in this patchwork quilt. Here . . . are remnants of that bright copper-plate cushion that graced my mother's chair. . . . Here is a piece of the first dress I ever saw, cut with what were called "mutton-leg" sleeves. It was my sister's . . . , and here is a fragment of the first gown that was ever cut for me with a bodice waist. . . . Here is a fragment of the first dress which baby brother wore when he left off long clothes. . . . Here is a piece of the first dress which was ever earned by my own exertions! What a feeling of exultation, of self-dependence, of *self-reliance*, was created by this effort.[15]

The quilt thus bears the marks of conflicting social structures: the materials of family-arity; the materials of self-dependence and wage labor.

And the quilt itself takes on a complex social life of its own. "Annette," its maker (probably Harriet Farley or Rebecca Thompson), after becoming a mill worker, gives the quilt to her sister for her marriage, thus returning it from the sphere "of self-dependence, of *self-reliance*" to the sphere of marriage. It is beneath this quilt that her sister dies, coughing up her medications, so that when the quilt is returned to Annette, there are "dark stains at the top of it."[16] The quilt is made up of pieces of cloth that bear the traces of her history; and, in its use, the quilt comes to bear the traces of others, of her sister, of death.

Elaine Hedges notes how widespread in the nineteenth-century United States was the transmission of fabrics that "bound together members of dispersed families." In 1850, Hannah Shaw writes to her daughter Margaret: "I have been looking for something to send you, but I could not find any-thing that I could send in a letter bitt [sic] a piece of my new dress." Other dress scraps are sent from mother to daughter, from sister to sister: "'Here is a piece of my gingham Lydia made me'; 'a piece of my dress of delanes'; 'a piece of my bonnet trimmed with green plaid ribbon'; . . . 'some pieces of my new dresses for patch work.'" Hannah writes to Mar-garet that her daughter Rebecca "will now peace [sic] up your grandmothers's dresses in quilts," after the grandmother had died. "Piecing" as "peacing": pieces that make peace between the living and the dead.[17] A network of cloth can trace the connections of love across the boundaries of absence, of death, because cloth is able to carry the absent body, memory, genealogy, as well as literal material value.

But it is striking that, as cloth loses its economic value, it tends to lose its symbolic value. There seems, for instance, to be a connection between the ability to sell or pawn secondhand clothes and the careful transmission of clothes through wills. In the Renaissance, from the pawnbroking accounts of Italy and England, it is clear that clothes were by far the commonest pledge, followed by tools. Clothes first, tools second. As late as the 1950s, in *Some Like It Hot,* Tony Curtis and Jack Lemmon pawn their overcoats, even though it is the middle of a bitter Chicago winter. Overcoats are still *worth* pawning; they can still be exchanged for the money with which one can survive.

A pawnbroker, indeed, will only accept pledges for which there is a market. One can pawn clothes only if they're worth something. In Renaissance England, a single livery for the court dwarf, Ippolyta the Tartarian, cost more than the highest salary for a court lady.[18] And when Philip Henslowe paid for plays by writers like Shakespeare, he usually paid about £6 for a play, whereas he paid £20 10s. 6d. for a single "black velvet cloak with sleeves embroidered all with silver and gold."[19] A single jerkin bought for the Earl of Leicester cost more than the grand house that Shakespeare bought in Stratford.[20] The sheer value of textiles until the manufacture of cheap cottons explains the extraordinary care with which they were itemized in early modern wills.

At one level, and particularly among the aristocracy, the leaving of clothes was an assertion of the power of the gift-giver and the dependency of the recipient. Such is the chilling implication of the Earl of Dorset's bequest of his wife's own clothes to her in 1624: "Item I doe give & bequeath to my deerlye beloved wife all her wearing apparel and such rings and jewels as were hers on her marriage and the rocke rubye ring which I have given her." His own apparel Dorset divided among his servants.[21]

The will of Dorset's wife, Anne Clifford, on the other hand, is far more detailed and moving in its association of clothes with memory: She leaves to her grandchildren "the remainder of the two rich armors which were my noble father's, to remaine to them and their posterity (if they soe please) as a remembrance of him." And to her "deare daughter," she leaves

my bracelett of little pomander beads, sett in gold and enam-
elling, containing fifty-seven beads in number, which usually I
ware under my stomacher; which bracelett is above an hundred
yeares old, and was given by Philip the Second, King of Spaine,
to Mary, Queene of England [and by her?] to my greate grandmother, Anne, Countesse of Bedford: and also two little peices
of my father and mother, sett in a tablett of gold, and enamelled
with blew; and all those seaven or eight old truncks and all that
is within them, being for the most part old things that were my
deare and blessed mother's, which truncks commonly stand in
my owne chamber or the next unto it.[22]

Here, the transmission of clothes is a transmission of wealth,
of genealogy, of royal connections, but also of memory and of
the love of mother for daughter.

And it was not only aristocrats who bequeathed their
clothing with such care. A typical legacy of a master upon his
death to his apprentice was the gift of clothes. Thus, Augustine
Phillips, an actor and sharer in the King's Men, left bequests
upon his death in 1605 not only to fellow sharers like Henry
Condell and William Shakespeare, but also to the boy actor
who had trained under him: "Item, I give to Samuel Gilborne,
my late apprentice, the sum of forty shillings, and my mouse-
colored velvet hose, and a white taffeta doublet, and black
taffeta suit, my purple cloak, sword, and dagger, and my bass
viol."[23] The clothes are preserved; they remain. It is the bodies
that inhabit them which change.

What are the implications we can draw out from these
wills bequeathing clothing? First, clothes have a life of their
own; they both *are* material presences and they *encode* other
material and immaterial presences. In the transfer of clothes,
identities are transferred from a mother to a daughter, from
an aristocrat to an actor, from a master to an apprentice.
Such transfers are, of course, staged within the Renaissance
theater in the many scenes where a servant dresses as his
or her master, a lover dresses in the borrowed garments
of another lover, a skull inhabits the clothes that have survived it. In *Twelfth Night*, brother is transformed into sister
and sister into brother through the costume identified as Ce-
sario/Sebastian. We here move closer to the narrower meaning
of "transvestism" as that term is used today to imply cross
gendering. But what I want to emphasize is the extent to which

the Renaissance theater, and the culture more generally, was fixated on clothes in and of themselves.

It is only, I believe, in a Cartesian and post-Cartesian paradigm that the life of matter is relegated to the trash can of the "merely," the bad fetish that the adult will leave behind as a childish thing so as to pursue the life of the mind. As if consciousness and memory were about minds rather than things. As if the real could only reside in the purity of ideas rather than in the permeated impurity of the material. It is about that permeated impurity which Pablo Neruda writes so movingly in *Passions and Impressions:*

> It is worth one's while, at certain hours of the day or night, to scrutinize useful objects in repose: wheels that have rolled across long, dusty distances with their enormous load of crops or ore, charcoal sacks, barrels, baskets, the hafts and handles of carpenters' tools. . . . Worn surfaces, the wear inflicted by human hands, the sometimes tragic, always pathetic, emanations from these objects give reality a magnetism that should not be scorned.
>
> [Our] nebulous impurity can be perceived in them: the affinity for groups, the use and obsolescence of materials, the mark of a hand or a foot, the constancy of the human presence that permeates every surface.
>
> This is the poetry we are seeking.[24]

A poetry of the worn and permeated surface; a poetry of clothes.

In *Landscape for a Good Woman*, an account of her working-class childhood, Carolyn Steedman writes about these permeated surfaces with pain and anger, as well as with love. Pain and anger, because in the erasure of the material is embodied the erasure of her mother's and her own lives from the significances of history. Things, she writes, "remain a problem": "it was with the image of a New Look coat that, in 1950, I made my first attempt to understand and symbolize the content of my mother's desire." But the New Look coat was precisely what Carolyn Steedman's mother could not afford. Her face was pressed against a store window through which she saw, but could not reach out for, what she desired:

> [My mother] knew where we stood in relation to this world of privilege and possession, had shown me the place long before, in

the bare front bedroom where the health visitor spoke haughtily to her. Many women have stood thus, at the window, looking out, their children watching their exclusion: "I remember as it were but yesterday," wrote Samuel Bamford in 1849, "after one of her visits to the dwelling of that 'fine lady'" (his mother's sister, who had gone up in the world): she divested herself of her wet bonnet, her soaked shoes, and changed her dripping outer garments and stood leaning with her elbow on the window sill, her hand upon her cheek, her eyes looking upon vacancy and the tears trickling over her fingers.

What we learned now, in the early 1960s, through the magazines and the anecdotes she brought home, was how the goods of that world might be appropriated, with the cut and fall of a skirt, a good winter coat, with leather shoes, a certain voice; but above all with clothes, the best boundary between you and a cold world.

As Carolyn Steedman puts it, her mother "wanted things. Politics and cultural criticism can only find trivial the content of her desires, and the world certainly took no notice of them. It is one of the purposes of this book to admit her desire for the things of the earth to political reality and psychological validity."[25]

Clothes, then, as memory, but also as the stepping-stones by which one walks away from an unbearable present—the present of childhood, for instance, when one is made over by one's parents. Jen White told me of a pair of shoes her parents bought her for school: sensible, practical shoes; shoes which, as the saying goes, she wouldn't want to be caught dead in. It is difficult to take seriously enough the agony of such moments: the rage, the anguish, the despair. An all-too-visible identity is there on your feet, mocking you, humiliating you. For you have been made up, made over by another, put into the livery of abject dependency. And it is the ecstasy of release from such livery that Annette so finely captures in her memories of "the first dress which was ever earned by my own exertions": "a feeling of exultation," she calls it.

Many of us sense that feeling most powerfully through its negation. When Sasha Jansen goes to Paris in Jean Rhys's *Good Morning, Midnight,* she thinks: "My dress extinguishes me. And then this damned fur coat slung on top of everything else—the last idiocy, the last incongruity." And later, working in a fashionable Parisian dress shop, she fantasizes about

40

buying the dress that will set all to rights: "It is a black dress with wide sleeves embroidered in vivid colours—red, green, blue, purple. It is my dress. If I had been wearing it I should never have stammered or been stupid. . . . I start . . . longing for it, madly, furiously. If I could get it everything would be different."[26] Sasha never gets the dress.

Allon White died at home, wearing his pajamas, in exactly the posture in which Lucas, the protagonist of the novel he wrote many years before but never published, died. "Lucas was on his left side with his knees drawn up tight and his hands pushed down between his thighs. A blanket was pulled up over his shoulder." A blanket: as Carolyn Steedman puts it, "the best boundary between you and a cold world." But it is hard for us to live with the dead, not knowing what to do with their clothes, in which they still hang, inhabiting their closets and dressers; not knowing how to clothe *them.* Florence Reeve, a Mormon, died on February 10, 1887. Alice Isso writes: "I went to assist in laying her out. On the 11th we made her clothes. We worked all day, then packed her in ice. On the 12th, in the evening we dressed and repacked her."[27] What will *we* do? How will we dress the dead? Not at all? In their most disposable clothes? In their best finery?

When Philip Roth's father died, his brother, searching a dresser, found "a shallow box containing two neatly folded prayer shawls. These he hadn't parted with":

> When the mortician, at the house, asked us to pick out a suit for him, I said to my brother, "A suit? He's not going to the office. No, no suit—it's senseless." He should be buried in a shroud, I said, thinking that was how his parents had been buried and how Jews were traditionally buried. But as I said it I wondered if a shroud was any less senseless—he wasn't Orthodox and his sons weren't religious at all—and if it wasn't pretentiously literary and a little hysterically sanctimonious as well. . . . But as nobody opposed me and as I hadn't the audacity to say, "Bury him naked," we used the shroud of our ancestors to clothe his corpse. . . .
>
> Then, one night some six weeks later, at around 4:00 A.M., he came in a hooded white shroud to reproach me. He said, "I should have been dressed in a suit. You did the wrong thing." I awakened screaming. All that peered out from the shroud was

the displeasure in his dead face. And his only words were a rebuke: I had dressed him for eternity in the wrong clothes.[28]

In the wrong clothes.

A necessary feature of transmission, if it is to take place at all, is that it can go astray: the letter does not arrive, the wrong person inherits, the legacy is an unwanted burden. Transmissions go astray. Yet even in the wildest of transmissions, something always does arrive at its destination. For the last two years or so, my mother and father have increasingly been thinking and talking about the pieces of furniture they treasure, about what will happen to them when they die, about who will want them. Who will take in the desk of my mother's mother? Who will care for it? Who will have the portrait of my father playing the recorder with his brother? At first, I found such questions tiresome. To a good post-Cartesian, it all seemed rather grossly material. But, of course, I was wrong, and they were right. For the questions are: Who will remember my grandmother, who will give her a place? What space, and whom, will my father inhabit? I know this because I cannot recall Allon White as an idea, but only as the habits through which I inhabit him, through which he inhabits and wears me. I know Allon through the smell of his jacket.

Notes

1. My thoughts are here indebted to C. A. Bayly, "The Origins of Swadeshi (Home Industry): Cloth and Indian Society, 1700–1930," in *The Social Life of Things: Commodities in Cultural Perspective*, ed. Arjun Appadurai (Cambridge: Cambridge University Press, 1986), 285–321.
2. William Shakespeare, *King Lear* (1608), 4.6.26.
3. I have written about this in "Worn Worlds: Clothes and Identity on the Renaissance Stage," in *Subject and Object in Renaissance Culture*, ed. Margreta de Grazia, Maureen Quilligan, and Peter Stallybrass (Cambridge: Cambridge University Press, 1996), 289–320.
4. John Murra, "Cloth and Its function in the Inka State," in *Cloth and Human Experience*, ed. Annette B. Weiner and Jane

Schneider (Washington, D.C.: Smithsonian Institution Press, 1989), 292, 293, 287.

5. Bayly, "The Origins of Swadeshi," 288; Bernard S. Cohn, "Cloth, Clothes, and Colonialism: India in the Nineteenth Century," in *Cloth and Human Experience,* ed. Weiner and Schneider, 303–53.

6. Nina Payne, "Old Clothes! Old Clothes!" (unpublished ms.), unpaginated.

7. On the history of the concept of the fetish, see William Pietz, "The Problem of the Fetish, I," *Res* 9 (1985): 5–17; "The Problem of the Fetish, II," *Res* 13 (1987): 23–45; "The Problem of the Fetish, IIIa," *Res* 16 (1988): 105–23. See also his "Fetishism and Materialism: The Limits of Theory in Marx," in *Fetishism as Cultural Discourse,* ed. Emily Apter and William Pietz (Ithaca, N.Y.: Cornell University Press, 1993), 119–51.

8. Vladimir Nabokov, *Look at the Harlequins!* (New York: Vintage Books, 1990 [1974]), 73.

9. Philip Roth, *Patrimony* (New York: Simon and Schuster, 1991), 31, 33.

10. Laurence Lerner, *Rembrandt's Mirror* (Nashville, Tenn.: Vanderbilt University Press, 1987), 19.

11. John Donne, "A Nocturnall upon S. Lucies Day, Being the Shortest Day," in *The Poems of John Donne,* ed. Sir H. J. C. Grierson (London: Oxford University Press, 1933), 40, l. 18.

12. Payne, "Old Clothes! Old Clothes!"

13. Christiane Klapisch-Zuber, *Women, Family, and Ritual in Renaissance Italy,* trans. Lydia Cochrane (Chicago: University of Chicago Press, 1985), 165–77; David Herlihy and Christiane Klapisch-Zuber, *Tuscans and Their Families: A Study of the Florentine Catasto of 1427* (New Haven, Conn.: Yale University Press, 1985), passim.

14. Elaine Showalter, "Piecing and Writing," in *The Poetics of Gender,* ed. Nancy K. Miller (New York: Columbia University Press, 1986), 222–47.

15. Benita Eisler, ed., *The Lowell Offering: Writings by New England Mill Women (1800–1845)* (Philadelphia: Lippincott, 1977), 152–53.

16. *Lowell Offering,* 154.

17. Elaine Hedges, "The Nineteenth-Century Diarist and Her Quilts," *Feminist Studies* 8 (1982): 293–99.

18. Janet Arnold, *Queen Elizabeth's Wardrobe Unlock'd* (Leeds: Maney, 1988), 107.

19. Andrew Gurr, *The Shakespearean Stage, 1574–1642* (Cambridge: Cambridge University Press, 1980), 178.

20. Gurr, *Shakespearean Stage,* 13.

21. George C. Williamson, *Lady Anne Clifford, Countess of Dorset, Pembroke, and Montgomery, 1590–1676: Her Life, Letters and Work* (Kendal: Wilson, 1922), 460, 462.

22. Williamson, *Lady Anne Clifford*, 467, 468, 469. On Anne Clifford's construction of a "matrilineal dynasty," see Alice T. Friedman's fine analysis, "Constructing an Identity in Prose, Plaster and Paint: Lady Anne Clifford as Writer and Patron of the Arts" in *Albion's Classicism: The Visual Arts in Britain, 1550–1660*, ed. Lucy Gent (New Haven, Conn.: Yale University Press, 1995), 359–76.

23. G. E. Bentley, *The Profession of Dramatist in Shakespeare's Time, 1590–1642* (Princeton, N.J.: Princeton University Press, 1971), 20.

24. Pablo Neruda, *Passions and Impressions*, trans. Margaret Sayers Peden (New York: Farrar, Straus, and Giroux, 1983), 128.

25. Carolyn Kay Steedman, *Landscape for a Good Woman: A Story of Two Lives* (London: Virago, 1986), 24, 38, 109.

26. Jean Rhys, *Good Morning, Midnight* (New York: Vintage, 1974), 15, 28, 32.

27. "Memoirs of Alice Parker Isso," *Utah Historical Quarterly* 10 (1942): 73.

28. Roth, *Patrimony*, 233, 234, 237.

2

Memory Confined

Liliane Weissberg

Mall Culture

At the Wittenbergplatz in the center of Berlin, a tablet calls upon memory: "Places of terror that we should never forget."[1] No colon gestures toward anything to follow, but ten slates, added to the first tablet, offer names: "Auschwitz Stutthof Maidanek Treblinka Theresienstadt Buchenwald Dachau Sachsenhausen Ravensbrück Bergen-Belsen." I have passed by this sign quite often, and I have, at times, wondered about the logic of the names' sequence. The names are not listed in alphabetical order, the places they designate are not limited to a specific geographical realm.[2] While the names of the places recorded have come to stand for the concentration camps established in these villages and towns, their choice seems to mimic the random selection of people who were sent to these sites. On the black slates, the camps' names are listed in letters as yellow as the sign of the star that Jews were forced to wear. "Auschwitz Stutthof Maidanek Treblinka": the slates, and individual names, can be replaced. I am asked to remember, like the Ten Commandments, ten concentration camps only, singled out by the mere act of naming.

Berlin's Holocaust memorial is located on a traffic island. Unlike any traffic sign, however, it is not placed in direct view of any driver, or in a pedestrian's path. Placed on a lawn, it stands sideways in front of the Wittenbergplatz subway station. Modest and nonintrusive, it does not beg for attention; it keeps its proper distance from a station which, like many others, served to transport Jews to various collection places. But the tablet, inscribed on both sides, is also situated in front of Berlin's largest and most luxurious department store,

45

2.1 Berlin, Wittenbergplatz (subway station). Courtesy of Almuth Finck.

the KaDeWe, a building advertised as a consumer's paradise. Places of terror we should never forget: the Holocaust memorial does not distract shoppers from their errands nor does it hint at KaDeWe's past as Berlin's *Kaufhaus des Westens*, "Department Store of the West," owned, before the war, by a Jewish businessman.[3]

The Holocaust memorial on the Wittenbergplatz appears itself forgotten and forlorn, a mark in thin air. In a city like Berlin, where places of past Nazi terror abound, only a few are publicly identified. Last summer, a debate ensued over whether to establish a memorial at the Grunewald commuter train station, from which hundreds of Jews were deported. A plan to establish a memorial in front of a desecrated synagogue in one of Berlin's business centers, Steglitz, was abandoned, as the sketch that won the competition suddenly seemed inappropriate to some politicians and many of Steglitz's citizens. We should never forget: but who does this "we" include?

The Steglitz memorial was to consist of a mirrored wall inscribed with a statement by a German-Jewish journalist,

**2.2 Berlin, Wittenbergplatz (KaDeWe department store).
Courtesy of Almuth Finck.**

Chaim Schneider, that refers to recent attacks against Turkish
guest workers and asylum seekers, some of whom were killed,
by right-wing gangs: "Now, like fifty years ago, one has to
regard oneself as a Jew, an asylum seeker, a foreigner."[4] The
discussion about the establishment of the selected memorial
did not center around this quotation, however, but on the
mirrored wall. According to the memorial's many critics, it
was deemed to:

> resemble a new Berlin wall
> be hostile to human beings, as it would be established in the
>   middle of a marketplace
> provoke traffic accidents
> define all Steglitz citizens as philistines who ought to look in
>   the mirror
> be placed in front of a synagogue that was not a place of
>   murder and deportation
> be unable to celebrate the achievements of Jews
> offer a surface for graffiti
> encourage anti-Jewish graffiti that would gain attention in

47

the national and international press and especially provoke
   Jewish responses
be unable, as a mirrored wall, to serve the blind.[5]

Convenient Recall

Holocaust memorials ask for remembrance: we should
never forget. In Germany, this "we" seldom includes former
victims, but addresses more often perpetrators, bystanders,
and their children and families. For many of them, memory
does not come easily. Indeed, for West Germans after the war,
remembering and forgetting have entered a peculiar dialectic. Constantly reminded of the Holocaust and the Nazi past
through television shows, newspaper articles, and a host of
books, many Germans have found a way to cope with the
past. They can forget while "remembering." Memory can be
drowned out in the vast number of allusions to the past, by the
mere evocation of the concentration camps' names. Naming
can replace working out. West Germany's new postwar identity
was forged by an economic miracle, moreover, which taught
West Germans how to compromise even in matters of naming,
and to proceed in these matters "economically." The city of
Hamburg, for example, moved a plaque designating the place
of its former main synagogue to another, neighboring site so
that a university high rise could be erected on the former
synagogue's ground.

There is a difference between terror's actual place and
memory's proper location. In Germany, as the weekly journal
Spiegel assures its readers, citizens want memory to be taste-
ful and discreet.[6] Memorials are, moreover, not demanded by
many Jews in Germany, who are often unable to face their
personal past and the past that is situated within recent Jewish history. For German Jews, too, a working out is neither
asked for nor encouraged. Germany's postwar reparation pay-
ments to Jews have not included funds for psychological aid.
While remaining German Jews may feel the guilt of survival,
their mere presence converts them into Holocaust memorials
for others. Declared as neither truly alive nor dead, they are
treated with caution.

The East German government did not regard itself as a successor to a fascist state, and thus placed the burden of memory on the West. In the West's imagination, in turn, all concentration camps—with the notable exception of Dachau—were situated somewhere in the Eastern bloc. Until recently, a barbed-wire frontier and a wall separated these camps from the daily concerns of West German citizens. Thus, actual camp sites in the West were ready for reuse. In 1948, a maximum security prison was erected next to the Hamburg-Neuengamme concentration camp, supplemented in the 1970s with a juvenile correction facility. Both institutions incorporated Neuengamme's guard towers, camp barracks, SS garage, and roll call square. Until recently, Neuengamme's slave factory, the *Klinkerwerke,* was leased to a builder of luxury yachts. A building of the Oranienburg camp outside Berlin was turned into a brewery. Other camp structures, there and elsewhere, are used today as office buildings and army training sites.[7]

Former concentration camps that were designated as memorials are now suffering a worse fate: that of actual disappearance. Funds to maintain Dachau as a memorial are scarce, and the Auschwitz-Birkenau camps in Poland are in such disrepair that the Polish government established an international commission to help decide Auschwitz's fate. Should a former concentration camp be refurbished? Should the structure be let to decline as a ruin for memory? Will anything remain to provide a history lesson for future generations? And, with 500,000 visitors to Auschwitz per year, how can the monument be preserved for a flourishing tourist industry? In May 1993, the Hessian radio station in Frankfurt am Main sponsored a one-week music festival, "Against Forgetting" (*Gegen das Vergessen*), that featured rock groups, opera stars, and folk singers in an attempt to collect money for Auschwitz's preservation. Estimates of the amount needed run to about forty million dollars, and the head of Germany's Jewish community, Ignatz Bubis, knows who should be willing to pay. The responsibility for the past must be taken: "The Federal Republic of Germany in specific is obliged to finance, together with Poland, the preservation and maintenance of the [Auschwitz] camps."[8] Germany may, therefore, build Auschwitz for a second time.

49

Museums

There is no Holocaust museum in Germany. Indeed, the founding of Holocaust museums in recent years, more than fifty years after the war in Europe ended, appears to be a particularly American phenomenon. While Israel has a Holocaust memorial, Yad Vashem, the building of American museums seems to have reached a competitive pace. In February 1993, the "Museum of Tolerance—Beit Hashoah" opened in Los Angeles. In April 1993, the Holocaust museum in Washington, D.C., opened its gates. A Holocaust museum in New York opened in spring 1997. All in all, the United States now boasts more than twenty local Holocaust museums, along with seventy-five Holocaust research centers, thirty-four Holocaust archives, and five Holocaust libraries.[9]

While the museums in Los Angeles and New York were planned as such, the United States Holocaust Memorial Museum in Washington was first conceived as a memorial and developed only later, under the guidance of the designer Ralph Appelbaum, into a full exhibition space. The building itself has undergone an evolution. Even after the final architectural plans were approved, exhibition areas were being constantly revised, and so were installations of exhibits.[10] Survivors visited the museum when it was still under construction and were encouraged to engage in discussions about the project's concept and design. Before the museum's completion and official opening, soil from thirty-eight concentration camps, ghettos, and villages was buried by survivors in the museum's Hall of Remembrance.[11] Symbolic acts abounded; even for the construction of the building and the installation of the exhibition, the United States Holocaust Memorial Council (established to oversee the construction) preferred to hire survivors, who in turn often volunteered.[12] The process of building the museum thus became part of a process of remembering.

The museum's constant rebuilding and rearrangement under Jeshajahu Weinberg's directorship inscribed the time of memory as one of constant revision; the museum's display, on the other hand, had as its primary objective the construction of a linear account. A visitor to the building would have to start his or her tour on the fourth floor and move symbolically "downward": beginning with the "Nazi Assault—1933–1939" (fourth floor), proceeding to the "Final Solution—1940–1944"

50

2.3 United States Holocaust Memorial Museum, Washington, D.C. Courtesy of Liliane Weissberg.

(third floor), and concluding the visit with "Aftermath—1945 to Present" (second floor). The move "downward" reflects the structure of another museum, New York City's Guggenheim. The sequence of documents exhibited suggests a progression of events, the logic of which the museum wants to teach even if this logic may defy reason. On the ground floor, opening the doors to the outside, the visitor will finally find a world that seems much more comforting and familiar: present-day America.

In its final shape, the United States Holocaust Memorial Museum bears the traces of its evolution, and it now wants to fulfill a triple function: to present a history of events, to provide memorial space in the Hall of Remembrance, and to offer a library as well as other educational facilities. These latter include theater and film rooms, spaces for special exhibitions, and a computer learning center that prides itself in representing "leading-edge efforts in digital video technology."[13] For the museum, however, the Holocaust itself turns into a learning tool. The first goal is to learn about the past events. But the museum also provides another lesson on history by teaching

51

2.4 United States Holocaust Memorial Museum, Washington, D.C. Courtesy of Liliane Weissberg.

past events as both example and warning to humanity. History may gesture toward the future: perhaps it may be able to repeat itself. On the outside walls of the Hall of Remembrance, there is thus inscribed "never again": "Out of our memory . . . of the Holocaust we must forge an unshakable oath with all civilized people that never again will the world stand silent. . . . We must harness the outrage of our own memories to stamp out oppression wherever it exists."[14]

This message is not different, only more general and discreet in tone from the urgent one with which Los Angeles's Museum of Tolerance implores potential Jewish donors. In recent months, I have received large black envelopes marked with white and red letters: "Outbreaks of a virulent new strain of antisemitism around the world confront *you* with a choice. URGENT: EARLY REPLY REQUESTED." For the director of its museum, Rabbi Marvin Hier, the next Holocaust could be just around the corner; the "lesson of history," he states in his fund-raising letter, has not yet been learned. It is not the world but the Jews who are in danger. The Los Angeles museum is advertised as an insurance policy for Jews, and Hier plays on their existential fears. Would I be able to save my own life by supporting a museum? Can museums prevent future Holocausts? What can be learned from the past?

In his essay "The Rites of the Tribe: American Jewish Tourism in Poland," Jack Kugelmass described organized visits of American Jews, specifically Jewish youth groups, to Auschwitz.[15] Supported by Jewish organizations and local synagogues, the itinerary of many of these tours combines a visit to Auschwitz with one to Israel. Thus, travel agents provide a historical narrative of "past" and "present" (or "future") that suggests the establishment of the Israeli state as a direct consequence of the Holocaust; it implies Israel's right of existence, its claim to "life," as founded on the six million dead. Israel is not simply a final destination for a trip that supports a Zionist ideology. Israel (as a place) as well as the Holocaust (as an event in time) have become references for the self-definition of American Jews as Jews. Indeed, within the context of such travel, the existence of Israel is necessary but secondary: it is the Holocaust, not religion, that provides the most important means of identification for American Jews—as much as for German ones.[16]

Holocaust museums, however, are able to bring Auschwitz "home," to replace the travel to concentration camp sites with a visit to an exhibition that can easily exchange Israel with the United States as a final destination. Did not those travelers mentioned return, after all, to New York Chicago Philadelphia Boston Los Angeles? Did they have a bad conscience, perhaps, over declaring America as their chosen land? The United States Holocaust Memorial Museum in Washington, bearing a national claim in its very name, does not only delimit the effort of journeying, but also that of having to consider another country, Israel, as a safe harbor for Jews. Visiting the museum, Jews should not feel like Jews but like American Jews or, simply, like Americans. At the same time, the museum creates a process of identification that is intended to turn every visitor into a Jew. The museum is not built to represent Jewish history. History becomes Jewish insofar as it becomes a victim's narrative. It becomes American by the very structure in which the story is told. Deportation and rescue: this is another version of the pilgrim's tale.

The lesson of Auschwitz genocide can travel. Gypsies, communists, homosexuals, religious groups, the mentally ill—they were persecuted as well. Elsewhere, other genocides have to be accounted for. While the Holocaust may be unique in its scale and modes of execution, the museum also takes pains to reduce its uniqueness by reference to other genocides. In the introduction to the book accompanying the permanent exhibition, Weinberg writes, in a sequence of "howevers":

> The museum consciously avoided including in its permanent exhibition or its Learning Center genocidal events other than those that occurred in the framework of the Holocaust of 1933–1945. This does not mean that the planners of the museum were unaware of the strong intellectual and moral relevance of many such events to the Holocaust. However, it was their mandate to build a Holocaust museum rather than a museum dealing generally with genocide in human history. However, by no means does this thematic distinction preclude the inclusion of materials pertaining to other genocidal events, such as the Middle Passage of African slaves, the Armenian massacres in Turkey in 1915, or the Cambodian events after the Vietnam war, in the museum's library and archives or in its educational activities.[17]

In the 1980s, several German historians engaged in a discussion—now known as the *Historikerstreit*—about whether the Holocaust constitutes a unique event in human history.[18] Within the considerations of the museum world, uniqueness is dependent on the sponsor's mandate (no further questions asked) and the confines of the museum's space. In direct contrast, the Los Angeles museum, despite its mailings targeted to American Jews, was forced to broaden its focus to receive further public funding.[19] It now includes exhibits and films on the Civil Rights Movement, the genocides in Armenia and Cambodia, and the trials following the beating of Rodney King; it has turned itself into a theme park on racism and ethnic strife. How would a museum be able to preserve the Holocaust's unique status and tell racism's general lesson as well?

In the Washington museum's context, the Holocaust provides the lesson that "liberty" should forge a united nation imbued with moral values. The site of the museum—close to the museum mall, with a view of both the Washington and Jefferson memorials—symbolizes the Holocaust's importance for American history and its task in promoting racial integration. And while the actual site of Auschwitz is in decay, a large number of its objects (as well as exhibits from other camps) have traveled to America's capital, to be collected in its new repository at the nation's center. The object's journey, replacing that of the people's, assures its authenticity. The authentic object provides the proper evidence of the events for those who would doubt the historical facts. The authentic object is able to stand for the site. It is also able, moreover, to replace the "original" location—much as the Getty Museum or Hearst's villa may duplicate Florentine palazzi. With the help of the United States government and the Holocaust Memorial Council, Auschwitz has come to you.

In his description of the museum's mission, Weinberg is eager to vouch for the proper origin of the objects displayed.[20] But the museum prides itself also on the great number of artifacts collected, not only at the new building in Washington but in several warehouses in the Maryland suburbs. The museum owns, or has on loan, more than thirty thousand Holocaust-related items and is the largest collection of its kind outside the actual camps.[21] A collection like this not only gathers and preserves, it establishes a "canon" of some sort that defines the scope of "Holocaust-related" articles. Thus, both the collection and the museum sponsor, and are a response to, the institutionalization of the field of "Holocaust research" which, in turn, supports the new discipline of "Holocaust studies" that is

promoted at many colleges and universities and represented
by several American journals dedicated to the subject. The
fifth floor of the museum houses a library that holds books
in this field and offers an "Encyclopedia of the Holocaust,"
now published in English, Hebrew, and German. It is available
in English, on line, in the museum's computerized Learning
Center.[22]

Victimization

Many survivors left the Displaced Person camps after
1945 to emigrate to the United States, and now the displaced
objects of the Holocaust have followed. Conservators ensure
that the objects' life expectancy will be much higher than
that of the survivors. At the end of the museum's permanent
exhibit, witnesses, interviewed on videotape, see their task as
one of telling a story that will survive them. They describe
their accounts as testaments of and for their families, and
for future generations far removed from the historical events.
The museum designers intend that these historical events
are not learned merely intellectually, but psychologically and
emotionally as well. After watching the witnesses' reports, I
look to my right and left, and see people in tears.

"The passport is the most noble part of a human being,"
Bertolt Brecht wrote in response to the persecuted persons'
need during the war to find a place of refuge.[23] Real or fake
or stolen, marked or unmarked with the letter "J" for Jew,
the passport was the single most desirable commodity in the
thirties and forties, assuring at least the possibility of survival
through escape. A passport could lead to another country or
to another identity. After the war, it became a symbol of the
survivor's struggle with his or her identity, or with his or her
desire for assimilation. In Germany, many Jewish survivors
and their children refused German citizenship or took foreign passports. Until recently, moreover, the Federal Republic
permitted its Jewish citizens to acquire Israeli passports,
thus providing an exception to Germany's single passport
rule. Even Jews remaining in Germany became foreigners,
in many ways.

Whereas it was difficult to acquire a passport during the
war, the museum has a more liberal approach: it offers false

2.5 United States Holocaust Memorial Museum, Washington, D.C. Courtesy of Liliane Weissberg.

papers to everyone, and without questions. These passports, however, adorned with the American seal and the Holocaust museum's logo—"For the dead and the living we must bear witness"—are not intended to rescue its holder. The passport is to help its holder to take the Holocaust personally, to identify with a victim. The story of the Holocaust will only be "true," the museum seems to imply, if seen from a specific perspective. To be able to take this perspective, I will have to become a victim, and rename myself.

Originally, the museum had installed twelve passport dispensers in the entrance hall and additional machines in two other exhibition areas. Once a visitor provided the machines in the entrance hall with some personal data, a computer program was supposed to match the individual with a "real life" victim of comparable age and experience, and he or she would follow the life of his or her alter ego like a detective in search of a life. For any visitor first entering the permanent exhibition, it would be unclear whether his or her victimized partner survived the war, although some life stories are narrated in the first person. "This card tells the story of a real person who lived during the Holocaust," the back of the passport reads. "Please carry it with you and update the story at each of the three printing stations located on the fourth and second floors of the exhibition." Soon after the museum's opening, however, the machines broke down and were removed. The last sentence on the identification card was eliminated, and the passports were made available to visitors in two cardboard boxes marked "male" and "female." Here, too, selections can be made at random.

I take this personally, even without much encouragement. I am a German Jew. My birth documents are false, my American citizenship acquired. Changing identities, adding passports, is nothing unfamiliar to me. But the museum does not want me to assume the sole role of victim. It asks me to be victim and victor at once. It is this latter role I may have fantasized about, but was not prepared for.

Already in the elevator to the fourth floor, chaperoned by a guide, I view a video clip that tells the story of the liberation of the death camps. As I enter the fourth-floor exhibition, films and photographs abound and offer documentation by British, Russian, and American soldiers who recount what they saw when they entered Auschwitz Bergen-Belsen Maidenek Dachau. In Somalia in 1992, arriving American soldiers were greeted by journalists with video recorders. In Europe after the war, the Allied soldiers liberated the death camps

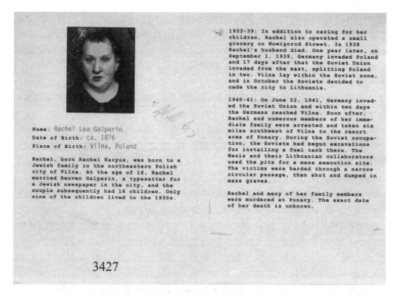

Name: Rachel Lea Galperin
Date of Birth: ca. 1876
Place of Birth: Vilna, Poland

Rachel, born Rachel Karpus, was born to a
Jewish family in the northeastern Polish
city of Vilna. At the age of 16, Rachel
married Reuven Galperin, a typesetter for
a Jewish newspaper in the city, and the
couple subsequently had 16 children. Only
nine of the children lived to the 1930s.

1933-39: In addition to caring for her
children, Rachel also operated a small
grocery on Nowigorod Street. In 1938
Rachel's husband died. One year later, on
September 1, 1939, Germany invaded Poland
and 17 days after that the Soviet Union
invaded from the east, splitting Poland
in two. Vilna lay within the Soviet zone,
and in October the Soviets decided to
cede the city to Lithuania.

1940-41: On June 22, 1941, Germany invaded the Soviet Union and within two days
the Germans reached Vilna. Soon after,
Rachel and numerous members of her immediate family were arrested and taken six
miles southwest of Vilna to the resort
area of Ponary. During the Soviet occupation, the Soviets had begun excavations
for installing a fuel tank there. The
Nazis and their Lithuanian collaborators
used the pits for a mass execution site.
The victims were herded through a narrow
circular passage, then shot and dumped in
mass graves.

Rachel and many of her family members
were murdered at Ponary. The exact date
of her death is unknown.

3427

2.6 United States Holocaust Memorial Museum, Washington, D.C. Courtesy of Liliane Weissberg.

with film cameras in hand. At the end of the permanent exhibition, I will see further films of the liberation, bringing the Holocaust's narrative to a structural close.

Unlike the Museum of Tolerance in Los Angeles, the United States Holocaust Memorial Museum does not offer video arcades, but it does rely on technology. Its rich treasure of tapes, films, and photographs have been made possible by Adolf Hitler's love for motion pictures and his propaganda ministry's prolific production of material. It has been further aided by the Allied soldiers who, though claiming not to have known what to expect, were willing to expect the worst—and to document it on film. The Russians, first to liberate the concentration camps, filmed whatever they saw. British soldiers added lectures to the footage that were delivered, in German, to the concentration camp guards. Some of the American film clips center on General Dwight David Eisenhower's visit and his reactions; these films already began to shape his political image and career at home. Remarkably, the American army clips are shot with color film—an unusual choice for documentaries, especially since the film was harder to come by, and more expensive. For Colonel George Stevens, recording the liberation of Dachau was just the first step in a film career involving the Holocaust. Previously known for his Hollywood comedies, he was to serve as director on *The Diary of Anne Frank* in 1959.

Only after facing the horror as well as the liberation— both the "truth" and the conclusion of the Holocaust—are visitors asked to consider the story chronologically. Here, the liberator becomes victim again. In the fourth-floor galleries, the installations are dense and the glass cases conform, indeed, only within an inch of the fire code. On the fourth floor, I don't need crowds of visitors to feel claustrophobic, although the museum guards, moving people along, are probably an accidental touch that confirms my role as a persecuted Jew. Space is structured to help me feel victimized. I will have to pass through corridors and rooms that, architecturally, allude to a ghetto or a selection ramp. I will walk through a boxcar, which is set on railroad tracks, and then enter a camp's barrack. I will finally face the greatest crowds before the video terminals that show films of medical experimentation or of the burying of the dead.

Why do these films attract these crowds? In my role as a victim, I cannot really feel drawn to them. They seem to play with the public's voyeurism the same way horror movies do. These film clips are superior to any slasher movie: they have the excitement of the "real thing." Small walls built around the video stations let me view the images from a skewed angle only; intended to protect children from these images, the architecture produces the effect of a peep show. I don't view the banality, but the obscenity of evil. At the entrance door, a sign warns visitors that the museum's exhibits may not be appropriate for children under eleven years of age. Would an eleven-year-old child be able to face these pictures? Many of the visitors do not seem concerned. On a Sunday afternoon, I see small children, babies, and a pet dog.

Witnessing

How can the story of the Holocaust be told? Descriptions and narratives reminiscent of history textbooks and school fairs abound on the upper floors. This didactic mode of story-telling, however, fosters another experience: the projection of visual images, or the installation of voice chambers, in which the recorded testimony of survivors can be heard. Here, the visitor is not asked to read and contemplate, but to witness. This is, indeed, the victim's role.

In presenting these images and voices, the installation does not provide a distanced, linear account, but rather the immediacy of moments experienced. In witnessing events, and witnessing the witnesses, my experiences are made to match those of people from another decade and another world. In a recent study, the literary critic Shoshana Felman and the psychoanalyst Dori Laub (the latter involved with the Fortunoff Video Archive for Holocaust Survivors at Yale University), have reflected on the use of documentary material for educational purposes. For Felman, it is not the transmission of "facts" that stands in the foreground, but rather the theorization of a concept of "testimony" and "witnessing" that rests, paradoxically, on the fact that the Holocaust cannot be told.[24] After watching the tapes from the video archives, Felman's students are left speechless, in search of language, isolated; at the same time, their experience has bonded them and they have formed a new community. This seems to me the effect the Holocaust museum wants to build on. It is an effect that marks the testimony's success and witnessing's crisis.

Subjective testimony, defying any "objective" historical account and often proper language itself, speaks in fragments and silences that mute language for the viewer and listener. To write poetry after Auschwitz, Theodor W. Adorno concluded, would be barbaric—if it would be possible at all.[25] Felman, on the other hand, turns to Paul Celan's poetry, which centers on a silence both explicitly expressed and implicitly incorporated in the text. Experience can speak, but only in a language of alienation and fragmentation:

> To stand in the shadow
> of the scar up in the air.
>
> To stand-for-no-one-and-nothing.
> Unrecognized,
> for you
> alone.

With all there is room for in that,
even without
language.[26]

Felman, a trained analyst, conducts her classes as analytic sessions that lead from shared experience to isolation and, finally, social restoration. In Washington, the museum designers take the psychoanalyst's position and try to produce a situation of transference through which a learning process may proceed. Psychoanalytic sessions are not limited to fifty minutes here, but the visitor has to leave the exhibit twice, once stopping to view abstract artistic renderings of the Holocaust, before continuing. For the dead and the living we must bear witness: The visitor, not the museum or its objects, must become witness par excellence.

Camp Aesthetics

Human beings give testimony. Testimonies are also given by objects. Piles of shoes and hundreds of pictures of a prewar shtetl near Vilnius are able to speak, in their silence, more powerfully than any historic marker could. These objects were used, looked at, and touched by persons no longer alive. This is the Holocaust's residue, a metonymic evidence for people about whom little more is known today.

Miles Lerman, national campaign chairman for the museum, recalls the transfer of artifacts from Poland in one of his fund-raising letters:

> I was asked to pose for a photograph with one of these items—a child's shoe. Let me tell you, when this little shoe was handed to me, I froze.
> Bear in mind that I am a former partisan. I was hardened in battle and I deal with this Holocaust story almost on a daily basis. But when I held in my hand that shoe—the shoe of a little girl who could have been my own granddaughter—it just devastated me.[27]

The museum wants this experience to be repeated. An object like a shoe should aid identification, and bridge the time— "could have been my own granddaughter." In the museum's

2.7 United States Holocaust Memorial Museum, Washington, D.C. Courtesy of Liliane Weissberg.

exhibition, however, this child's shoe is not singled out. It is the sheer number of shoes, a fraction of the surviving pairs found in Auschwitz, that give evidence of the enormity of the crime. These were shoes sorted by prisoners once their owners had been selected for the gas chambers, but they were not used again: sandals, walking shoes, children's slippers.

In an essay published in 1936, Martin Heidegger reflects on a painting by Van Gogh depicting a pair of shoes; he speculates on the picture's origin.[28] The shoes represented are able to tell Heidegger of the soil they have touched and the feet they protected; they provide him with a description of their owner and his occupation. The shoes in the Holocaust museum offer and resist to give such information. They have turned into a uniform gray, a color that masks their individual shapes. Once worn by living human beings, they are now evidence of their deaths. Unique and homogenized into a pile, these shoes, too, however, have turned into art. Placed in a room on their own, they resemble an installation by a modernist artist and resonate not only with other period objects in the museum's collection, but also with Ellsworth Kelly's paintings

2.8 United States Holocaust Memorial Museum, Washington, D.C. Courtesy of Liliane Weissberg.

(*Memorial*) and Sol Le Witt's installation (*Consequence*) located in the lounges on the third and second floors.

The photographs in the "Tower of Faces" also provide more than a documentation of the Lithuanian shtetl Ejszyszki. They offer an overwhelming visual experience. Names of places that have lost all or most of their Jewish population are engraved in alphabetical order in straight lines on the glass walls of a corridor; the first names of victims are engraved on the glass wall of another. These corridors evoke the Vietnam memorial, with its seemingly endless rows of victims' names. Rendered in glass, however, the museum's inscriptions do not bear the heaviness of a gravestone. Like smoke from chimneys, these names seem to dance in air and, at the same time, diffuse the light and provide an oblique view of the floor below. The museum's architect and designer were intent on producing these fractured views on every level; the architecture of the building itself offers multiple angles and refracted light. Thus, the architecture alludes not only to the architectural models of ghetto and concentration camp, but also to the refraction through which we are now forced to view

2.9 United States Holocaust Memorial Museum, Washington, D.C. Courtesy of Liliane Weissberg.

the historical events. Originally, even the installation bars that secured the texts and images were to be installed on an angle.[29] And while noting the horror of its subject, the viewer will have to come to terms with a troubling aspect of this museum. This is not a building for the blind. The arrangement of the collection provides aesthetic pleasure. The building is able to stage the Holocaust as a work of art.

"The Holocaust in its enormity defies language and art, and yet both must be used to tell the tale, the tale that must be told," declared Elie Wiesel, a driving force behind the museum's construction, in 1986. The occasion was the announcement of the selection of the museum's architect, James Ingo Freed. Much has already been written on the museum's design, and Freed has been widely celebrated for his building. But the difference between the "use" of art and the Holocaust's representation as art has not been sufficiently reflected upon. In a review published in the *New York Times,* Herbert Muschamp praised the building as defying us to separate "esthetics from morality, art from politics, form from content."[30] The *Architecural Record* praised the design as a

65

challenge to "literal architectural interpretations of history." For this journal's critic, however, another disjunction could occur. The Holocaust museum could function without its objects. Ironically, the symbols of American democracy could be arranged to signify otherwise:

> At first glance, the U.S. Holocaust Memorial Museum, designed by Pei Cobb Freed in association with Notter Finegold + Alexander for a site adjacent to the Washington mall, appears to mirror the built symbols of American democracy that surround it. PCF design partner James Ingo Freed, however, organizes these elements into a cathartic evocation, even without exhibits, of the physically and psychically disturbed world.[31]

Freed's building, praised for a design that allows for multiple points of view and interpretation, can tell a story as well: that of the ambiguity and transformation of references and symbols, that of the move from camp to liberty—and back again.

Would the museum structure itself then suffice as a memorial? Are the "authentic" objects themselves nothing else but a further, decorative touch? Is art, thus entered and inhabited, sufficient to become a Holocaust monument and a memorial in itself? At the information desk in the grand entrance hall, the "Hall of Witnesses," I was handed a brochure, published by Freed's architectural firm, that gives minute details on the museum's plan and construction. It is a description of an object fully mastered by its creators and is longer, and more extensive, than any descriptions of the exhibits.

Art and politics, aesthetics and morals may not be separated. However, Freed's steel and glass construction of corridors not only tells the story of ghetto bridges and railroad tracks but also turns them into a thing of beauty. In Freed's architecture, the story of the Holocaust is told by an abstraction that parallels the installation of the room of shoes or the tower of faces. New museum buildings have been praised elsewhere for their appropriateness, innovative design, and visual gratification. What are the risks involved, however, in turning the Holocaust museum and its displays into objects of aesthetic contemplation?

In a book of essays and photographs, *In Fitting Memory*, Sybil Milton raises, implicitly, a similar question in regard to Ira Nowinski's illustrations. Nowinski's photographs,

66

which document memorial sights, communicate a melancholy mood, work with oblique lighting, and search for new and unconventional vantage points. "His documentary style discloses the unexpected and the haunting natural beauty that exists even at sites of humanity's evil," Milton writes (271). For her, these are images that "enable the reader to access the visual heritage of the Holocaust" (271). However, these are not images witnessed by victims; on the contrary, these are images that presuppose their death and our sorrow. The camp aesthetics is that of the still life. It transforms trees into weeping willows and machines into a landscape of remnants. It completes, paradoxically, the work of a technology that had death as its primary imperative, turning human beings into objects in the first place. Objects can be easily removed. This aesthetics thrives on absence.

America

Tickets to the Holocaust museum are available, for a small fee, through Ticketmaster, a ticket outlet that serves the arts; they are also available at the museum's own "box office." In the bookstore, located on the first and second floors, visitors can learn about the further commercialization of the Holocaust. Videotapes of the witnesses' filmed accounts are not available (they are United States government property), but mourning candles with the Holocaust museum's insignia are for sale, and books are sold in Holocaust museum shopping bags. In the cafeteria, housed in the adjacent museum annex building, one can order bagels and matzo ball soup, items from an Eastern Jewish culture lost in the Old World, but partially integrated into the New. Like any other museum, the United States Holocaust Memorial Museum offers membership benefits. Like any other museum, it is in need of money, but it is already one of the most richly endowed enterprises on the Washington Mall. The bookstore offers a special full-color issue of a United States Holocaust Memorial Museum publication, dated summer 1993, that documents the museum's dedication and publishes pictures of President Bill Clinton, Secretary of Defense Les Aspen, and other government and religious luminaries who were present. They too, seem moved

2.10 United States Holocaust Memorial Museum, Washington, D.C. Courtesy of Liliane Weissberg.

by the museum and its mission. Not only am I expected to respond emotionally to the exhibition, I learn, but my emotions
are socially acceptable. Among the newly made victims, I am
in good company.

After reaching the end of the permanent exhibit, I look into my new passport. It relates the story of a happy ending. My chosen guide survived, and has become an American. The museum offers, then, not only the story of a victim, but a lesson about the making of an American as well. To become American is a rags-to-riches American success story that deals with the economy of revival in the strictest sense. To become American means to appreciate the values of liberty, but it is also an experience of religious dimensions. And like the catharsis in a Greek drama, it is not easily won.

The Hall of Remembrance is dedicated to the victims of the Holocaust and offers an eternal flame as well as space for contemplation. Memorials for unknown soldiers and unknown victims are alike. On its outer limestone walls, former American presidents have left their endorsements and signatures: Eisenhower, Carter, Ronald Reagan. The Holocaust museum may want to remember the dead, but it also attempts to celebrate America. America, in turn, appears as a construct that easily transcends all party lines.

In his study of Holocaust memorials, James E. Young tells the story of the Washington museum's conception (335–37). In 1980, the U.S. Holocaust Memorial Council was established by an act of Congress and charged with fostering Holocaust remembrance in the United States. President Carter advised the council to create a "living memorial"[32] that would be built on donated public ground, but with private funds. Carter's dictate and the choice of the museum's location clearly declare the remembrance of the Holocaust as an important act for American citizens and an important part of their history. In his account of the events, Young follows the official story as disseminated by, for example, Michael Berenbaum in his history of the Holocaust, which serves as the museum's catalog.[33] The Americanization of the Holocaust and its remembrance were the result of a political balancing act, however.

In the late seventies, Jimmy Carter planned to sell F-15 fighter jets to Saudi Arabia, but was worried that this deal would elicit protest from American Jewish organizations. Supporting an Arab state with war technology could be seen as threatening Israel's dominant military position in the Middle East. As a solution to this dilemma, Ellen Goldstein, a Presidential advisor, conceived of creating the United States Holocaust Memorial Council, which was to be charged with building an official U.S. memorial. Goldstein's plan was accepted, and Carter succeeded: the American planes were sold, the Holocaust museum was built.

While Young does not seem to question the justification for a Holocaust museum near Washington's Mall, Milton tries to catalog the reasons for its location in America, and in this nation's capital:

> America was a country of asylum to the survivors
> Americans liberated camps
> America became a new home for survivors and some of the perpetrators
> America played a role in the Nuremberg and subsequent Nazi trials (14)

Henryk Broder, on the other hand, wonders about the project and its location. In an article written for *Der Spiegel*, he sees the U.S. government's concern with the Holocaust as a case of adoption. Only the commercialization of the Holocaust would constitute its typically "American" characteristic as a "Shoah business" that could easily result in a museum as Disney World. According to Broder, the exhibition of the Holocaust's story serves, moreover, as a deflection from, and purification of, American history. As long as the Holocaust was considered a genocide planned by others, Americans could assume a position of innocence. The stories of the Vietnam War, the American slave trade, and the genocide of Native Americans remain, moreover, untold within its context (256). It is interesting to note, however, that Broder's own remarks were incorporated into German "purification" rites. A few months earlier, *Der Spiegel*'s American correspondent, Matthias Matussek, reviewed the Los Angeles museum positively.[34] It was left to the German-Jewish journalist Broder to provide the newsmagazine with the more extensive, and more critical piece on Holocaust museums, and America's—not Germany's—inability to deal with its own past.

In contrast to Broder's account, the U.S. Holocaust museum offers a more complex view of history. With its symbolic architecture and presidential inscriptions, it celebrates the United States. On the other hand, the presentation of some artifacts complicates the issue of guilt. In 1984, David Wyman published his seminal study, *The Abandonment of the Jews*,

2.11 United States Holocaust Memorial Museum, Washington, D.C. Courtesy of Liliane Weissberg.

which documented the U.S. government's unwillingness to aid Europe's Jewish population during the war.[35] Washington's Holocaust museum chronicles this unwillingness, beginning at an even earlier date. For German and other European

71

Jews, immigration to the United States—as well as to other countries—was already made nearly impossible in the thirties. In 1939, German refugees boarded the ship the *St. Louis*, which set out for Cuba. The ship was denied harbor there as well as in the United States, and had to return to Europe. Most of the refugees perished—and the *St. Louis*'s inability to receive permission to anchor was used by Hitler for his propaganda machine. Hitler had a point: even as he regarded Jews as an undesirable element of the German population, Jews were not wanted elsewhere, either.

By August 1, 1942, the U.S. government was informed about the Final Solution. A telegraph to an American Jewish organization carrying information about the death camps was intercepted by the American Secret Service. Despite the information at hand, the U.S. government refused to take action. While the chemical plants in nearby Buna were bombed, Auschwitz was not. The museum exhibits a photograph taken from an American fighter plane that shows Auschwitz-Birkenau's barracks and gas chambers; it documents that the U.S. government had been clearly informed not only about the concentration camp's existence, but also about its function. Not even one bomb was spared to target the railroad tracks leading to the camps.

After the war, the American military erected Displaced Person camps but did not immediately separate Jewish victims from Nazi soldiers under investigation. Immigration quotas limited the number of Jews who could receive U.S. entry papers. Ironically, the American passport, liberally distributed at the museum's entrance, was a rare commodity after the war.

The U.S. Holocaust museum tells this other story of American (non)involvement, but tells it hesitantly. Little is made of the reluctance of American Jews to help their poorer Eastern European brethren. Not mentioned are the former Nazis who gained easy admission to the United States after the war. Unaccounted for are the deals made with former Nazi officials who would again structure political life in the postwar West German state. Too soon after World War II, the cold war had begun. Ultimately, the United States benefited not only from the influx of wealthy and well-known Jewish and political refugees of the Third Reich, but also from Hitler's scientists who, like Werner von Braun, came to America after the war.

2.12 United States Holocaust Memorial Museum, Washington, D.C. Courtesy of Liliane Weissberg.

The Holocaust museum's place in Washington can be justified only as a repository of this specific story of American's own violation of its ideals of liberty and equality for all. It would provide the museum with its raison d'être as a memorial as well. This story of implicit and explicit guilt is difficult to tell, however, from a victim's point of view. The visitor may not have to experience his or her role as victim alone, but work out his or her role as a bystander or supporter of the events as well. In regard to the history of the Holocaust, everybody's innocence is lost. What the United States Holocaust Memorial Museum can and should produce is a revisionist history of the genocide—not one that denies its existence, but one that questions America's role as a shining hero and victorious liberator. In the general war effort, I learned, the Holocaust had not been worth even the slightest consideration.

Entering the Hall of Remembrance at the tour's end, I look at the American passport that the museum handed to me, and that was given to me, really, for a second time. And I think: Mourning can now begin.

Notes

I would like to thank Ann and Rocky Adriance for our conversations about the U.S. Holocaust museum, and Ivy Gilbert for her assistance in preparing this chapter for publication.

1. "Orte des Schreckens, die wir niemals vergessen dürfen."
2. In his study of Holocaust memorials, James Young mentions the Berlin sign and seems to detect from the order that "German camps are listed last." James E. Young, *The Texture of Memory: Holocaust Memorials and Meaning* (New Haven, Conn.: Yale University Press, 1993), 54. Subsequent page citations appear parenthetically in the text.
3. Some of Berlin's major department stores were owned by Hermann Tietz and "Aryanized" in the thirties. The KaDeWe is now part of a national chain of stores that includes the Hertie department stores.
4. "Wie vor fünfzig Jahren fühlt man sich als Jude, als Asylant, als Ausländer"; see Klaus Hartung, "Steglitzer Spiegel," *Die Zeit* 34 (August 27, 1993), section Länderspiegel, 7.
5. See Hartung, "Steglitzer Spiegel," 7.
6. [Matthias Matussek], "Die Hölle als Erlebnispark" (Hell as Theme Park), *Der Spiegel* 11 (March 15, 1993), 213–14.
7. See Sybil Milton and Ira Nowinski, *In Fitting Memory: The Art and Politics of Holocaust Memorials* (Detroit: Wayne State University Press, 1991), 10. Subsequent page citations appear parenthetically in the text.
8. "Gegen das Vergessen," *Skyline* 5 (1993): 28–29, here 28.
9. These statistics are taken from Henryk M. Broder, "Das Schoah-Business," *Der Spiegel* 16 (April 19, 1993), 248.
10. This process is also recorded in a television documentary on the Holocaust museum, "For the Living," which aired on public television on September 20, 1993.
11. See Carol Horner, " 'Make Sure We're Not Forgotten,' " *Philadelphia Inquirer* (March 28, 1993), L, 1, 8.
12. James Ingo Freed, the museum's architect, is a survivor from Germany, as is the head of the engineering company in charge of the installation, Gerhard Vogel, who left retirement to join the project.
13. This triple function is advertised in all of the museum's brochures. The description of the museum's computer equipment is taken from the flyer "Background: United States Holocaust Museum's Wexner Learning Center," available on the museum's second floor.

   At the time of my visit the museum offered two special exhibits: "The Story of Daniel," representing the life of a Jewish child during the Holocaust, and "Assignment: Rescue—The Story of Varian Fry and the Emergency Rescue Committee" in France.

14. This is an excerpt from President Jimmy Carter's statement, inscribed on one of the outer limestone walls of the Hall of Remembrance, Raoul Wallenberg Plaza.

15. Jack Kugelmass, "The Rites of the Tribe: American Jewish Tourism in Poland," in *Museums and Communities: The Politics of Public Culture*, ed. Ivan Karp, Christine Mullen Kraemer, and Steven D. Lavine (Washington, D.C.: Smithsonian Institution Press, 1992), 382–427.

16. Julius H. Schoeps, "Jüdisches Leben im Nachkriegsdeutschland: Von den Jahren des Aufbaus bis zum Ende der Teilung," *Jüdische Lebenswelten: Essays*, ed. Andreas Nachama, Julius H. Schoeps, and Edward van Voolen (Frankfurt am Main: Berliner Festspiele/Jüdischer Verlag im Suhrkamp Verlag, 1991), 358–61.

17. Jeshajahu Weinberg, "From the Director," in Michael Berenbaum, *The World Must Know: The History of the Holocaust as Told in the United States Holocaust Museum* (Boston: Little, Brown & Co., 1993), xv.

18. See the documentation *"Historikerstreit": Die Dokumentation der Kontroverse um die Einzigartigkeit der nationalsozialistischen Judenvernichtung* (Munich: Piper, 1987).

19. The history of the museum is documented in Young, *Texture of Memory*, 305–9.

20. Weinberg, "From the Director," xv.

21. See the description in Berenbaum, *The World Must Know*, 235, and Horner, " 'Make Sure We're Not Forgotten,' " 8.

22. The project of the "Encyclopedia of the Holocaust" was supervised by Israel Gutman, in cooperation with the Holocaust Memorial, Yad Vashem, Jerusalem. Its individual language editions differ and are adapted to their "national" reading public. The German edition—*Enzyklopädie des Holocaust: Die Verfolgung und Ermordung der europäischen Juden*, ed. Eberhard Jäckel, Peter Longerich, and Julius Schoeps (Berlin: Argon)—appeared in January 1993, shortly before the U.S. Holocaust museum's opening.

23. "Der Paß ist der edelste Teil von einem Menschen." Bertolt Brecht, "Über Pässe/Über die Ebenbürtigkeit von Bier und Zigarre/Über die Ordnungsliebe," in *Flüchtlingsgespräche* (Frankfurt am Main: Suhrkamp, 1967), 7.

24. Shoshana Felman, "Education and Crisis, or the Vicissitudes of Teaching," in *Testimony: Crises of Witnessing in Literature*,

75

Psychoanalysis, and History, ed. Shoshana Felman and Dori Laub (New York: Routledge, 1992), 1–56.

25. Theodor W. Adorno, "Engagement," in *Noten zur Literatur, Gesammelte Schriften* 11 (Frankfurt am Main: Suhrkamp, 1974), 422.

26. STEHEN, im Schatten
des Wundemals in der Luft.

Für-niemand-und-nichts-Stehn.
Unerkannt,
für dich
allein.

Mit allem, was darin Raum hat,
auch ohne
Sprache.

Paul Celan, *Atemwende,* in *Gedichte* II (Frankfurt am Main: Suhrkamp, 1975), p. 23. I have quoted here the translation by Michael Hamburger: Paul Celan, *Poems* (New York: Persea Books), 181.

27. Miles Lerman, undated letter mailed to potential donors, spring 1993.

28. Martin Heidegger, "Der Ursprung des Kunstwerks," in *Holzwege. Gesamtausgabe* I, 5, ed. Friedrich-Wilhelm von Herrmann (Frankfurt am Main: Vittorio Klostermann, 1977), 7–68.

29. In one of the ongoing revisions of the museum's design, Weinberg decided against the original plan of installing all exhibits at an angle, and for a straight installation of the steel beams.

30. Herbert Muschamp, "Shaping a Monument to Memory," *New York Times* (April 11, 1993), section 2, 1, 32; here 32.

31. "U.S. Holocaust Museum Challenges Literal Architectural Interpretations of History", "Design News," *Architectural Record* (May 1993): 27.

32. U.S. Code Annotated, Title 36 (Patriotic Societies and Observances), Chapter 46 (United States Holocaust Memorial Council), Section 1401. Quoted in Young, *Texture of Memory,* 335.

33. See Berenbaum, *The World Must Know,* quoted above. Young's description of the U.S. Holocaust museum was written before its opening, and before the publication of Berenbaum's book.

34. See Matussek, "Die Hölle als Erlebnispark," 207–14, quoted above. The article was published anonymously.

35. David S. Wyman, *The Abandonment of the Jews: America and the Holocaust, 1941–1945* (New York: Pantheon, 1984).

3

From Calendar Custom to National Memory: European Commonplaces

Dorothy Noyes and Roger D. Abrahams

Imagined communities, invented traditions, *lieux de mé-moire:* the burgeoning scholarship on national memory in recent years has convinced us that nations are neither primordial bodies nor constitutional arrangements, but ideological constructs wrought by intellectuals into symbolic forms that model their eternity for the benefit of the general population.[1]

How do they become commonplace, taken for granted, too sacred or too banal to bear the weight of interrogation? How do they become common places, shared realities? Reiteration does its work, to be sure, and today a national holiday like Thanksgiving, which became national only though clerical and magazine campaigns and an eventual presidential proclamation in 1863, is seen by most of us as inevitable. As much nuisance as pleasure, it is nonetheless an interruption we cannot comfortably do without: those who, from dislocation or familial disruption, fail to celebrate Thanksgiving rarely go undisturbed by its omission.

But there is a longish interval for any commemorative practice between the charm of novelty and the status of "from time immemorial." During this interval, the would-be tradition may take root and spread or lose its initial impetus and sink into desuetude. In this chapter, we argue that the most successful formulations of Euro-American national memory are those that build on preexisting local performances. American examples are many: take Thanksgiving, which, however imbued with New England unionism, resonated with local harvest celebrations in a still agricultural nation; or, more recently, the Vietnam Veterans' Memorial, designed to provide a centralizing site for vernacular practices of grave visiting and decoration.

It is never easy to explain why you deliberately eat too much or caress a name engraved in granite, experiences far more moving and memorable than the Thanksgiving sermon or the speeches on Veterans Day. A symbolic approach treating culture as text will not account for these bodily techniques of incorporation, in which memory is made material and inalienable, something that cannot be transmitted to an outsider in words. Consider George Eliot's Adam Bede, sitting in his village church in the north of England on the day of his father's burial, listening to the singing and glancing from time to time at the pink cheeks of the woman he loves in a neighboring pew:

> But Adam's thoughts of Hetty did not deafen him to the service; they rather blended with all the other deep feelings for which the church service was a channel to him this afternoon, as a certain consciousness of our entire past and our imagined future blends itself with all our moments of keen sensibility. And to Adam the church service was the best channel he could have found for his mingled regret, yearning, and resignation: its interchange of beseeching cries for help, with outbursts of faith and praise—its recurrent responses and the familiar rhythm of its collects, seemed to speak for him as no other form of worship could have done; as, to those early Christians who had worshipped form their childhood upward in catacombs, the torchlight and shadows must have seemed nearer the Divine presence than the heathenish daylight of the streets. The secret of our emotions never lies in the bare object, but in its subtle relations to our own past: no wonder the secret escapes the unsympathising observer, who might as well put on spectacles to discern odours.[2]

We see here community and synchronicity emerging from synesthesia: a coherence attained in the body rather than articulable in language or logic. The individual's experience of tradition is laminated and complex: it cannot be reduced to language, but rather builds toward it.

By extension, this essay proposes a four-stage model for

the transition of communal memory from local practice to the more highly theorized invented traditions of the state. While these stages vary in their degrees of systematicity, susceptibility to entextualization,[3] and accommodation to hegemonic ideologies, we find conscious agency in each of them and do not see the common people as purely reactive to the more deliberate constructions of the powerful. Rather, memory comes up from the very bottom of the body social. Following recent interpretations, we understand hegemony as a two-way street[4]: The nation wins the mass support it requires by convincingly resonating with local *Heimatgefühl,* as Hans Kohn long ago pointed out.[5] We take most of our examples from Catalonia, whose small size offers unusually rapid transitions and visible links between the local and the national. But we hope that our framework will encourage broader explorations of the cultural influence exerted by the periphery on the center and the lower classes on the upper.

Central to our exploration is the notion of calendar custom. This body of observances repeated from year to year on a given date in a given place constitutes a specific form of European collective memory: memory *of* the collective. Calendar customs are powerful sensory experiences undergone in common, consensual in both the usual sense and the etymological one: felt together.[6] It is this experience in common that creates in important ways the European idea of community—a bounded group of people connected over time to a bounded place—and that therefore lies at the foundation of attempts to foster popular identification with larger collectivities such as the nation-state.

Customary Memory

The first level of community memory might be called customary or occasional memory. It is the mindfulness of the body, the incorporation of past experience in forceful ways that both allow the body to reproduce it and call the conscious mind to a realm of feeling usually left unarticulated. It differs from the everyday bodily habitus in being bound to an occasion, to Custom with a capital *C*, the calendar customs beloved by the early survivalist folklorists. And it differs in the object it creates: While everyday disciplines of the body create the reality of social categories in the individual—class, gender, race—the calendar custom creates the collectivity as an objective entity that can be remembered. The characteristic elements of calendar observances—noise and crowding, music and dancing, masking, eating and drinking, physical risk-taking, and the demarcation of community space—work powerfully on the bodies of participants and, furthermore, impose participation on all present. Unified in practice, the community creates a unity in feeling.

Calendar custom often provides founding memories for the individual as a cultural being. In Berga, Catalonia, a Corpus Christi festival called the Patum has since the early seventeenth century furnished a unifying motive and nearly the only stable point of reference for an often bitterly divided body politic, one that has been subject to major political upheavals almost once a generation in a four-hundred-year period. The built environment of the city has been burned down repeatedly, in the War of the Reapers, the War of Spanish Succession, the Napoleonic invasions, the Carlist wars, and the Spanish Civil War; the central space in which the Patum is celebrated was long known as the Plaça Cremada, the Burned Square. The population feels itself to be diverse, and no common historical identification—religious, class-based, ideological, ethnic, or linguistic—can be ascribed to all the members of the community. One of the few things all Berguedans have in common, diachronically or synchronically, is the Patum, which annually renews the community in an explosion of noise and fire locally understood as all the crises of the life cycle in one: generation, death, and rebirth.

Berguedan children learn the Patum in the same way American children are taught to recognize and imitate animal noises: where the American child learns the categories of nature and culture through toys of farmyard animals he or she may never see in reality, the Berguedan child learns the categories of self and other—really self and deeper selves—though the dancing effigies of the Patum, some awe-inspiring, some approachable, others violent. Parents lift their babies to touch the hand of the Black Giant, help a child just learning to walk to dance the dwarves as they hum the music, or give a two-year-old a burning stick with which to chase the neighbors in the guise of the festival's flaming mule.

80

As children grow up inside the Patum, getting annually closer and closer to its dangerous center of fire and motion, they take in its rhythms and gestures with less conscious effort. "We carry the Patum in our blood," say Berguedans, but they are alluding to practice rather than inheritance. Through the eyes, the skin, the mouth, the feet, they assimilate its elements. In the five days of the Patum, as the dances are repeated, participants have less and less sleep every night and more and more to drink every day, as the festival masters the body. On Monday morning, the Berguedan at last can go to bed, but the vertigo will not let her rest: the drum's "Pa-tum," now in a kind of syncopation with her heartbeat, will jerk her out of sleep for the next week at least.

So memorably incorporated, the Patum emerges from Berguedan bodies on a wide range of joyful occasions: after a victory by the Barcelona football team, or when a group of Berguedans in exile reunite. "The Patum of the Poor," as this spontaneous Patum is called, has been danced in Barcelona, Oviedo, Paris, Amsterdam, a British summer language camp, an army installation in North Africa, and, we are told, Franco's prison camps after the civil war.

The Patum is anticipated annually not as a unique performance (as we folklorists have preferred to view our data in recent years), but as a congeries of familiar sensations, relived with nostalgia. Days are counted to the first beat of the drum announcing the festival, to the testing of the firecrackers that will bring the first whiff of Patum. The maternal symbolism used to describe the Patum—the suckling of mother's milk, a return to the womb—expresses both the comfort Berguedans find in the festival and the sadness that edges their joy: their yearning will not long be satisfied, for the festival will end and cast them out again.

On the first day of the Patum in 1989, on the Wednesday when the giants come out at noon to parade though the streets of Berga, Dorothy Noyes followed the celebration in the company of Ritxi, the director of the municipal music school who was born in the working-class heart of the old city. When the carriers paused for a rest, they also stopped for a drink, and Ritxi's smile turned melancholy. "Look at them," he said, waving his glass out the door to the four giants lined up in the street. "Aren't they beautiful? You know, I've seen them come out every year of my life. And they're always the same, always beautiful. You and I grow old; I'm getting bald"—he patted his head ruefully. "They never change."

This sense of dissonance between the reproduction of the festival and the loss and change of everyday life is not unique to Berga. It is most acute in cases of violent dislocation: "How shall we sing the Lord's song in a strange land?" But gradual changes, though less anguished, may be more disconcerting. C. P. Cavafy made this the subject of his lyric "The Poseidonians," taking an epigraph from Athenaios:

> [We behave like] the Poseidonians in the Tyrrhenian Gulf, who although of Greek origin, became barbarized as Tyrrhenians or Romans and changed their speech and the customs of their ancestors. But they observe one Greek festival even to this day; during this they gather together and call up from memory their ancient names and customs, and then, lamenting loudly to each other and weeping, they go away.[7]

Closer to home, we may consider how the 1994 Winter Olympics in Lillehammer became an occasion to contemplate and mourn the fate of Sarajevo, site of the games ten years earlier. The event was the same; even many of the athletes participating were the same. But the context had changed irrevocably: Where had all the flowers gone?

The eternal return of the festival brings the passing of time into focus, for the time of calendar custom is out of phase with everyday time. Of course the festival is not immobile; it is affected by the changes taking place in everyday time as well as by more deliberate alterations and reforms. Still, in addition to the festival's status as "tradition," which stresses the necessity of continuity and exact reproduction, there is the fact that it is practiced only a few days a year, compared to the three hundred and sixty-five in which we dress and cook, for example. Consumer economies with their constant novelties accentuate the gap between the two cycles of reproduction.

The extreme dissonance between cycles may be seen in the Mediterranean votive festivals that are celebrated at ten-year intervals, or sometimes even less frequently. In Berga, the 1916 canonical coronation of the Mare de Déu de Queralt, the local Madonna image, has been followed by commemorations at twenty-five-year intervals. The coronation took place under a conservative Catholic local regime and was attended

3.1 Courtesy of Luigi, Berga.

by a Spanish Infanta; very much under clerical and official control, the celebration was dominated by processions and masses, and the popular contribution consisted of the most submissive forms of folk religion—the erection of altars in the street, sayings of the rosary, and so forth.

The twenty-fifth anniversary took place in 1941; two years after the defeat of the Spanish Republic in 1939 and in the midst of still ferocious reprisals, it blended the national Catholicism of the Franco regime with aggressive military display. In 1966, for the fiftieth anniversary, the military elements were downplayed, but the processions and altars—now definitely anachronistic—continued to center the celebration. In 1991, for the first anniversary celebrated under democracy, the municipal government and the people had no model for the occasion except the old Catholic one from 1916, 1941, and 1966. The continuing community devotion to the Mother of God—closely identified with the mountains behind the city, where her image was said to have been discovered—was by then habitually exercised in picnic-pilgrimages and the exploration of the landscape rather than in rosary-saying and altar-building. Even the practicing Catholics of the community had

83

been largely socialized out of these old-fashioned devotions by a clergy schooled under the Second Vatican Council. So the processions, the altars, and the banners over the streets reading "Salve Maria" looked wholly out of place in contemporary Berga.

The intense degree of popular participation in these now unfamiliar practices astonished the clergy, the municipality, and the people themselves. Some Berguedans attempted to explain the strange behavior by attributing it to the Andalusian immigrants, considered to be a few generations behind the Catalans in the attainment of modernity.[8] Indeed, the decorations of the immigrant quarter were exuberant, but for once they were in harmony with the rest of the city. What amazed the more self-aware among the natives was their own unsuspected ability to reproduce an anterior situation, the degree to which the Francoist past could rise within them and take shape again. The most progressive and secular-minded members of the community were profoundly disturbed. "It's 1940 all over again!" fumed one woman who, in the face of Berga's backwardness, had long since moved to Barcelona. Dorothy Noyes came upon her raging through the garlanded streets; ignoring her parents' pleas, she returned to the metropolis that same evening.

Rarely is the experience of time out of phase brought so fully to consciousness. But the relative stability of calendar custom does provide a locus from which to examine change. Conversely, the conservatism of custom is not merely claimed at the discursive level: intensely lived custom plays a role in the actual conservation of practices.

Practical Traditionalizing

The discourse of memory is, of course, more easily grasped by outsiders than is bodily memory, and this discourse has hitherto been the focus of scholarly attention to community memory and traditionalizing practices. Such groups as the Occitan school of ethnohistorians[9] and American scholars in the ethnography-of-speaking tradition[10] have provided rich accounts of the construction of "bygone days" in conversation. The use of landscape as mnemonic and the construction of sites of memory have also been richly mined

84

since Halbwachs's account of the Holy Land.[11] Other folklorists have observed these community inscriptions of the past in material culture.[12] We would like to note a fourth arena of this second level of memory—what we call "practical traditionalizing"—in the manipulation and reshaping of custom.

We use *practical* because the inscription of the past in narrative, art, or custom is not merely a way to pass the time or even to give satisfying aesthetic shape to identity. Rather, as all these scholars have learned from their local teachers, the consensual account of the community past becomes the interpretive authority for present actions and events. These native metacommentaries are practical not only as they are imbricated in community practice, but as they respond strongly to contemporary problems and pressures: they are strategically engaged in the defense of local community.

Such practical traditionalizing seems to have reshaped a wide variety of collective activities in Europe with the introduction of a market economy and the consequent transformation of community relations. When the reproduction of the community as a relatively stable set of arrangements regarding the distribution of resources and responsibilities in a given place became unsettled, those arrangements were brought to the fore and defended as "custom": practiced "since time immemorial" (that is, since before the memory of the oldest inhabitant), practiced commonly in the present, and specific to the place.

This is the first stage, elaborated most fully by E. P. Thompson in regard to seventeenth- and eighteenth-century England.[13] The transition to industrial capitalism entailed the redefinition of property not as specific rights to certain exploitations of communal resources, but as the absolute possession of enclosed land. The relationship of elites to plebeians was redefined not as a multistranded personal bond, echoing the sacred order of the universe as a single hierarchical body under God, but as a simple contractual exchange of wages for labor, with no further commitment on either side. Time itself was redefined from a collective rhythm structuring common activities to a succession of homogeneous units of value with no autonomous meaning.

These attempted redefinitions did not go uncontested: the innumerable bread riots, "Saint Mondays," and invasions of enclosed land in the early modern period testify to the slow pace by which the new order imposed itself. In these protests came the link of calendar custom and customary law—the language of communal festivities and the claims to common rights. Maskers who normally emerged from the collective memory only on holidays came out to speak for the community in enclosure riots and house attacks; the customary distribution of food to the poor on holidays was cited as evidence for the elite's acknowledgment of the people's right to bread; and the old calendar rose up against the commoditization of time in the work place.[14] Not all plebeian invocations of calendar custom in these struggles were threatening or carnivalesque: many revived old ceremonies of respect. While accepting the terms of paternalism and their base position in the hierarchy, the lower class here called on the upper to abide by its own rules—to live up to its own promise;[15] it offered deference and social tranquillity in exchange for material concessions. The invocation of the past as custom became as powerful a tool as the threat of present disorder in the struggle of the lower class to preserve its prerogatives. And custom became increasingly the province of the lower class.

Further on in the nineteenth century, with the more complete entry of local communities into large market economies, and with the increasing mobility of the landless labor force, we find a wide variety of popular manipulations of custom in the creation, defense, and marketing of local identity. Practices were increasingly defined by their practitioners (and not simply by the observing elites) as common, local, and/or ancient. Utz Jeggle and Gottfried Korff describe how itinerant peddlers from the Zillertal in Austria enhanced the attractions of herbal oils and, later, imitation chamois gloves with picturesque accounts of their beautiful valley and its quaint customs, creating in narrative and song the authenticity lacking in the product itself.[16] Tamás Hofer and others explain the localism of costume and various popular arts in nineteenth-century Europe not as the survival of age-old village particularisms holding on against homogenizing influences but, on the contrary, as an innovation responding to increasing contact with metropolitan, exotic, and neighboring others.[17] Rather than copying metropolitan models, newly prosperous rural communities developed local ones intended both to valorize difference and advertise uniqueness.

Calendar customs also responded to social change with increasing self-consciousness and elaboration. Martin Lovelace suggests that the texts of the British mummers' plays, long assumed by folklorists to be the degeneration of pre-Christian or medieval forms, were in fact a latter-day development of a simpler, luck-visiting custom, created as a showy performance that would elicit generous donations from the gentry.[18] Anthony Green musters impressive evidence to situate the northern English mummers' play not among the peasantry, but among nineteenth-century rural proletariats and industrial working classes in the towns.[19] Again, the play was probably an intensification of a preexisting custom of more gestural luck-visiting. The text of such plays as that of the Antrobus Soulcakers may be seen to describe the conflicts of the nineteenth-century community, with its many marginal characters: the old soldier, the tramp, the idiot, the widow. The play integrates these threatening persons into the community, not least the mysterious Wild Horse effigy, which becomes "a metaphor of the tradition."[20] Contemporary players define the importance of the horse by its great age and the general significance of the mumming by its transmission from generation to generation: it has become "a small community's self-definition" and its perpetuation. Folklorists did not discover the mummer's play in the nineteenth century because nationalist or evolutionist ideology told them to go out and look for relics of the past: rather, the folk themselves pointed up the importance of the custom's continuity in a time of community disruption by devoting additional intellectual and material resources to it, and this enhancement caught the attention of the elite.

With the expansion of a consumer economy, the twentieth century sees a continuation in Europe of this "aesthetic compensation for economic backwardness."[21] As the old acquires scarcity value, community practices are increasingly reified as ancient, unchanged, authentic. Their consequent rise in value is evident, negotiable not only as tourist attraction but as "a culture," the possession of which confers the dignity of an identity as bounded entity.[22] But, as Bendix among others has discovered,[23] the display value of "tradition" is not all that is at stake: putting on shows for the tourists creates involvement and interaction among the participants, making more viable the continuity of a community that may be much threatened by economic and social change. Indeed, the practice of the tradition may become so satisfying in itself that the tourists are resented as superfluous, and the tradition itself becomes sufficient reason for staying in the community.

This development took place in the Patum of Berga, as in many other European festivals. The festival was given increasing economic support by the municipality since the 1880s as a way of encouraging summer tourism, and it was also given astonishing freedom under the Franco regime, in the hope that this state accommodation to local tradition would be met with equal local accommodation to state control in larger matters.

In fact, the Patum became the focus of implicit, then explicit, resistance to the Franco regime: the one occasion on which public refusal of the official definition of the situation was possible. The rigidly hierarchical social body originally defined by the church in the Corpus Christi procession had become a model for the Franco regime, which made frequent use of Eucharistic imagery and appropriated visual and gestural aspects of the procession in outdoor masses, military parades, youth groups, and numerous everyday rituals of social control. In Berga, the population attacked this distorted reproduction of the body social at the source by intensifying and sacralizing the disorderly Patum that countered the procession. Direct participation in the Patum had been the province of lower-class males before upper-class and female spectators. Now the whole population swarmed in the *plaça*, and the Patum grew longer to accommodate the public's desire to dance in the streets, filling five days with almost no intervals for sleep. The crowned eagle and the elegant giants of the dances yielded their place in popular emphasis to the makers of chaos, the fire and smoke of the dancing mule-dragon and the devils. The mule pushed its way into the Guardia Civil barracks and burned Spanish flags "by accident"; many of its carriers became radical independentists. The devils simply multiplied, from twelve to eighty or ninety at a time. By the 1960s, so many people wanted to be devils that the city had to find a place for them to be dressed—formerly something that happened in the *plaça* before the eyes of the public.

This instrumental problem, resolved by the councillors in assigning an empty space beneath City Hall to the dressers, was soon elaborated by Berguedans into "a whole ritual," an "initiation" into full Berguedan identity. Now the would-be devil must descend a long stair behind the *plaça* to the bottom of City Hall, pass a half-door over which a shadowy old man peers and grants—or refuses—entry, feel her way in the dark along a narrow corridor, then fall into an open space covered with *vidalba,* the clematis vine from the mountains above town that is wrapped around the devil's head to shield her from the falling sparks. "Red- and green-smocked figures among the vines, the 'dressers,'" pull her into a heavy costume, force her to kneel, push the mask over her head, tie slow-burning firecrackers on her horns and tail, tug and tie the vines around her—beetles crawling down her back and snails up her devil's horns—and deliver her, almost blinded, swaddled like a baby or wound like a corpse, to an "accompanist," who leads her back to the *plaça.* There she and seventy or eighty like her are set alight, the crowd pressing among them to receive the marks of the falling fire, to hop from foot to foot around the *plaça* until everything has exploded. The lights go back up; they pull off her mask to let her breathe; she gasps and sees again, as the smoke clears, the church, City Hall, her friends, the world.

This, the Berguedans say, is the descent into hell and the subsequent resurrection; this is the darkness of the womb and the violence of expulsion—but also the release of orgasm. This dark place is the Cove of Can Maurí in the mountains where the Moors first fought the Berguedans and whence the Patum's mule and leafy devils are said to have emerged. For this experience they stay in Berga; they cultivate the friendship of the twenty old men—miners and truck drivers, many of them— who control access to the costumes, bringing them brandy on their saint's days and, it is said, doing them occasionally more substantial favors for the privilege of being a devil. Some people are able to do it every year, but everyone is supposed to do it at least once, and the whole crowd "accompanies," dancing through the trails of sparks. This collective regression to the womb of the community, to the primeval Berga that preceded all their present quarrels, is the experience of perfect oneness that can be attained nowhere else—that gave the community the strength to fight for democracy in the sixties and seventies and that today makes it worth resisting the better jobs and more varied pleasures of Barcelona. Self-evidently, this is the oldest part of the Patum, its invention in living memory notwithstanding—and here we see how practical traditionalizing works off of the body's customary memory, making it more explicit and controlled. The Patum is old because it feels old: it is deep in the community and the landscape because it is deep in the body, lived as much in the guts and the genitals as in the eyes and ears. It is also biographically deep, recalling earliest childhood and the first consciousness of bonded and separate identities. The changes in the Plens, as the devils are called—it means "the full ones"— became the occasion for a metacommentary on and an experiential encapsulation of the community descent into the Patum and the necessary reemergence into contemporary life.

Should it be said again? This and many other "folklorisms," as the Germans call them[24]—deliberate elaborations and reforms of customary practice—are not in the least imposed from above by a more self-conscious elite aware of dimensions in the metropolis. They are the strategies of local actors in response to changing circumstances. They do not destroy the authenticity of the practice, as earlier folklorists maintained, but create it, asserting the community's wholeness and its continued agency against external threats to both. Using the language of origins, they make an argument for persistence into the future.

Ideological Traditionalizing

Practical traditionalizing frequently provokes an elite epiphenomenon, a translation of community metacommentaries into hegemonic terms, which we call "ideological traditionalizing." Although the "traditional intellectuals," as Gramsci called them[25]—the teachers, notaries, clergy, and so on— receive their training in the metropolis and represent the metropolis to the people, it should not be surprising to find them in fact often making common cause with their communities of origin. In the first place, in provincial communities the resources of elites are often less than their positions would ideally command: they have neither sufficient force nor sufficient capital to impose themselves entirely on their inferiors. Rather, the fortunes of a provincial professional class ride largely on the fortunes—and the goodwill—of the common people. Second, the political capital of provincial professionals with metropolitan ambitions is their ability to represent—to speak for and interpret—their localities.[26] They are in fact often better equipped to bring the periphery to the center than to do the reverse.[27]

Local custom can be an important part of their capital. A community such as Berga has little claim to national attention or support in its population, its architecture, its notable citizens, or its natural resources; rather, its recognition comes from its ability to embody the national past. "The town has nothing in particular to distinguish it from others," wrote the municipal councillors of 1789 in response to a royal questionnaire, "except for the festival."[28]

What the festival meant, of course, depended greatly on who was asking. The Patum's central opposition of figures of order and figures of chaos in a series of combats with no clear outcomes has been understood primarily in class terms in local metacommentaries for as long as we can trace—back to the early seventeenth century. In the hands of elite interpreters, the Patum became variously an allegory of the victory of Christians over Muslims, orthodoxy over heresy, spirit over animal nature, Spain over France, Carlists over Liberals and vice versa, Catalonia over Spain, the people over their feudal lords, true Spain against infidel Reds, democrats against Franco, and doubtless other sets of antagonists. Narratives of origin situated the roots of the festival in whatever epoch and social context was used to legitimate the present order. The conservative romantic nationalists of the 1890s declared the Patum a late-fourteenth-century institution of the Berguedan elite as a homage to the Catalan king of Aragón, a kind of elaborated tournament; one went so far as to fabricate a document to prove this.[29] Thus the Patum came to birth under Catalan autonomy, in the chivalric aristocratic realm so beloved of the nineteenth-century Renaixença. Catholic interpreters saw the festival emerge as a spontaneous popular homage to the sacrament out of the medieval Corpus Christi festival. For the Hispanicizers of the early Franco regime, the Patum was a simple *auto sacramental*, part of a larger Spanish tradition of devotional drama. For the consensus-building democratic nationalists of the 1970s—who drew their conclusions from the devils—the festival emerged from pre-Christian fertility and fire rituals: it was thus inalienably popular and inalienably of

91

the place, antedating any particular political label. With the exception of the Francoists, all these groups tended to posit the Patum's uniqueness, conveniently ignoring a plethora of mules, giants, and devils to be found in neighboring Catalan festivals.

The Invention of Tradition

It is in these ideological traditionalizings, inscribed in appropriate genres such as police reports, sermons, magazine articles, tourist brochures, memoirs, and local histories,[30] that local memories reach the center. They reassure the center of the periphery's submission to hegemonic definitions; sometimes they even win the center's support and validation, in the form of special permissions, declarations of historical importance, subventions, or simply tourists. At the same time, they provide the center with a vocabulary with which to speak to the periphery. "Customs" or "traditions" can be invented, following preexistent local models, and returned to the periphery as an integrating device.[31] The success of these invented traditions depends on the sensitivity of elite readings. Some invented traditions, articulating closely with local practice, are embraced and maintained—on occasion even after the center would prefer they be discontinued. Others, such as the Francoist appropriation of the most hieratic aspects of the Corpus Christi procession, receive public acquiescence, are ignored or mocked in private, and cease to be practiced when the center turns its eye elsewhere.

Local traditions move laterally with the encounters of marketplace, labor migration, pilgrimage, and courtship. But they spread faster and more widely when mediated by the center. The national and nationalist ceremonial often assembles signs of the local to mark its scope, as did Ludwig I of Bavaria when his officials sought marriageable couples in local costume from each Bavarian province to participate in the royal wedding of his heir. Some regions went well prepared with costume; others had to invent one in response to the royal imperative: thereafter, all had an official local costume to employ on such occasions of display.[32] Similarly, the nationalist organizers of the 1902 Festes de la Mercè in Barcelona invited towns from all over Catalonia to contribute their giants to the festival and place them in competition with each other. Giants thereafter became recognized emblems of the local, and those municipalities lacking them hastened to create them.

"National" dances are often local dances that know how to advertise. The "Catalan" *sardana*, a round dance with complex timing, was the festival dance of the Empordà and other northeastern counties in the early nineteenth century. In the second half of the century, the Renaixença writers of that region celebrated the *sardana* in novel, poem, and essay as an innocent communitarian entertainment (as distinct from the lascivious waltz, for example) and as an emblem of unity with its ever-expanding ring. The musician Pep Ventura reformed and regularized the *sardana cobla* (orchestra); composers such as Enric Morera devoted themselves to producing new *sardanes*, often named after localities of the Empordà, and these *cobles* with their new *sardanes* began to travel to Barcelona and to the *festes majors* of towns without *cobles*. Local composers in *sardana*-less towns then began to respond to the need, and town bands converted themselves into *cobles*. The *sardana* acquired such a presence as to be called national. Now the poets of Barcelona began to write nationalist lyrics for sung *sardanes*; now treatises were written, societies formed, monuments erected, and new rules created. Most important among the rules was the obligation to open the ring of dancers to anyone wishing to enter, emblematic of the achieved character of national identity in a region economically dependent on immigration.[33]

Under the Franco regime, the *sardana* became a sign of nationalist resistance, acknowledged as such even by southern and western Catalans. Its pacific and "folkloric" character kept it from being outlawed entirely. Later, with more aggressive resistance to the regime, the flaming mules and devils of the Patum of Berga and a few other festivals entered nationalist allegory; their music was appropriated by Catalan rock groups; and fire in the less violent form of bonfires and traveling torches became the key symbol of the new "national" festival of St. John's Eve. After the lifting of restrictions with the restoration of democracy, devils and mules were "recovered" in Barcelona and in towns throughout the country; local ethnologists scoured the archives for early references which, if not found, were posited or invented.

A still newer "national" symbol derived from calendar custom is the *castell,* or human tower, found in a few towns in south-central Catalonia. Emigrants from these towns created new groups in other towns; television and tourism added to the interest in the original groups. Young people found the towers, with the crowding and danger of their erection, more exciting than the *sardanes.* Groups multiplied and are now well-established in the Barcelona region and moving north. Just as the *sardana* was seen as an emblem of Catalan voluntarism, order, inclusiveness, and business sense (given the metrical calculations necessary to its correct performance), so the *castell* was celebrated as embodying the nation's spirit of collaboration, youthful dynamism, and vocation for architectural design.

Sardana, devils, and *castells* all took part in the long-negotiated opening and closing ceremonies of the 1992 Summer Olympic games in Barcelona. Interlocked *sardanistes* formed the Olympic rings; the *castells* demonstrated native athleticism; and devils and fireworks closed the games, along with a not-yet national emblem, the Catalan-Cuban-gypsy-Andalusian rock 'n' roll rumba of Barcelona. Socialist politicians, whose voters reside primarily in the industrial districts of Barcelona and its province, have tried to construct this local memory of immigration and hybridization as a national tradition: Catalonia as "terra de pas," interstitial, cosmopolitan, Mediterreanean, founded on the *mestissatge* of Frankish immigrants with a local population already composed of indigenous tribes and Phoenician, Greek, Roman, and Arab invaders.

All these customs have become nationally available, aided by the mass media and improved roads as well as by the charismatic historical moment of the transition to democracy. While their local origins still give them different weight in the counties, their resonances are becoming as ideological as they are geographic among the youngest generation: all are Catalan, but they construct different Catalonias.

Catalonia does not lack invented traditions of metropolitan, elite origins: the Floral Games created in the late nineteenth century on the model of Toulouse are a notable example. But these poetic competitions, which persist in Barcelona (in rather ossified form, as many professional poets complain) and also at the local level—sponsored by schools, Catholic shrines, and municipalities—do not call forth the mass participation or induce the ineffable but indisputable sensation of recognition, of belonging, of permanence that is created in collective bodily performance repeated from year to year.

This four-stage process of exchange between the local and the national may be short-circuited with the increasing circulation of media and populations, especially in times of popular political mobilization. In the transition to democracy in Catalonia, the most basic forms of movement and melody, derived from local festival and ultimately from children's taunts (perhaps the first arena for the formation of collective self and other) entered directly into collective events defined as national: matches of the Barcelona Football club, concerts of Catalan New Song, and political demonstrations. Participants from throughout Catalonia attended these events, bringing their forms of the local with them. When messages of national revolt were appended to tunes and gestures calling up the first memories of community, they were more easily performed but, more importantly, more deeply felt. Potentially controversial details of the message could be postponed or ignored in the enjoyment of physical unity, a sensation frequently denied by the regime's controls on public assembly and made the more powerful by the size of the new community that was brought together, with its old, long-unspoken name: Catalonia.

This successful linkage of old memories of attachment to new possibilities of enlargement, effected without elite mediation by the physical assembly of the nation in the streets of Barcelona, made Catalonia an emotional reality. In turn, it may be argued that this charismatic memory ultimately made Catalonia a constitutional reality in 1979. Without the popular pressure visibly exerted in the streets, which multiplied as participants sought over and over to renew the sensation of strength in unity, the Catalanist negotiators in Madrid would have had little leverage. Calendar custom has long been a channel through which the vox populi can make itself known to the authorities. Mobilized and carried to the center, the materiality of the memory it both transmits and creates gives the nation the reality in individual feelings that ensures its success as a political project.

Notes

Dorothy Noyes would like to thank the National Endowment for the Humanities for a Summer Stipend in 1995 supporting her fieldwork in Catalonia.

1. See Benedict Anderson, *Imagined Communities: Reflections on the Origin and Spread of Nationalism*, 2d ed. (London: Verso, 1991); Eric Hobsbawm and Terence Ranger, eds., *The Invention of Tradition* (Cambridge: Cambridge University Press, 1983); Pierre Nora, ed., *Realms of Memory: Rethinking the French Past*, trans. Arthur Goldmann (New York: Columbia University Press, 1996).

2. George Eliot, *Adam Bede* (New York: Rinehart, 1948 [1859]), 202–3.

3. Cf. Richard Bauman and Charles L. Briggs, "Poetics and Performance as Critical Perspectives on Language and Social Life," *Annual Review of Anthropology* 19 (1990): 59–88.

4. See E. P. Thompson, *Customs in Common: Studies in Traditional Popular Culture* (New York: Free Press, 1993). Also see James C. Scott, *Domination and the Arts of Resistance: Hidden Transcripts* (New Haven, Conn.: Yale University Press, 1990).

5. Hans Kohn, *The Idea of Nationalism: A Study in Its Origins and Background* (New York: Macmillan, 1944).

6. James Fernandez, "'Isn't There Anything Out There That We Can All Believe In?' The Quest for Cultural Consensus in Anthropology and History," paper read at the Institute for Advanced Study School of Social Science, Princeton, N.J., December 15, 1988.

7. C. P. Cavafy, *Collected Poems*, trans. E. Keeley and P. Sherrard (Princeton, N.J.: Princeton University Press, 1975), 181.

8. Cf. Johannes Fabian, *Time and the Other: How Anthropology Makes Its Object* (New York: Columbia University Press, 1983).

9. See Jean-Claude Bouvier, ed., *Tradition orale et identité culturelle* (Paris: CNRS, 1980), for the programmatic texts; James Fentress and Chris Wickham, *Social Memory* (Oxford: Basil Blackwell, 1992), provides some English-language summary.

10. See Samuel Schrager, "What Is Social in Oral History?" *International Journal of Oral History* 4 (1983): 76–98; Charles Briggs, *Competence in Performance: The Creativity of Tradition in Mexicano Folk Art* (Philadelphia: University of Pennsylvania Press, 1988); Kathleen Stewart, *A Space on the Side of the Road* (Princeton, N.J.: Princeton University Press, 1996).

11. Maurice Halbwachs, *La Topographie légendaire des Evangiles*

en Terre Sainte (Paris, 1939). Also see Henry Glassie, *Passing the Time in Ballymenone* (Philadelphia: University of Pennsylvania Press, 1982); Mary Hufford, *Chaseworld: Foxhunting and Storytelling in New Jersey's Pine Barrens* (Philadelphia: University of Pennsylvania Press, 1992); Kent C. Ryden, *Mapping the Invisible Landscape: Folklore, Writing, and the Sense of Place* (Iowa City: University of Iowa Press, 1993).

12. See Mary Hufford, Marjorie Hunt, and Steven J. Zeitlin, *The Grand Generation: Memory, Mastery, Legacy* (Seattle and Washington, D.C.: SITES and University of Washington Press, 1987). Also see Barbara Kirshenblatt-Gimblett, "Objects of Memory: Material Culture as Life Review," in *Folk Groups and Folklore Genres: A Reader,* ed. E. Oring (Logan: Utah State University Press, 1989), 329–38.

13. Thompson, *Customs in Common,* passim.

14. For the customary form of these revolts, see also Dorothy Noyes, ed., "Façade Performances: Public Face, Private Mask," *Southern Folklore* special issue (1995).

15. Scott, *Domination and the Arts of Resistance,* passim.

16. Utz Jeggle and Gottfried Korff, "On the Development of the Zillertal Regional Character: A Contribution to Cultural Economics," in *German Volkskunde,* ed. J. R. Dow and H. Lixfeld (Bloomington: Indiana University Press, 1986), 124–39.

17. Tamás Hofer, "Changes in the Style of Folk Art and Various Branches of Folklore in Hungary During the 19th Century—An Interpretation," *Acta Ethnographica* 29 (1980): 149–65. Also see Tamás Hofer, "The Perception of Tradition in European Ethnography," *Journal of the Folklore Institute* 21 (1984): 133–47.

18. Martin Lovelace, "Christmas Mumming in England: The House-Visit," in *Folklore Studies in Honor of Herbert Halpert,* ed. K. Goldstein and N. Rosenberg (St. John's: Memorial University of Newfoundland, 1980), 271–81.

19. Anthony Green, "Popular Drama and the Mummers' Play," in *Performance and Politics in Popular Drama,* ed. D. Bradby, L. James, and B. Sharratt (Cambridge: Cambridge University Press, 1980), 139–66.

20. Green, "Popular Drama," 158.

21. Jeggle and Korff, "Zillertal Regional Character," passim.

22. Richard Handler and Jocelyn Linnekin, "Tradition, Genuine or Spurious," *Journal of American Folklore* 97 (1984): 273–90. Also see Richard Handler, *Nationalism and the Politics of Culture in Quebec* (Madison: University of Wisconsin Press, 1988).

23. Regina Bendix, "Tourism and Cultural Displays: Inventing Tra-

ditions for Whom?" *Journal of American Folklore* 102 (1989): 131–46.

24. Hermann Bausinger, "Toward a Critique of Folklorism Criticism," in *German Volkskunde,* ed. Dow and Lixfeld, 113–23. Also see Regina Bendix, "Folklorismus: The Challenge of a Concept," *International Folklore Review* 6 (1989): 5–15.

25. Cf. Fentress and Wickham, *Social Memory,* 103.

26. Cf. Pierre Bourdieu, *Language and Symbolic Power* (Cambridge, Mass.: Harvard University Press, 1991).

27. Provincial elites are never the sole brokers, of course, much as they may struggle to be; but urban migration and the advent of mass and interactive media render them largely superfluous in this role of mediator.

28. Dorothy Noyes, "The Mule and the Giants: Struggling for the Body Social in a Catalan Festival Drama," Ph.D. diss., University of Pennsylvania, 1992, 343.

29. Noyes, "The Mule and the Giants," 221–26.

30. Cf. the "autoethnographies" of John Dorst, *The Written Suburb* (Philadelphia: University of Pennsylvania Press, 1989).

31. Cf. Edward Shils, *Tradition* (Chicago: University of Chicago Press, 1981).

32. Regina Bendix, "Moral Integrity in Costumed Identity: Negotiating 'National Costume' in 19th Century Bavaria," unpublished ms., 1997.

33. For an account of the *sardana* as invented tradition, see Stanley Brandes, "The Sardana: Catalan Dance and Catalan National Identity," *Journal of American Folklore* 103 (1990): 24–41.

4

Sites of Memory: Discourses of the Past in Israeli Pioneering Settlement Museums

Tamar Katriel

Heritage museums have become a pervasive feature of the cultural landscapes of contemporary Western societies. Recognizing their emergence as increasingly important arenas for cultural production and ideological assertion, scholars have directed considerable scholarly attention in recent years to the examination of the role of the "heritage industry" in the context of nationalism and touristic practices.[1] As Dean MacCannell has argued, museums and historical sites serve to anchor the "secular pilgrimages" undertaken by modern tourist-pilgrims.[2] Through a process of "sight sacralization,"[3] museums and sites thus become cultural enclaves whose aura of timeless stability stands in sharp contrast to a world marked by an ethos of change and the "acceleration of history."[4]

Despite the enormous thematic and presentational variations found among heritage museums in different countries and regions of the world, they all share some basic features in their orientation toward a collective past. It is to the exploration of this shared orientation that this chapter is devoted. The main conceptual point to be explored relates to an analytic distinction elaborated by historians in recent years between what they see as two fundamentally opposed orientations to the past: The first is a "memory orientation," which involves the invocation of the past through ritualized actions designed to create an atemporal sense of the presence of the past in the present—in other words, the past mythologized. The second is a "historical orientation," which involves a reflective exploration of past events considered along an axis of irreversible, linear temporality, with a view to understanding their situated particularity, their causes and consequences. Historians Natalie Zemon Davis and Randolph Starn summarize the difference between these two orientations: "Against memory's delight in similarity, appeal to the emotions, and arbitrary selectivity, history would stand for critical distance and documented explanation."[5]

A closer look at actual history-making practices, however, suggests that the analytic categories of "history" and "memory" can be viewed as dialectically related: a historical orientation both builds on and transcends individual memory, and a memory orientation both incorporates and refashions historical knowledge in making it part of an encompassing, commemorative project. In what follows, I will try to show how these two orientations combine to produce richly textured discourses of the past in Israeli pioneering settlement museums. In so doing, I draw on the basic insight of historian Pierre Nora, who elaborated the analytic distinction between the categories of memory and history, yet pointed out their interdependence:

> Memory is life, borne by living societies founded in its name. It remains in permanent evolution, open to the dialectic of remembering and forgetting, unconscious of its successive deformations, vulnerable to manipulation and appropriation, susceptible to being long dormant and periodically revived. History, on the other hand, is the reconstruction, always problematic and incomplete, of what is no longer. Memory is a perpetually actual phenomenon, a bond tying us to the eternal present; history is a representation of the past. Memory, insofar as it is affective and magical, only affects those facts that suit it. . . . History, because it is an intellectual and secular production, calls for analysis and criticism. . . . Memory takes root in the concrete, in spaces, gestures, images and objects; history binds itself strictly to temporal continuities, to progressions and to relations between things. Memory is absolute, while history can only conceive the relative.[6]

These very different orientations to the past coexist as part of our cultural consciousness, and each contributes differentially to our experience of both past and present. In considering the role played by the heritage industry as a major institutionalized form for representing the past in contemporary societies, we must, therefore, attend to the inherent tension associated with the memory-history dialectic, and with the localized inflections it assumes in particular sociocultural contexts. Historiographical research addresses issues related to the representation of the past in the context of history writing. From a cultural perspective, however, an interest in the role played by the past in the present must clearly take us beyond the context of official history writing and explore other social contexts in which the past is reinvoked or re-presented. Heritage museums and sites are good candidates for such an exploration.

Notably, the dialectical tension between memory and history that has concerned contemporary historians has also been a central theme in modern Jewish thought.[7] As Yosef Hayim Yerushalmi reminds us, in the case of the Jews, knowledge of the past has been traditionally transmitted in a significant way by means of communally shared ritual practices rather than by means of the historical narrative. This array of ritual practices has not served to represent events of the shared past from a stance of critical reflection, but rather to reinvoke a series of timeless existential states that participants are invited to relive. This idiom of personal identification is reflected, among other ways, by the use of the first person singular on some of these liturgical occasions. (For example, in the context of the Passover ritual celebration, the Seder, each participant speaks of himself or herself as having personally come out of Egypt.) In traditional Jewish thought, therefore, the main interest lies in the significance of past events rather than in the concrete details of their unfolding, and the particularity of new events is subordinated to well-recognized archetypal patterns.

The secularization of Jewish history in the wake of the Jewish Enlightenment movement of the nineteenth century has marked a rupture in Jewish cultural experience, which involved a shift toward the historicity of the past rather than its eternal, ritualized presence. As Yerushalmi points out,

> Western man's discovery of history is not a mere interest in
> the past, which has always existed, but a new awareness, a

101

perception of a fluid temporal dimension from which nothing is exempt. The major consequence for Jewish historiography is that it cannot view Judaism as something absolutely given and subject to *a priori* definition. Judaism is inseparable from its evolution through time, from its concrete manifestations at any point in history.[8]

The kind of past the historian can provide, therefore, cannot adequately respond to the persistent quest for collective memory in a secularized world. In the context of contemporary, secularized Jewish tradition, this quest leads to the emergence of newly constructed, ritually enclosed memory-building practices, which in Israel form part of the "civil religion" of nationhood.[9] Nora's discussion of the basic features of what he calls "sites of memory" (or *lieux de mémoire*) is, therefore, of interest here:

> These *lieux de mémoire* are fundamentally remains, the ultimate embodiments of a memorial consciousness that has barely survived in a historical age that calls out for memory because it has abandoned it. They make their appearance by virtue of the deritualization of our world—producing, manifesting, establishing, constructing, decreeing, and maintaining by artifice and by will a society deeply absorbed in its own transformation and renewal, one that inherently values the new over the ancient, the future over the past. Museums, archives, cemeteries, festivals, anniversaries, treaties, depositions, monuments, sanctuaries, fraternal orders—these are the boundary stones of another age, illusions of eternity . . . they mark the rituals of a society without ritual; integral particularities in a society that levels particularity; signs of distinction and of group in a society that tends to recognize individuals only as identical and equal.[10]

Thus, traditional memory's spontaneity has been lost; its traces are experienced as deliberate constructions and as an externally imposed duty to remember. This transformed sense of memory expresses itself through an archival obsession, an attempt to conserve the present and preserve the past as fully as possible, a goal for which the "houses of memory" of modernity have been erected.[11] Thus, heritage museums, wherever they are found, are prime examples of modern memory's archival sensibility, with its reliance on "the materiality of the trace, the immediacy of the recording, the visibility of the image."[12]

102

The meaning and texture of these sites of memory, how-ever, are shaped by the historicized context in which they are located. This study thus becomes an exploration in the uses of history and the reclamation of memory as part of a complex and persistent contemporary process of cultural invention.

For Nora, *lieux de mémoire* are largely "cultural re-mains," pale testimonials to a past suffused with "living mem-ory." His main concern is with the way memory has been affected by its passage through history. I believe there is more than a trace of nostalgia in this scholarly treatment of the memory-history dialectic. Subjecting the processes of the pro-duction of "sites of memory" to critical-historical analysis, we can also bring out the ways in which history is affected and de-flected by our persistent quest for memory. This latter empha-sis highlights the reconstructive, largely discursive "work" that goes into the production of *les lieux de mémoire*. In each such reconstruction, the memory-history dialectic is shaped and reshaped in particular ways. Thus, going beyond an initial, oppositional definition of "memory" and "history," this chapter explores some of the forms the process of cultural production takes in the context of Israeli pioneering settlement museums, and what can be learned from it in a more general way.

Attempting to develop a discourse-centered perspective on the study of museums as "sites of memory," I ground my analysis in selected dimensions of the museums' representa-tional practices, exploring the kinds of orientations they em-ploy toward the past. In so doing, I focus on what Nora refers to as "the push and pull that produces *lieux de mémoire*— moments of history torn away from the movement of history, then returned. No longer quite life, not yet death, like shells on the shore when the sea of living memory has receded."[13] Thus, the narrative performances of tour guides as they rou-tinely lead audiences along the museum path will form the basis for exploring the ways these museums are discursively constructed as culturally focal sites of memory. Although one distinctive feature of the museum encounters I have studied is that they may become occasions for shared reminiscing, the personal uses of the public museum text will not be consid-ered here. It is in a less obvious, more general sense that I wish to consider settlement museums as "sites of memory" in the context of this essay. I begin with an account of Israeli pioneering settlement museums as culturally situated sites of

103

memory, then move on to explore the uses of history in the museum context. Next, I analyze the rhetorically evocative power of the museum's object narratives, posing an indexical relationship between them and the museum's master narrative, and I discuss some issues related to the recontextualization of objects in the museum setting. I conclude with some self-reflexive comments on the cultural significance of the study of *lieux de mémoire* as a form of autoethnography.

Israeli Pioneering Settlement Museums

Israeli historical museums that focus on prestate (pre-1948) history have become prominent features of the Israeli cultural landscape only in the past decade or so. Many of them (over 50 in number)[14] are devoted to the story of the pioneering settlement era, and each in its own way tells and retells the Zionist version of Israeli foundation mythology, which celebrates the ideological roots of Jewish resettlement in the Land of Israel in the past hundred years.[15] Established through local initiatives, often by a core group of volunteers, the museums then gain public recognition and support both directly, in the form of regional or national development grants, and indirectly, through a variety of institutional endorsements. The Ministry of Education and Culture, in particular, sponsors and channels the visits of schoolchildren to these museums, and students are estimated to account for more than 60 percent of the two million visitors who frequent the museums annually.[16]

The most outstanding feature of the discourse of these museums is the explicitness and the directness of its ideological assertions. I was told on numerous occasions by museum personnel that the mission of the museum is "to teach Zionism," or "to cultivate the children's roots in the land," or to counteract young people's growing desire to emigrate. One museum guide, for example, in preaching the return of direct ideological assertion, opened the tour of a group of university students with the following words: "Our parents made a mistake. They thought that if they gave us lots of orange juice to drink, we'll become rooted in the land, but it hasn't worked out that way, with all the emigration of young people that's going on now. We have to speak about our Zionism out loud."[17] Another guide similarly used the idiom of "roots" to talk about the museum's educational mission, saying: "It's the idea that we have to deepen our roots in this land, in this people, that's why we have gone to all this trouble of preserving the 'Old Courtyard' . . . to take this place and use it as an educational tool. Preserving the place is not a goal in itself, and the educational tools—the experience, the story, the direct impression, the touching, are an attempt to reach into the very root of things." He was, however, more attuned to the pedagogical problematics involved in this ideological project. Elaborating on the "roots" metaphor, he said: "We don't know exactly if the educational goal we set out to accomplish of cultivating our roots in the land is attained, but we know we shouldn't overdo it, take out the roots all the time, and check how they're doing, and in plowing the land around them, educationally speaking, we should take care not to get too close to the roots so we don't cut them."[18]

Indeed, the emergence of heritage museums and sites as newly designed arenas for the deployment of such explicit ideological discourse in contemporary Israeli society must be considered in the context of the demise of the socialist values and communal ideals they rearticulate and revive in a "museumified" version.[19] One of the museum guides succinctly summarized this situation in responding to a question concerning the shape he thought the museum would take in years to come: "Thirty years from now? Let me tell you this, I'm not sure the kibbutz will exist then, but I can assure you the museum will."[20] Clearly, were the values and ideals so painstakingly invoked within the museum walls still alive, there would be no need to enliven and celebrate them in these specially designed *lieux de mémoire*.

As sites of memory charged with a particular persuasive task of representing the past, these museums fulfill their rhetorical mission by merging the authenticating force of memory and the objectifying thrust of history in a compelling, culturally legitimating idiom. Throughout my discussion, I will attempt to foreground the tentative balance of identification and critical distance, of memory and historical sensibility, which is recreated anew in every museum encounter. This negotiated balance is more complex than the oppositional model proposed by the aforementioned historians.

The ethnographic project of which this study is a part has investigated the representation of the pioneering era in two Israeli settlement museums, both of which focus mainly on the 1920s and 1930s. Both are located in Israeli collective settlements, or kibbutzim. The first museum, established in 1972, is located in kibbutz Yif'at, and the second, established in 1987, is located in kibbutz Ein-Shemer. While museums, as *lieux de mémoire,* are culturally designed contexts for material display, their overall "story" or "message" is largely conveyed and mediated through verbal renderings in the form of written labels and/or museum guides' oral interpretations. In the case of the museums explored in this study, the tour guides' oral performances are central to generating the desired "museum experience." Much of this "experience" relates to the aforementioned nexus of memory-history as interpreted and presented by the guides, and as relived by the audience. Placing itself between memory and history, then, the museum guided tour embodies the "push and pull" that produces *lieux de mémoire.* The "texts" spoken on those tours, documented either by audio or video, thus offer interpretive sites in and through which the discursive construction of memory—in a world that organizes its past in terms of a historical consciousness—can be fruitfully explored. In this exploration, I consider the museum tour as a cultural performance, highlighting the role of the different narrators and their stances toward various aspects of the narrative construction of the museum story.

Memory and History in Settlement Museum Discourse

Settlement museums are suffused with a "rhetoric of history." Framing the museum story within the notion of history, which involves the idea of a sequence of causally related events, serves to "naturalize" the museum's version of "the past" with a powerful idiom of factuality. The material "remains" that make up the museum display are clearly congruent with this overall idiom. That the telling and retelling of a particular version of the past is self-consciously part of a larger ideological project of considerable social significance is brought out by the oft-cited dictum that "a people who do

106

not know their past will have no future."[21] This dictum is spoken from the standpoint of a historical consciousness that decrees that "learning about the past"—whether in museums, in schools, or by other formal means—is not an end in itself but a necessary means for self-knowledge at the societal level, in the service of "the future." Notably, however, the idea of "learning about the past," as it is interpreted within the folk-historiographical perspective grounding settlement museum practice, tends to appeal to a rather restricted sense of historical knowledge. Throughout the museum tour, emphasis is placed on the fragmented re-creation of the "facts of the past" rather than on the cultivation of a historical understanding of the unfolding of past events. The museum context is, of course, conducive to a fragmentary and ahistorical presentation as events of the past become chronicled in the spatial language of objects. It is thus in the name of historical facticity that themes, material items, and stories find their way into the museum space. All this allows the museum to sustain the fiction that the past is told "as it really was," and to ignore questions of point-of-view and ideological inflection in narrative constructions of the past, which would point to the possibility of alternative or oppositional readings of it. Controlling the representation of the past in the museum context is therefore a matter of unacknowledged cultural politics, which is, in its own turn, spoken of in the Israeli cultural idiom as a contemporary way of "making history."[22]

The museum's version of the past becomes naturalized through the use of the concept of "history." Even when arguments about the contents of or representational strategies in a museum are raised, they tend to be formulated as a matter of contested facticity, involving charges of historical ignorance, inaccuracy, or fanciful fabrication. Thus, while tour guides never waver in their claim to be representing the past, they vary in the subtler nuances of their claims to facticity. At one end are the "scholar" types who become upset by any deviation from strict factuality: for example, the guide who objected forcefully to the display of the sickle in the kibbutz museum, arguing that it was never in use in kibbutz agriculture and therefore had no place there.[23] This attitude is countered by a much looser attitude toward representational practices that speak in a generic sense about "traditional agriculture" and "early agricultural practices" so that such fine factual distinctions become irrelevant. More explicitly, I have repeatedly heard versions of the claim: "It doesn't really matter if it happened here or elsewhere, the point is something like this really happened."[24]

One prominent example of a vexing point of contested facticity that is framed as an argument between the claims of scholarly writings and the museum's representation of the past relates to the highly publicized debate over the swamps of the Jezreel valley. As depicted in school books and other sources of folk-historical knowledge, the Jezreel valley, among other parts of the country, was covered with swamps when the Jewish pioneers arrived. These had to be drained both because they were breeding grounds for malaria, which took many lives, and to prepare cultivation areas for agriculture. Thus, "draining the swamps" became a symbol of the pioneers' mythic struggle against the hostile forces of nature that threatened the success of their nation-building enterprise. An article published in 1983 by two Haifa University historical geographers claimed that the popular view regarding the wide expanses of swamps in the Jezreel valley in the early 1920s was highly inaccurate, and that it was propagated to uphold the pioneering mythology.[25] Apart from the scholarly argument it triggered—relating both to the credibility of historical sources and to the conceptual definitions of the notion of "swamps"— this article became a symbol in its own right. It came to stand for the academic scholars' disaffected drive to demythologize the pioneering past, to belittle the accomplishments of the pioneering era, in this case by claiming that they were not as great as Israelis have been made to believe. Thus, standing on the top of the hill of the Yif'at museum, facing the expansive view of the cultivated, lush fields of the Jezreel valley, the museum guide delivered a celebratory exposition of the great accomplishment symbolized by this view which often carried an argumentative dig against alleged detractors. Stories about the swamps, the Arabs' dread of them, and the Jews' heroic and successful efforts at draining them would be prefaced by a somewhat sneering allusion to the people in the university who claim there were no swamps in the valley and a promise to show definitive pictures of them later on. The guided tour thus becomes another round in the ongoing argument in the debate about the swamps, the visiting group another audience whose adherence to the museum version of the story is to be gained.

Notably, the debate is framed as a matter of factuality, while what is at issue is the underlying ideology that gives shape to the stories. The factual argument concerning the swamps, in attempting to set the record straight, also serves to modify the mythologizing tendencies that mark official representations of the pioneering past. Providing a recycled yet revitalized version of this kind of discourse, heritage museums may thus find themselves embroiled in the wider cultural debate surrounding the settlement ethos and its symbolism, which has long been a centerpiece of the Israeli cultural politics of nostalgia.[26] A conference held at the University of Haifa on March 16, 1993, marked the publication of an important new collection of essays that explored the role of the Jezreel valley as both historical site and cultural myth. It included a talk by Yoram Bar-Gal (the first author of the famous article on the Jezreel valley swamps) entitled "The Jezreel Valley Swamps: Between Myth and Reality," which offered a historiographical treatment of the swamps theme in Israeli textbooks. Although the presentation was quite low-key, B., one of the long-time guides from the Yif'at museum who had expounded the story of the swamps in front of the breathtaking view of the valley countless times, fidgeted in the chair next to me. He claimed the presentation was inaccurate, that the speaker did not take into account a particular spring B. had known firsthand, which had given rise to many swamps. Unimpressed by the academic ambiance and the learned talk, he concluded with a statement I had heard from old-timers before: "The trouble with these people is they work out of documents, they don't really know how things are on the ground, so they make mistakes."[27]

Indeed, it is precisely the position that the past is to be cherished for the sake of the future, that its ideals and values are (or should be) relevant to the present and serve as a cornerstone for the education of the young, that seems to motivate the "demythologizing" practices undertaken in the name of historical facticity. It is precisely the museum's ideological role in providing compelling models *for* social action that requires that the pioneering story be cut down to human size. A similar point was made in an earlier study that explored Israeli pioneering mythology in a variety of pedagogical materials whose central settlement narrative recounted the story of the operation known as Tower and Stockade (*Homa Umigdal*), which established fifty-five new Jewish settlements in British Mandate Palestine between the years 1936 and 1939. Discussions regarding the rhetorical uses of this narrative of heroic settlement pointed out that "pedagogically the message of the story is problematic: only great deeds are worthy of mythologization, but the greater their grandeur the more difficult they are to emulate. Therefore, the elevation of the deeds and accomplishments of the pioneering era . . . involves an ambiguous message. This message simultaneously engenders a sense of possibility and impossibility, an uneasy balance of empowerment and self-doubt."[28]

The drive to "humanize" the larger-than-life image of the pioneering era to retain the essential validity of its ideological claims has greatly colored the texture of museum representations in other ways as well: alongside heroic tales of selfless commitment, arduous labor, and great accomplishments, there emerged a genre of "little stories" describing the day-to-day experiences of the early pioneers in a way that generated interest and amusement rather than awe, and invited identification rather than admiration.

These stories, whether presented in the first person as a form of reminiscence or recited as part of a communally shared anecdotal fund, expand the definition of what counts as "historical knowledge" by introducing new areas and items of relevance that are woven into the construction of the museum's version of the past. Notably, this expansion of "historical knowledge" is often accomplished by mobilizing and legitimizing personal memories as a source of "historical data," whether they are found in documentary materials or drawn from the guide-interpreter's autobiographical experience. This is yet another way in which the dialectics of memory and history plays itself out in the museum context.

The rhetoric of facticity comes into play here as well, but in a different way. While in the aforementioned discussion it was demonstrated that arguments concerning historical factuality are designed to place constraints on the spinning of pioneering myths and relocate them within a human context, the appeal to anecdotal bits of information concerning the pioneers' way of life, which are often not verifiable through standard historical research procedures, serves to legitimate a broad narrative base. Interestingly, this, too, is done in the name of factuality: the anecdotes are said to represent

110

a "hidden" history, a past often ignored in official versions promulgated by the historians.

Humorously presented, many of these stories in fact give voice to the "dark side" of events, thereby combining the two functions of narrative factuality discussed earlier: they expand the factual base of museum narratives to include domains that have been traditionally excluded from official histories, and at the same time they demythologize the idealized and nostalgic version of the past by introducing "negative" materials. For example, the general ideological emphasis on the warmth of communal life is counteracted by stories recounting the tensions introduced into intimate family relations; the wholehearted celebration of the new way of life in the land of Israel is counteracted by stories concerning individuals' acute longings for the families they left behind in the diaspora, and so on. These folk-historiographical deliberations find their expression in the culturally constructed opposition between "the historians" and "the storytellers," the former being committed to the transmission of researched, officially authorized "facts," while the latter enjoy the license of "folklore" by contributing to mythmaking and giving voice to "hidden" histories. In this battle, the "storytellers" are often on the defensive, having to legitimate the "intrusion" of materials at the fringes of verifiable history into the museum tale. At the same time, the considerable audience appeal these materials have, at both the ideological and entertainment levels, is widely recognized. An explicit elaboration of the tension between official history and folk expression can be found in the introduction to a collection of stories related to the history of settlement, appropriately titled *In the Beginning*,[29] which was written by an arch storyteller and historian of the period, Muki Zur:[30]

> Memory appears in different ways. It is the internal censorship which silences what is remembered, it is the confession that gives voice to events that never happened. Thus, the masters of memory, the writers and the historians, argue among themselves. They all remember, but in different ways. The historians claim that they are objective, and that the storytellers only decorate the cake and sometimes add things to it that they should not. When you come across the storytellers you are surprised to find that it is they who hold keys to a history that has been hidden away. It was hidden because it was feared that it would threaten the precarious balance between the pain

111

and disintegration and the great accomplishments that became a model for days to come. The personal testimonies add an important dimension to the story and the history.[31]

The personal experience stories are thus claimed not only to broaden the scope of historical representation, but also to introduce the seeds of a critical perspective toward the past. Pitting the facts of an expanded version of history grounded in story and testimony against the restricted versions of "the historians" is a step toward counteracting the aggrandizing attitude associated with a nostalgic and ideologically motivated representation of the past. It is a step, however, taken within a broader context of basic ideological consensus regarding the versions of history being told and retold within the museum walls. Therefore, the museum's rhetoric of history and factuality is framed by a discourse oriented toward the enhancement of memory. Another central feature of this discourse will be discussed in the next section.

The Play of Indexicality in Museum Narratives

Museum displays are constructed out of "memory objects" and their attendant narratives. The dialectical tension of memory and history can be seen in relation to both objects and narratives. Remembered meanings and values are invoked and the visitors' "sense of history" is rekindled by the sheer materiality of the display and the claims to facticity accompanying the museum tale. The museum story is constructed to combine two very different layers of narrative construction: the first is the "master narrative" that grounds the museum's ideological message and frames its display, and the second is made up of localized "object narratives" that are woven into the museum tour and concretize its message. In the settlement museums I have been studying, the master narrative encapsulates the ideological stance of Labor Zionism. It runs roughly as follows: The Jews of the diaspora were dispersed and dislocated. They had no territory of their own and therefore could not engage in agricultural labor and were condemned to unwholesome occupations as traders and middlemen of all sorts. Throughout the ages their greatest dream was to come to the land of Israel and become farmers.[32] The early pioneers fulfilled this dream, leaving religion and diaspora living patterns behind them, seeking to become New Jews in the Land of Israel. The beginnings were full of the hardships of a new and unaccustomed way of life (in kibbutzim the difficulties of communal living are specifically highlighted), a difficult climate, and a hostile natural and sometimes human environment. Despite the hardships, they succeeded in establishing flourishing agricultural communities, like the one that houses the museum.

Emphases vary between one rendering of the story and another, and the master narrative as such is not usually articulated in full, as its story line—which is congruent with hegemonic versions of Jewish-Israeli history commonly found in history textbooks—is well known to most museum visitors. In the context of the guided tour, it may be briefly alluded to in an explicit way, or, more frequently, it is indirectly invoked through the elaboration of "object narratives" spun together as the tour moves along the museum path. A relatively explicit, if fragmentary allusion to the museum's master narrative is found in the following excerpt from a guided tour given to a group of Arab schoolteachers:

> At the end of the last century the Jews understand that the return to the land of Israel, a national revival in the land of Israel, has to begin from the land, from agriculture. This is the basis for the nation's existence. . . . The Jews who arrived in Israel understood that they had to go back to the land, from which Jews had been cut off. In the diaspora they were not farmers, except for some exceptional cases. . . . They come here and they have no idea of how to go about it, but they have a strong will and understand that this is the way to do it.[33]

Each of the "object narratives" that makes up the museum tour serves as a sign indexing some component(s) of the master narrative, both amplifying and concretizing its ideological message. In other words, each "object narrative" stands in a metonymic relation to the master narrative and the ideological world associated with it.[34] In fact, narrative segments are legitimized as part of the museum tale to the extent that they index some aspect of its grounding master narrative through a localized criterion of narrative relevance. Also, the master narrative may dictate features of the spatial display—for example, in the Yif'at museum the corner devoted to traditional agriculture, which contains Arab implements, is located at the entrance because, as is repeatedly pointed out in the tours and interviews, this is what the pioneers found when they came to the Land of Israel.

Let me briefly illustrate the metonymic nature of "object narratives" by means of two narrative segments, both of which index and concretize the themes of the powerful hold of communal values, the hardships associated with the pioneers' adaptation to communal demands in a context of extreme poverty, and the resourcefulness they mobilized to deal with them. Both stories are typical in that they jointly express and diffuse the sense of hardship they wish to convey through a humorous description of some of the conditions and practices associated with the pioneering past.

The first example concretizes the problematics associated with communalism through the story of a newcomer to the kibbutz group, a girl named Sonya, who caused so much consternation by refusing to become part of the shared clothing arrangement natively known as *shituf* (i.e., partnership), that the group was convened by Ya'acov, the kibbutz secretary, to discuss the issue in the communal dining hall. The tour guide recounts:

Imagine, a newcomer boy or girl arrives, they came straight from home. New clothes. Shoes, beautiful clothes compared to the worn, torn and patched up clothes the group had. These were what we call now "grade A" clothes, Sabbath clothes. They were put aside, and anybody who went out to town would wear the beautiful clothes and the pretty shoes, that's what you'd wear to go to Tel Aviv. For example, you want to go to Tel Aviv so you go to the wardrobe, and you see—hey, someone has already gone to Tel Aviv. So never mind, you go to the railway station, there, near Gan Shmuel, near Hadera, you wait. And when she comes back from Tel Aviv, you both go behind the bushes, exchange clothes, you give her your work clothes, and put on the good clothes, and travel *farandji* [well-dressed], as they say, in good clothes. But she, Sonya, refuses. What does Ya'acov say? "She refuses to give her shoes to the *shituf*. She has the newest shoes. All the girls in the group will have to go to Tel Aviv and Haifa in their worn-out shoes, they'll have no shoes to wear. This is a matter of principle. If you don't give your things to the *shituf*, listen, if you

114

4.1 Reconstructed pioneers' dining hall. Courtesy of Yair Gil.

don't play our game, go to another place. It can't work this way, or the group will fall apart. The *shituf,* it starts with shoes, then it'll be the clothes, then they'll take a tea-kettle to their rooms, then they'll start reading their newspapers in their rooms, and all the companionship and equality will fall apart." This is what Ya'acov explains, it all begins with one shoe, but it's a matter of principle.[35]

The second story is one of many told about the peculiar living arrangement whereby a third person was made to join the living quarters, tent or cabin, of a conjugal couple. The third person came to be nicknamed "primus" (after a common three-legged kerosene stove), and the stories are told about the misunderstandings and discomfort created by this arrangement:

The problem was that there was a shortage of living space, and if there was a couple who were living in here, they would add another person [to the tent], because there was no other place. The third person's nickname was "primus." Say there's a couple here who are married, or at least living together—they weren't so strict about getting married those days—they're lying here in

115

bed, each in his or her own bed, and are waiting for the third person to lie down and fall asleep, so they can be together for a while. He [the third person] doesn't want to disturb them, so he doesn't come in, and walks around outside, to pass the time.[36]

These stories, informative and entertaining as they are in and of themselves, draw their full significance from the pathos associated with the museum's master narrative. Localized events of the pioneering past are recharted onto the grand tale of Zionist redemption in such a way as to diffuse the particularity of the historical circumstances surrounding them, transforming the tokens into types. Indeed, this approach to the events of the past echoes a familiar strategy in traditional Jewish thought, which, as mentioned earlier, was more concerned with timeless meaning rather than the fleeting shape of historical events. As Yerushalmi points out with reference to the medieval Jewish chronicles, they "tended to adapt the flow of events to longstanding and stable conceptual frameworks. . . . It is important to understand that there is no real interest in finding novelty in the passing events. On the contrary, there is a clear tendency to adapt important new events to well-known archetypes."[37]

I would like to argue, then, that the narrative reconstruction of the past in these settlement museums marks a return to deep-seated patterns of memory-building, which have little to do with contemporary notions of history. In a culturally intelligible, ritual gesture of material and narrative inscription, individual acts, events, and persons of the past thus become generic elements in the play of indexicality that turns the different textual layers of the museum story into a credible site of memory. Another strategy for turning the historically distinctive into the generically remembered involves the recontextualization of Arab objects within the narrative frame of the Zionist enterprise, as described and analyzed in the next section.

Transcending Factuality

As is well recognized, the material conservation of valued objects that are associated with a cherished past for the

4.2 Enlarged photograph of dancing pioneers. Courtesy of Yair Gil.

purpose of commemoration, in whatever context,[38] involves a moment of decontextualization and recontextualization.[39] Removed from their original contexts of use, objects considered unusable in their day-to-day existence are relocated and rearranged in the confines of the museum space in a way that creates a new context for their secondary, museum life. The spatial organization of the display provides part of the new meanings that attend the recontextualization of objects in the museum; for example, linear, sequential organization is often used to represent chronological progression, and thematic arrangement in distinct locations in the museum is used to crystallize experiential areas in a quasi-mimetic sense. The attending verbal interpretation complements the spatial recontextualization through the use of labeling (or naming) procedures and through the recounting of "object narratives." Both these aspects of recontextualization—the naming of the objects on display, and the little stories spun around them—reflect (and reinforce) the museum's approved version of the past by indexing the master narrative that grounds its discourse. In the regular run of events, this practice goes un-

117

noticed, as the museum's "rhetoric of history" naturalizes ideology. When visitors approach the museum with a completely different version of the past in mind, however—as is the case for Arab visitors who come to visit Jewish settlement museums—the recontextualization of the objects along the lines of the museum's master narrative may be interpreted as an unacceptable act of historical appropriation, and thereby as highly problematic.

As a matter of fact, Arabs are not frequent visitors to Israeli pioneering settlement museums. Of the two museums discussed here, only the Yif'at museum receives Arab visitors on a regular basis. Despite the left-wing ideological leanings of kibbutz Ein-Shemer, which are reflected in the guides' passing comments about amiable, neighborly relations with nearby Arab villages, it does not cater to Arab visitors. Most of the guides I have approached about this issue expressed their regret about this fact, but also said that if they began to receive Arab schools, for example, they would need to change the story they were telling. They did not specify what these changes would entail, beyond noting that they would skip the room displaying the kibbutz arsenal, which is the only place in the museum where the Arab-Jewish conflict is brought to the fore. I did not push as I realized that they were too thoughtful to give me quick answers, and my observations in the museum in Yif'at, which has been receiving groups of Arab educators and schoolchildren from nearby villages and towns for many years, have alerted me to the complexity of the narrative accommodations Arab visitors "invite."

The general, unspoken interpretive "policy" taken on these occasions of intergroup contact is for the tour to be heavily focused on the "traditional agriculture" corner, which displays the main point of contact between Arabs and Jews in the museum's rendering of the history of settlement. This corner displays the traditional agricultural tools used by Arab farmers and therefore initially also used by the Jewish settlers when they came to the Land of Israel around the turn of the century. Having started their agricultural venture with these tools, the Jews are said to have improved them and then replaced them by technologically more sophisticated implements and machines. The Arabs are thus credited with having taught the Jews how to work, but are also said to have greatly benefited from the technological progress introduced by the

118

4.3 Traditional agriculture on the museum wall. Courtesy of Yair Gil.

Jews. Interestingly, however, this part of the linear story of cultural contact and technological progress is never contested, but another part of it—the claim that the tools the Jews found in use among nineteenth-century Arabs were the ones used by their forefathers in biblical days—is not as readily accepted.

The scene of narrative action is the "traditional agriculture" corner of the museum shed in Yif'at. A variety of agricultural implements made of wood and iron are hung on the wall or laid on the ground along it. As is the case throughout the museum, there is sparse labeling, all in Hebrew and English. Although this corner of the museum is devoted to the Jews' encounter with traditional Arab ways, and the objects themselves have been brought in from Arab villages, the object names on the labels hark back to biblical times. Even when the oral interpretation makes mention of the object's Arabic name, it is given as a footnote that demonstrates the narrator's immersion in local speechways, thereby enhancing his or her credibility as a cultural broker, or as a curiosity. ("In Arabic it has a funny name" is a phrase I have heard more than once.) The renaming of the object as a biblical

119

item makes a great deal of sense within the Zionist version of Jewish historiography, which sees the return to the Land of Israel as marking a reconnection to biblical times. A favorite strategy of the tour guides is therefore to locate the item they have identified on the wall within the textual space of the Old Testament by demanding of the audience: "Where in the Bible is it mentioned? Yes, the Book of Judges, and who used it? Does anybody remember the exact phrasing?" And so on. The literalness with which this strategy is pursued is brought out clearly in the following excerpt from a guided tour:

> I'll tell you a story, do you remember the story about the Patriarch Abraham? Oh, he was quite a man! Phee [Wow], he had lots of cows and sheep and lots of people working for him, and he used to wander from place to place, and he lived in the desert. He was the first Bedouin, the Bedouins weren't there yet, but he was there already. He was sitting in a tent, what was his wife's name? Sara. Sara sat with him in the tent, and three angels are coming, they are going around in the desert, and they see some old man sitting with a young and beautiful woman, so they say: "Let's go visit them." So they come, so Abraham says to them: "*Tefadalu*, please, come in and be our guests." So he says, what does he say to Sara? He whispers a loud whisper in her ear: "Go get three measures of flour [*seot kemah*]." Here are the measures [pointing to the wall], *from the Bible straight here on this wall.* You see, this is what they used to measure in, imagine, the Patriarch Abraham in his time. How many years already? Oh, it's impossible, I wasn't there, you weren't there, your parents weren't there, and he was already using this to measure with this.[40]

To Jewish audiences this kind of story sounds like a playful elaboration of a well-known biblical tale, which is retold here as elsewhere by way of reiterating a largely accepted ideological claim concerning the historical depths of the Jews' roots in the Land of Israel (despite the two thousand years of the diaspora). Renaming Abraham as the first Bedouin, or recent Arab tools as biblical items, cannot be subsumed under the museum's commitment to factuality, which includes an accurate specification of the objects' provenance but is intelligible in terms of its larger mission of reinventing Jewish collective memory.

To Arab audiences, for whom the traditional agriculture corner provides an occasion for animated personal reminisc-

4.4 Reconstructed pioneers' baby cabin. Courtesy of Yair Gil.

ing as visitors identify objects they remember from their childhood or objects they own to this day, the strategy of endowing
these objects with an imaginary, biblical career is an act of
cultural appropriation, even of symbolic violence. Arab visitors rarely, if ever, express their negative reactions openly. At

121

one time, when a grade-school child from a nearby Arab village openly showed his dissatisfaction with the claim that the valley had been an empty, swampy terrain before the arrival of the Jewish pioneers, he was hushed by his teacher, who said to him: "The Palestine we know is not the Palestine of the Jews." This strategy of avoiding any potential open conflict over the interpretation of the past is dominant. I once asked a group of Arab teachers who assured me they felt the museum was telling their story more than the Jews' story (pointing to the many Arab-made objects found in the traditional agriculture corner) if they wouldn't prefer "their" museum to be located in an Arab village rather than a Jewish kibbutz; my question met with multiple evasions. Several teachers said it didn't matter where the museum was; they assured me they were glad they could bring their school kids over to see the implements that had until recently been in use in Arab villages. Arab children nowadays no longer see the tools, since they are part of a vanishing tradition. In so saying they not only reaffirmed their cultural ownership of the "traditional agriculture" corner of the museum, but also gently reminded me that contemporary Arabs are very different from the traditional figure of the Arab, which tends to be depicted as a Timeless Other in the settlement museum display.[41] One teacher suggested that a separate corner in the museum be devoted to olive growing and olive-oil industries, which have been central to traditional Arab agriculture and life in the area. The suggestion met with general approval by her colleagues, and I felt that if the museum were to follow it (my inquiries suggest it is unlikely), this would be interpreted as a gesture of incorporation toward Arab visitors, enhancing their tentative sense of the museum space as an island of political neutrality where Arabs and Jews can meet as children of the earth, producers and consumers of agricultural goods. A comment by another teacher, however, brought the discussion back to reality. He waved my question aside, saying there are many more important things the Arab population needs; they'd rather have proper medical services and schools before they were given museums. His colleagues responded with chuckling sounds of approval, but at the same time some of them were quick to check his protest with re-straining, light-hearted calls of "no politics here."

Here and there, though, voices of contestation neverthe-less sifted through. An entry written in the museum's visitor

4.5 Children's activity in the Museum. Courtesy of Yair Gil.

book by an Arab teacher reads, "It's a pity the Arab contribution to the settlement of the land has not been highlighted sufficiently"; and one Arab schoolteacher muttered a
sarcastic comment that encapsulated the problematics of the
tool display from the standpoint of Arab visitors: "The tools
belong to father and grandfather, and the stories belong to
Moshe and Haim [both Hebrew names]."[42] It is only on rare
occasions, however, that Arab visitors become openly con-
frontational, and these become memorable and "reportable"
events. One case was recounted by B., a long-time guide who
speaks Arabic and is therefore usually assigned groups of
Arab visitors. He told me the story in private conversation
and then repeated it to a group of university students (both
Jews and Arabs), who had come to the museum as part of my
ethnography class. Obviously agitated by the memory of this
encounter, he related in detail the argument he had recently
had with a group of Arab visitors who inquired about the
present whereabouts of the Arab villagers who had lived in
the pre-1948 village of Mjedel, where Yif'at is now located.
Posing this question was interpreted as a political provoca-
tion, which it probably was, and B., a great sympathizer with

123

Arab culture and cause, was clearly disturbed by this direct confrontation. He told us at length how he had explained to the Arab visitors that the villagers of Mjedel and the other pre-1948 villages in the area had fled of their own accord during the Israeli War of Independence, having been misled by the Iraqi army leaders who had urged them to leave, and that by the time they were ready to return, the kibbutz had already absorbed many Holocaust survivors who had nowhere else to go. He concluded his story by saying: "They saw I was right and said nothing in response." I later asked my Arab students if they had found B.'s account equally persuasive. Not contesting any of the details of B.'s account, they burst into laughter and said that the silence with which it was received had nothing to do with accepting his argument. Not getting into an argument, they pointed out, is a matter of respect; it is a way of doing *musayara,* or going along with the other.[43] As museum visitors, they regarded themselves as guests bound by the rules of proper conduct, which are culturally interpreted as enhancing harmony and avoiding confrontation.

The nonconfrontational, self-effacing strategies generally employed by Arabs in the context of settlement museum encounters (and elsewhere) contribute to the undisturbed, unself-conscious reproduction of the hegemonic version of the Zionist master narrative in their discourse. In sharing my sense of this largely suppressed problematics with museum personnel, most of whom have struck me as thoughtful, creative, and open-minded people, I found their responses depended on their overall vision of the museum's role. The general attitude, it seems to me, is that settlement museums have been established to tell the story of the Jews, not of the Arabs, and that it is therefore legitimately told from the perspective of Zionist ideology. Even when conceding the role of the museum as an arena where contacts between Arabs and Jews could be fruitfully highlighted and explored, museum professionals insisted that this was only a secondary matter, and that the primary focus should be on celebrating the Jews' culture and nation-building mission. There is no argument with the aforementioned statement that the Palestine of the Jews and the Palestine of the Arabs represent two different geographies of the mind. Let the Arabs tell their version of the story, I was told again and again.[44]

Note, however, that the museum story—that is, the story of the early socialist-Zionist pioneers who came to the Land of Israel from Europe in the 1920s and 1930s—is enshrined as "the story of the Jews," as opposed to "the story of the Arabs." It is presented as a national myth of beginning, to be embraced by all Jewish visitors to the museum. Identifying with these mythical roots may come easy to descendants of the pioneers, and perhaps to other Jews of European provenance (Ashkenazi Jews), but about half the Jewish population of Israel are Jews who came from Middle Eastern and North African countries (Mizrahi Jews), who arrived mainly after the establishment of the state in 1948, and for whom the Ashkenazi-based ethos of the pioneering days has been a major source of feelings of cultural and social exclusion for many years. Indeed, some of my students of Ashkenazi and Mizrahi origin, who had grown up in the development towns established in peripheral areas in the 1950s to accommodate the many immigrants to the land, openly told me they felt a strong sense of alienation when visiting settlement museums as part of our course and would not have chosen to go there otherwise. The notion of pioneering is still strongly associated with the socialist-Zionist beginnings, and recent extensions of the category to other social groups (as found in revised history textbooks) are not echoed in the settlement museum displays. The elevation of the newcomers of the 1920s and 1930s as nation-builders, agriculturalists, and culture-makers, and the symbolic marginalization of later immigrants, including those from North Africa who established agricultural settlements in the late 1940s, feeds on and into the widespread sociocultural bifurcation between the ideologically driven "pioneers" as dreamers and doers and the new "immigrants" who were forced to come to a ready-made homeland. The perception of the prestate era as the "cradle of the nation" and of the nation-building process as having been largely completed by 1948 clearly reinforces the sense that the immigrants' contribution to nation-building was minimal, that their story can be readily subsumed by the hegemonic version of the museum narrative. This diffuse symbolic incorporation of all social groups in Jewish Israeli society into one and the same narrative framework was never explicitly remarked upon, but it was nevertheless sufficiently powerful to silence other potential versions of nationhood and cultural identity in the museum context.

4.6 Old tractor. Courtesy of Yair Gil.

In discussing the uses of history in settlement museum discourse in the previous section, I have tried to show that the museums' "rhetoric of factuality" serves as a powerful memory-building strategy. This section has taken us beyond the simple case of consensual narrative framing and into contested sociocultural terrain. Here, it seems, history is both appealed to and transcended in allowing memory to do its ideological work.

Concluding Remarks

The conceptual point of departure for this study has been the argument developed by Nora and Yerushalmi (among others) concerning the coexistence of two fundamentally opposed orientations toward the past: one referred to as "memory" and the other referred to as "history." In elaborating this analytical opposition, Nora concludes: "At the heart of history is a critical discourse that is antithetical to spontaneous memory. History is perpetually suspicious of memory, and its true mission is to suppress and destroy it."[45] Interestingly, Nora has also pointed out that we have now come to a point at which a central part of our history is a history of *lieux de mémoire*.

In this view, then, *lieux de mémoire* are both enclosed cultural enclaves for the preservation of memory traces and objects for historical (and, I would add, anthropological) inquiry. If history's "true mission is to suppress and destroy" memory, what can we make of the historians' and other social scientists' obvious fascination with memory discourses as sites for scholarly scrutiny? In other words, are our metadiscourses of the past, in the form of histories or ethnographies of *lieux de mémoire*, another step in history's mission to suppress and destroy memory? Can we argue for a more complex picture, one that is grounded in a view of "memory" and "history" as dialectically related orientations to the past rather than independently defined, antithetical ones?

While my analysis has necessarily addressed the specifics of the Israeli case I have been studying, the representational practices I have identified, which both enact and mediate the history-memory opposition in sites of memory of various kinds, are of much broader relevance. In fact, they speak to an even more encompassing dialectical tension that is basic to modern life: the tension between the isolating, intellectual stance of critical reflection, which Nora would assign to the realm of "history," and the all-consuming moment of ritual, communal bonding, which he would assign to the realm of memory.

Museums, then, whatever else they do in terms of the local sociocultural scene, also serve as cultural sites for the articulation of the basic tension between history and memory as they jostle for cultural position. The ethnographic approach I have proposed for the study of the discursive production of sites of memory therefore highlights their negotiated and strategic dimensions. What I have tried to show in my discussion of Israeli settlement museums is that history and memory orientations interpenetrate in producing multilayered discourses of the past. Thus, museums, as *lieux de mémoire*, invoke a rhetoric of history that may both utilize and dissolve claims to factuality. At the same time, museums, like other *lieux de mémoire*, increasingly invite critical inquiry, leaving us with self-reflexive questions concerning the role of our metadiscourses about the discourses of *lieux de*

127

4.7 A primus—three-legged stove. Courtesy of Yair Gil.

mémoire and their processes of production. To what extent does studying the discourses of *les lieux de mémoire* become another ritualized, nostalgia-filled invocation of a world of "living memory" that no longer is? To what extent do our scholarly voices, suspicious of memory, remain part of the world that surrounds and contains it within the boundaries of *les lieux de mémoire?*

As I turn to the road that takes me up the hill to the Yif'at museum, or glimpse the top of the two old trees that pridefully announce one's approach to the Old Courtyard in kibbutz Ein-Shemer, my heart fills with a surge of unspeakable longing, a longing I have come to recognize in the voices of other visitors as they sight long-forgotten childhood objects in a museum corner, for a moment transfixed in time and place. Yet the only way I can truly listen to the museum narrative is by lending it a skeptical ear, by interrogating the representational practices employed, by attending to the silences around its edges—that is, by producing a critical ethnography.

Much has been written in recent years about the critical turn in ethnographic inquiry,[46] and some has been written about the autoethnographer's peculiar stance.[47] My conflicted participation in my chosen *lieux de mémoire* therefore comes as no surprise. My ongoing ethnographic exploration in a culture in which I live and work,[48] whose celebratory moments as well as repressive practices are part of the very fabric of my life, has also prepared me for the ever-present tension that is part of the autoethnographer's position as professional, if not cultural, outsider.[49]

The autoethnographer's self-conscious participation in his or her own cultural world, including its *lieux de mémoire,* may suggest the possibility of a new form of cultural enactment, one that transcends Nora's perspective on sites of memory as in-group oriented, affective, and magical enclaves that celebrate the essence of life in a world dominated by the sign of history. It invites a more complex attitude that interweaves memory and history, critical reflection and ritual enactment, in an ever-shifting yet productive tension. For such an alternative reading to make sense, we may need to relinquish our nostalgia for the "living sea of memory," and put greater faith in the meaningfulness of a reflective attitude. The history that is a living history of *lieux de mémoire* may in itself be a new cultural form that suggests the possibility of critical attention grounded in cultural affirmation.

It is, indeed, through the ethnographer's fascination with *lieux de mémoire* as significant cultural arenas that their vulnerability to critical interrogation is most clearly brought to light. Should we think of the ethnographer's task in this context as the production of *lieux de histoire*? Whether we can concede such a formulation or not, it appears that the memory-history dialectic speaks to more subtle and rich possibilities of cultural enactment than was originally suggested by the oppositional model that launched the present exploration, and that case studies such as the one offered here can help to illuminate some of the empirical and conceptual issues involved.

Notes

This research was supported by the Basic Research Foundation, administered by the Israel Academy of Sciences and Humanities.

1. Cf., for example, Robert Hewson, *The Heritage Industry: Britain in a Climate of Decline* (London: Methuen, 1987); Donald Horne, *The Great Museum: The Re-Presentation of History.* (London: Pluto Press, 1984); Michael Wallace, "Visiting the Past: History Museums in the United States," *Radical History Review* 25 (1981): 63–96; Ivan Karp and Steven D. Lavine, *Exhibiting Cultures: The Poetics and Politics of Museum Display* (Washington, D.C.: Smithsonian Institution Press, 1990); Tamar Katriel, "Remaking Place: Cultural Production in an Israeli Settlement Museum," *History & Memory* 5 (1993): 104–35.
2. Dean MacCannell, *The Tourist: A New Theory of the Leisure Class* (New York: Schocken Books, 1989 [1976]).
3. MacCannell, *The Tourist,* 39–56. Cf. also Elizabeth Fine and Jean Speer, "Tour Guide Performances as Sight Sacralization," *Annals of Tourism Research* 12 (1985): 73–95, and Tamar Katriel, "Performing the Past: Presentational Styles in Settlement Museum Interpretation," *Israel Social Science Research* 9 (1994): 1–26.
4. Pierre Nora, "Between Memory and History: *Les Lieux de mémoire,*" *Representations* 26 (1989): 8.
5. Natalie Zemon Davis and Randolph Starn, "Introduction," *Representations* 26, special issue, "Memory and Counter-Memory" (1989): 4.
6. Nora, "Between Memory and History," 8–9.
7. Yosef Hayim Yerushalmi, *Zakhor: Jewish History and Jewish Memory* (Seattle: University of Washington Press, 1982).
8. Yerushalmi, *Zachor,* 91–92.

9. Charles Liebman and Eliezer Don-Yehia, *Civil Religion in Israel: Traditional Judaism and Political Culture in the Jewish State* (Berkeley: University of California Press, 1983).

10. Nora, "Between Memory and History," 12.

11. Frances A. Yates, *The Art of Memory* (Chicago: University of Chicago Press, 1966).

12. Nora, "Between Memory and History," 13.

13. Nora, "Between Memory and History," 12.

14. The number of these museums runs between 50 and 60. Variations in counting are related to the fact that many of them grow out of local exhibitions and/or local archives, and it is not always clear when they can be properly referred to as museums. Another issue relates to the fact that quite a few are site-museums, which are located in historical sites that have undergone restoration. Given the rather negative popular associations of "museums" as the deadly instruments of high culture, some site museums reject the title and opt for some alternative. "Site" (*atar*) seems to be the most common. As the idea of open-air museums became more familiar, more and more pioneering settlement museum sites became a part of the professional museum scene, and a separate division for the settlement museums was established with the framework of the Israeli Museum Association in 1989.

15. Other Israeli heritage museums focus on such historical themes as clandestine immigration during the British Mandate or selected chapters of the military struggle for independence, for example.

16. These figures were given to me for the years 1990 and 1991 by Mr. Yosi Feldman, chair of the Society for Historical Preservation, which has been quite active in the preservation of many of these site-museums.

17. Z., guided tour, clandestine immigration heritage site in Atlit, May 3, 1991. All translations from Hebrew-language field materials in this chapter are my own.

18. R., interview, Ein-Shemer museum, October 15, 1991.

19. This process is now referred to as "the capitalization of the kibbutz."

20. A., discussion with university students, Yif'at, November 8, 1991.

21. This dictum is often cited as part of the guided tour itself, and I have heard it variously attributed to different Zionist personalities, most often to Yigal Allon. It is also inserted into the guides' discourse not as a citation but as a kind of proverbial truth.

22. The idiom of museum-making is subsumed in the Israeli cultural idiom of history-making and place-making, which are

typical of descriptions of the pioneering era. "Frame" stories told about the enterprise of the "crazy few" who initiated and established the museums echo the stories about the "crazy few" who pioneered the Jews' return to the land and established the places where the museums are now housed. This narrative isomorphism clearly "models" the cultural continuity the museum seeks to effect.

23. Group discussion with museum personnel, Ein-Shemer, December 10, 1991.

24. G., guided tour, Ein-Shemer museum, September 28, 1991.

25. Yoram Bar-Gal and Shmuel Shamai, "The Jezreel Valley Swamps—Legend and Reality," *Cathedra* 27 (1983): 163–79 (in Hebrew). Subsequent issues of the journal carried a variety of responses to this article. Also, Yoram Bar-Gal, *Moledet and Geography in a Hundred Years of Zionist Education* (Tel Aviv: Am Oved, 1993 [in Hebrew]).

26. Cf. Tamar Katriel and Aliza Shenhar, "Tower and Stockade: Dialogic Narration in Israeli Settlement Ethos," *Quarterly Journal of Speech* 76.4 (1990): 359–80; Fred Davis, *Yearning for Yesterday: A Sociology of Nostalgia* (New York: Free Press, 1979).

27. B., comment after lecture, University of Haifa, March 16, 1993.

28. Katriel and Shenhar, "Tower and Stockade," 368. Cf. a similar presentational dilemma in discourses of ordinary families regarding the extraordinary family of British royalty, discussed in Michael Billig, "Collective Memory, Ideology and the British Royal Family," in *Collective Remembering*, ed. David Middleton and Derek Edwards (London: Sage, 1990), 60–80.

29. Zvi Karniel, *In the Beginning* (Kibbutz Ramat Yochanan, 1992, [in Hebrew]).

30. Muki Zur is a central figure in the kibbutz movement as ideologue, educator, and politician. He is the author of several books relating to the pioneering era and a champion of storytelling. His collection of kibbutz stories is used, inter alia, as resource material in many museums. A one-day conference of the Israeli Museum Association settlement museum chapter was held when the museum in kibbutz Yif'at celebrated its twenty-year anniversary in August 1992. Muki Zur served not only as keynote speaker, but also as one of three people who conducted guided tours of the museum (the other two were the director and a senior guide).

31. Karniel, *In the Beginning*, 7.

32. The farmer image of the Zionist pioneer (*halutz*) was central to the Labor-socialist branch of the Zionist movement, but not to all Zionists. They were culturally and politically dom-

inant throughout the nation-building era, even if outnumbered by newcomers to the land who became city- and small-town dwellers. In the settlement museums I have observed, it was the dominant image—to the point of rewriting all of Jewish history, as indicated in this passage; the religion-based yearnings for Zion that accompanied the Jewish people in the diaspora through the ages have become reinterpreted as the yearning to cultivate the land as farmers. Religious Zionists, on the other hand, reinterpret the Zionist revival as one more indication of the Jews' age-old attachment to the land of Israel.

33. I., guided tour, Yif'at, October 13, 1991.

34. Cf. Charles Briggs's discussion of the notion of "triplex signs" in *Competence in Performance* (Philadelphia: University of Pennsylvania Press, 1988).

35. R., guided tour, Ein-Shemer museum, October 15, 1991.

36. I., guided tour, Yif'at, October 13, 1991.

37. Yerushalmi, *Zakhor*, 56.

38. Whereas museums and archives are our major conservation institutions in the public domain, there are also less institutionalized contexts of memory-building that make use of "material remains" in private contexts. Cf. Tamar Katriel and Thomas B. Farrell, "Scrapbooks as Cultural Texts: An American Art of Memory," *Text and Performance Quarterly* 11 (1991): 1–16.

39. Cf. Susan Stewart, *On Longing: Narratives of the Gigantic, the Miniature, the Souvenir, and the Collection* (Baltimore: Johns Hopkins University Press, 1984), and Barbara Kirshenblatt-Gimblett, "Objects of Ethnography," in *Exhibiting Cultures: The Poetics and Politics of Museum Display*, ed. Karp and Lavine, 386–443.

40. B., guided tour to a group of grade-school children, Yif'at, August 1, 1989.

41. Cf. Johannes Fabian, *Time and the Other: How Anthropology Makes Its Object* (New York: Columbia University Press, 1983).

42. A side remark made by a female teacher during a video-taped guided tour with B., October 4, 1991.

43. For an elaboration of this cultural communication pattern, see Yusuf Griefat and Tamar Katriel, "'Life Demands *Musayara*': Communication and Culture among Arabs in Israel," *International and Intercultural Communication Annual* 13 (1989): 121–38.

44. Indeed, they increasingly do. In museum-land the Arab version of the story of Palestine can be gleaned in the recently established first Palestinian Heritage Museum, located in the Galilean village of Sakhnin. It already receives many Arab as well as Jewish school groups and other occasional visitors.

Its director explained its establishment as being partly a response to the appropriation of Arab material culture in settlement museums, which he referred to as the Jews' "stealing" Arab heritage. Notably, the invisibility of the Jews is even more pronounced in the Sakhnin museum than is the absence of Arabs in the settlement museums. Although the director told me he defined "heritage" as going 30 years back, i.e., well into the establishment of the State of Israel, there is no trace of the Jews' presence or any intergroup contact in the museum display. The labeling, sparse as it is, is in Arabic and English (as is the business card of the museum director, who is fluent in Hebrew). A detailed comparison of the representation strategies employed in the Jewish and Palestinian museums takes us beyond the confines of this chapter. However, let me point out that in both cases the museum becomes an arena for the cultivation of an ahistorical, essentialist view of culture (Jewish-Israeli or Palestinian, as the case may be), a view that fits well with the museum's mythologizing agenda.

45. Nora, "Between Memory and History," 9.
46. Important books and articles that discuss the critical turn in ethnographic research and writing have appeared in recent years. See George Marcus and Michael Fischer, *Anthropology as Cultural Critique: An Experimental Moment in the Human Sciences* (Chicago: University of Chicago Press, 1986); James Clifford and George Marcus, eds. *Writing Culture: The Poetics and Politics of Ethnography* (Berkeley: University of California Press, 1986); James Clifford, *The Predicament of Culture: Twentieth-Century Ethnography, Literature and Art* (Cambridge, Mass.: Harvard University Press, 1988). In the communications field, Dwight Conquergood has advocated a critical stance toward ethnographic research; see, e.g., "Rethinking Ethnography: Toward a Critical Cultural Politics," *Communication Monographs* 58 (1991): 179–94, and "Review Essay: Ethnography, Rhetoric and Performance," *Quarterly Journal of Speech* 78 (1992): 80–97.
47. Of special interest in this connection is Smadar Lavie, *The Poetics of Military Occupation: Mzeina Allegories of Bedouin Identity Under Israeli and Egyptian Rule* (Berkeley: University of California Press, 1990). In this richly textured and sensitive analysis, Lavie discusses her positioning vis-à-vis the Mzeina culture on the one hand and Israeli culture on the other. As her title suggests, however, hers is only secondarily an autoethnography. Different as our studies are, they share a concern with the consequences of power and domination. My main focus here is on the role of representational practices in maintaining

hegemony, which from the standpoint of the dominant Jewish culture is a celebration of roots. Her main focus is on Mzeina performances of identity that wrestle with the cultural consequences of political domination.

48. Tamar Katriel, *Talking Straight: Dugri Speech in Israeli Sabra Culture* (Cambridge: Cambridge University Press, 1986), and Katriel, *Communal Webs: Communication and Culture in Contemporary Israel* (Albany: SUNY Press, 1991).

49. An exchange between John Fiske and Donal Carbaugh, "Forum: Writing Ethnographies," *Quarterly Journal of Speech* 77 (1991): 327–42, was devoted to the issue of critique in ethnographic research, suggesting the two general alternatives of consensus-oriented research on the one hand (Carbaugh) and conflict-oriented research (Fiske) on the other. I believe my research sidesteps this argument by applying a conflict approach (attention to silences) to the study of consensus-building practices (discourses of the past). Like Carbaugh, I am interested in the discursive production of community, but like Fiske, I am attuned to the exclusions that are inevitably involved, and am interested in the ways in which they are negotiated.

5

The Liberation of Buchenwald: Images and the Shape of Memory

Barbie Zelizer

Our language lacks words to express this offense,
the demolition of man. — *Primo Levi*

The world of Auschwitz lies outside speech as it lies
outside reason. — *George Steiner*

I n her review of the Hollywood movie *Schindler's List, New York Times* film critic Janet Maslin anchored her discussion of the film to the status of photographs about the Holocaust.[1] She began by telling the story of a steel tin of photographs that had been buried secretly in a park outside Vienna and unearthed decades later. That "real photographic record," she argued, provided the basis for the Spielberg film, allowing him to present "the subject as if discovering it anew." In this tension—between the familiar and the rediscovered—the "Holocaust threatens to become unimaginable because it has been imagined so fully." Therein lies the power of its photographic images. In a way that often privileges them over other recording devices, photographs have permeated nearly every recollection of the Holocaust—in part, in full, in confirmation, in denial. As one of the few bodies of visual documentation that remains available from the time of the Holocaust itself, the privileged status of photographs becomes entwined in our capacity to remember. Maslin's review, however, leaves unanswered many questions about the centrality of photographs in memory. What does it mean to remember the Holocaust through photographs? What part do they play in our memory, and can we rely on them? Do we remember independent of photographs? What is the status of the activity by which photographs were originally recorded? Have we forgotten, erased, denied it? And, finally, does it matter in our appropriation of its images today, more than fifty years later?

This chapter, part of a larger project exploring the photographic record of the liberation of the European concentration camps, addresses the initial recording of Buchenwald in images in the British and U.S. popular press during the spring and summer of 1945.[2] With an eye to exploring how that record has inflected memories about the camp's liberation, the essay interrogates the movements of two kinds of documenters—reporters and photographers—at the core of memory. For those who did not experience the Holocaust firsthand, their movements vis-à-vis each other molded collective recollection of one of the most gruesome moments of contemporary history.

The Shape of Memory

What do we mean when we speak of memory? In contemporary academic discourse, the increasing number of labels for the sharing of memory has suggested a growing interest in the term that has in turn complicated its invocation in unanticipated ways. From public memory and social memory, on the one side, to popular memory and cultural memory, on the other, the labels converge only on the fundamental point that they offer an approach to the past that is distinct from history. To some extent, this has had to do with what Pierre Nora claimed was memory's location in the archive. Memory, he said, relies "entirely on the materiality of the trace, the immediacy of the recording, the visibility of the image."[3] By way of its materiality, it takes on patterned and identifiable forms.

But memory has many shapes, dependent on its builders. Maurice Halbwachs was among the first to characterize collective memory as a strategic activity shaped by those invested in remembering.[4] Primarily through their membership in national, religious, ethnic, class, or professional groups, he claimed that people remember similar pasts in different ways. As James Young observed, "Both the reasons for memory and the forms memory takes are always socially mandated."[5] In any event of public life, then, there exist many forms of remembering an event, and each form offers but partial perspectives on the events that it records—partial both through its recording at the time and its recollection years later. This difference between literal memory and cultural memory—or that which is remembered through experience and that which has been culturally inscribed as memory—is not easily evident or predictable, however. And perhaps nowhere was this as obvious as with the liberation of the concentration camps in 1945. When considering the story of the camps' liberation and the larger terrain of Holocaust retelling, "the issue of history in relation to memory—the issue of what is needful to remember—refuses to disappear."[6] Difficulties in articulating this particular moment in history have made it into what Saul Friedlander has called "an event which tests our traditional conceptual and representational categories, an 'event at the limits.'"[7]

At the time of the liberation of the camps, the distinction between literal and cultural memory was complicated by tensions within the world of journalism. The distinction rested on the capacity of the institutions of journalism for recording what they learned: Not only was there a need to represent the atrocities to a skeptical and distant public, but news organizations had to report accurately, rapidly, and authoritatively. It was not clear, however, through which representational codes the memory of the liberation took shape. For at the time of the liberation, these same institutions of journalism were facing their own ambivalence surrounding the status of the image in news. Although the photograph had been around for nearly one hundred years, it was not yet considered an appropriate tool for documenting the events of daily news. Photographers were still called "pictorial reporters" instead of photojournalists, and images were seen as adjuncts to words rather than autonomous carriers of information.[8] They needed the intervention of journalists to make sense.

When news organizations faced the liberation of the camps, these tensions came to a head. News organizations needed to establish an authoritative record of what they were seeing, and it was on that point that images became central. Images were needed to help convince disbelieving audiences that what the liberating forces were seeing was real. They thereby played an instrumental role in establishing the record of the particular series of events that we call "the liberation."

138

Yet were they ready to do so? This chapter argues that they were not. News organizations had not sufficiently thought out how to process images as news and make them into autonomous carriers of information. Neither had photographers sufficiently coalesced into the kind of professional group that knew how to accommodate the demands of daily news. Thus, the record of the liberation posed interesting questions from the vantage point of journalism, which left little space for negotiating internal tensions within the world of journalism, despite the fact that such tensions figured both into the record and its recollection. Those tensions took on a particular shape surrounding the negotiation between reporters and their primary rivals—photographers. For in remembering the Holocaust fifty years later, certain photographic images "are everywhere, 'impossible to topple and destroy.' "[9] Yet how did they get there? Through what kinds of incongruities and tensions were they produced?

Images as Documentation

The use of images to document the liberation was characterized by two sets of tensions. One was an issue of professional expectation: What were images expected to do in news? Photographs offered the journalistic community a tool of documentation with its own authoritative features: photography's strength seemed to derive from its positioning as a medium of record. The photograph, long assumed to "tell it like it is," acted like a "transcription from reality."[10] It possessed a certain indexical, denotative, referential force, an aura of verisimilitude, that made it seem as if it captured things *as they were* in the real world.

For news organizations needing to account for events of the war, the referential force of photographs was crucial. Photographs met journalism's own aspirations of objectivity by appearing to extend the adage that "the camera does not lie" to journalism's primary recorders—the reporters.[11] If referentiality figured in the establishment of a news organization's own credibility, went the reasoning, then images would certainly enhance that credibility. Faced with recording military action on a front that stretched across five continents, news organizations recognized that photographs would help authenticate their record of events and establish journalism's authority for telling the story of the war.

But there was another quality to the image that news organizations overlooked, and that was its universality, its ability to represent more than a distinct and identifiable referent in the real world.[12] This quality of generalizability, connected loosely with functions of connotation and interpretation, was assumed to be beyond the bounds of "picture-getters," who, in one early view, were "not required to be picture makers."[13] They were seen as adjuncts, not substitutes, to the written word.

The second set of tensions surrounded the practices for using photographs in news that developed during wartime. As in any wartime situation, editorial staffs were expected to coordinate a vast and steady influx of material recorded under difficult and unpredictable circumstances.[14] The incorporation of photographs, however, at times constituted a challenge for the daily and weekly press.[15] The practices that developed— concerning credits, captions, the formula for positioning images alongside texts—were thereby highly uneven. Often images were presented without captions, with the wrong captions, without credits, or as depictions of events not presented in the accompanying texts. Photographs sometimes bore precise documentation—including definitive captions and credit lines—but other times they were presented without any documentation at all, failing to make available the dates, places, or circumstances under which the images were taken.[16] Photographs sometimes appeared as visual images without any precise delineation of what they were or how they connected to the news they were expected to depict. Photographers lamented the lack of standards for using images in daily news but were generally powerless to have an impact. They continued to debate as late as 1946 whether and in what form they should even use captions in newspapers and newsmagazines.[17] Similar complaints were recorded in the late forties about the failure of news organizations to give photographers credit for their images.[18]

The unevenness of these practices had a direct effect on the aforementioned referential force of the photograph. The sloppiness it produced in some of the war's visual documentation, a sloppiness that appears to have been rarely attended to as the war's urgent events pressed photographers to continue documenting, deprived many photographs of their referential status for depicting events of the war. Yet at the same time the second function of photographic images—that of universalization—was inadvertently highlighted. Photographs emerged as markers of universality rather than referentiality, and this would have particular effect when the journalistic community faced the atrocities of the camps.

Articulating Memory: Recording the Liberation of the Camps

How was the liberation of the camps recorded by the institutions of journalism? There were three issues of credibility that came to the fore as members of the journalistic community entered the concentration camps. One had to do with the magnitude of the atrocities they found there. For journalists in word and image, recording the liberation of the camps was a challenge probably unequaled in their professional experience.[19] Although the public in Allied countries had been informed of the existence of the camps, and of Nazi intentions to eliminate the Jews, no rumor or other verbal description offered by persons who escaped confinement had conveyed the full extent of horrors associated with the camps. It was only with their liberation that the public grasped the magnitude of what had been happening in Nazi-occupied Europe. As one news editor of the time admitted, "the occasional trickle of news, the testimony of fugitive eyewitnesses, seemed somehow exaggerated."[20] Thus, on seeing the camps, journalists in both word and image needed to report the essentially unbelievable. As the *New Republic* said shortly thereafter, "Only now, after Allied correspondents report what has been going on behind the walls of these Nazi camps, are all the hideous stories, doubted for so long, confirmed."[21]

A second issue of credibility had to do with the earlier reports of journalists concerning accounts of atrocities in the camps *before* their liberation. Earlier accounts of news organizations had understated the atrocities and had been too infrequent to have much of an effect on the public. They had made the story into a sidebar, in part due to the sheer number of

141

victims, the lack of uninterested (i.e., objective) eyewitnesses, earlier experiences with false World War I atrocity stories, and the difficulty of obtaining confirmation from impartial sources.[22] In trying to "modulate the tone of reports so as not to be accused of fomenting hysteria," the press had also tended toward moderation rather than toward what it regarded as overstatement or exaggeration.[23] Moreover, the coverage that did appear rarely incorporated photographs. Published photographs were usually ill-focused images that readers were told portrayed shaded extermination buildings or mounds of corpses, hardly sufficient to convince a disbelieving public of the horror of the camps. One such photograph, taken in the early forties, showed a close-up shot of a Nazi guard facing down a group of prisoners. The caption told readers of "The concentration camp! The rule of the rubber truncheon! The rule of the barbed wire fence. Inside the Third Reich alone, there were 100,000 victims in concentration camps in 1938. Now there are camps all over Europe."[24] Nowhere did the caption specifically mention a certain camp, a certain action, a certain date. In retrospect its almost civilized pose of Nazi guard and prisoners conveyed little of the horror that came to characterize photographic images of the camps. Thus, in both word and image, to report the liberation involved contradicting, repairing, or undoing earlier accounts of the camps.

A third issue of credibility had to do with the aforementioned status of photographs in daily news. Photographic documentation of the liberation was vast but uneven. Sometimes professional or semiprofessional photographers accompanied the troops liberating the camps. Photographs were taken in an official capacity by members of the Signal Corps of the British Ministry of War Information as well as by professional and semiprofessional photographers attached to the various military divisions. Civilian photographers were allowed to take pictures, as were representatives with the U.S. Surgeon General's office, the American Field Service, and HIAS (Hebrew Immigrants Aid Society). Soldiers also simply snapped photographic shots with their own private cameras, and, as one letter from a soldier later claimed, the photographs he shot of the liberation of one camp "are dim, for I was not a photographer."[25] Even the wide range of photographic documenters, however, did not constitute enough of an impetus to generate explicit standards for processing images as news. Yet images were increasing in popularity, and news organizations necessarily relied on them as documents. They thereby awaited the records of photographers as they entered the camps alongside their word-colleagues.

Recording the liberation thus tested the capacity of journalism in general. But the tension between image and word came to a head, for it was to the image that news organizations would turn in trying to convince a disbelieving public that what they were learning was real.

Recording the Liberation of Buchenwald

The liberation of Buchenwald took place on April 11, 1945, when American liberating forces met some 20,000 mostly male inmates of a camp normally inhabited by 50,000. On April 8, the Germans, anticipating the arrival of the Allied forces, had marched many of the inmates to other camps and sites, leaving behind only a fraction of the prisoners, including some 4,000 Jews.[26] Shortly thereafter, the Germans too had fled, leaving the emaciated prisoners to greet the Allied troops.

Reporters and photographers entered the camps shortly after General George Patton's troops. Among them was *Time* correspondent Percival Knauth, who later said that certain details he witnessed "I don't even remember writing at the press camp."[27] The narratives he and others wrote were structured as eyewitness reports. One reporter, admitting that he had not intended to write about Buchenwald, said he ended up doing so anyway because "I merely wanted first-hand knowledge so that if anyone ever asked me about German concentration camps, I could tell them the unexaggerated truth."[28] The eyewitness report was a helpful way to achieve that aim, for it underscored a reporter's authority derived simply from having been there. For reporters, eyewitnessing was contextualized as professional practice of the first order.

The Power and Insufficiency of Words

Reporters tried to bolster their credibility for what they were seeing by mapping the territory and citing witnesses

143

in their eyewitness reports. They concretized the atrocities by mapping the physical territory in which they took place. Taking their readers on detailed word-tours of the camps, correspondents gave concrete descriptions of particular details of their terrain. Their tours generally focused on a camp's places of torture and the routes taken to reach them. As one *New York Times* reporter said,

> The deathhouse had been built conveniently close. It is a neat brick building. To enter it you walk through a courtyard where stand the gibbets on which a dozen men could be hanged at once. . . . At the side of the death house is a stairway leading into a basement. This basement is paved with concrete sloping toward drains and equipped with hoses. Beside the stairway a chute led down into this basement on the outside.[29]

These tours of the territory were important, for they delineated concrete details against which the stories of the atrocities could be shaped. Whether they focused on torture chambers or strangling rooms, there appeared to be an almost uncomfortable relief at being able to focus on physical terrain, as it was one set of particulars that helped reporters document the depravity of the camps.

There was a similar focus on witnesses, who were cited not only for the information they could supply but for their silent presence as well.[30] Standing in for the witnessing activity of the general public, witnesses lent depth and legitimated narratives by virtue of their mere presence. The most authoritative, though most distanced, witnesses were the reporters themselves, who underscored the depravity of what they witnessed. Yet because the depravity was so overwhelming, reporters needed witnesses of a closer degree to authenticate their accounts. Four kinds of witnesses were used: prisoners and victims of the camps; German nationals, including civilians who lived nearby and former SS officials; soldiers with the liberating troops; and the officials of foreign governments and news organizations.[31] The eyewitnessing activity provided by all four groups took place during the first week or two after the camps had been liberated, but each signified a different kind of witnessing activity.

Prisoners and victims of the camps constituted first-order witnesses, whom journalists quoted whenever possible.

Particular attention was focused on persons who had achieved stature in their prewar lives—doctors, university professors, authors, diplomats, military officers—a technique facilitated by Buchenwald's status as a camp for the intelligentsia. One reporter, after detailing the anonymity of the masses in the camps, noticed a sign of vitality among the living dead, "a white-haired Frenchman, 73 years old, who had been a captain of marines in World War I and had been picked up by the Germans in Paris four years ago because he was in the French resistance movement. He told of punishments inflicted by the SS guards so depraved and so obscene that I could never tell them except to other men in whispers."[32] When interviewed, the prisoners were sometimes identified by status and country of origin but often remained unnamed.

Another group was the second-order witnesses embodied by the German nationals. These persons, either perpetrators or silent observers, were generally rendered voiceless in reporters' narratives.[33] When civilians were brought forcibly into the camp by the Allied forces as part of its denazification campaign, reporters focused on their reactions: "Twelve hundred men and women of Weimar walked unwillingly through [Buchenwald] and wept, retched, fainted," observed one reporter.[34] Harold Denny of the *New York Times* recounted the actions of one young German member of the Hitler Mädchen organization, who, made to sit before the camp's open furnace doors, cried, trembled, and moaned. When fleetingly given a voice, she referred to the horrific nature of what "they" had done. At that point, Denny muted her voice, observing that the "girl showed no sense of personal responsibility, though she had been a sworn supporter of the regime."[35]

Another second-order witness was the soldiers, who were called "G.I. sightseers."[36] This type of witnessing was important because it signified a military response to the events made evident by the camps' liberation. Percival Knauth of *Time* told of his entry into Buchenwald nine days after it was liberated:

We came up from the cellar and passed into another yard fenced in by a high wooden wall. There was a pile of bodies there, stacked more or less the way I stack my firewood back home, not too carefully. . . . Their mouths were open as though in pain and little streaks of blood flowed from their noses. "Some kind of hemorrhage," said a medical corpsman. "Hell, those guys died of starvation," said another G.I. He stared and stared and couldn't get that thought out of his mind, repeating it over and over."[37]

Readers were told how the "G.I. wept," the "G.I. turned his head," the "G.I. stared vacantly." Observations about this kind of witness stood in for the embodiment of human response to the atrocities.

Yet a third-order witness was created by positioning officials in the news accounts. These witnesses experienced the camps firsthand when they came to view what had happened after the liberation. In April 1945, Eisenhower brought nearly thirty U.S. congressmen to inspect the camps, and their function, in one newsmagazine's view, was "to look at horror"—a pure act of witnessing.[38] Once there, they "got shocked eyewitness proof" of the atrocities.[39] Asked to "see for yourselves and be the spokesmen for the United States," these officials went on from Buchenwald to see more camps.[40] Other delegations of congressional representatives or British parliamentarians were similarly tracked, and their testimony authenticated the earlier accounts of reporters and military personnel. Said one MP: "There has been no exaggeration. It beggars description."[41]

After Eisenhower assembled a fact-finding mission of eighteen American newspaper and magazine editors to the camps, the press also printed extensive accounts of their tour.[42] The *Bulletin* of the American Society of Newspaper Editors (ASNE) devoted the first few pages of its June 1945 issue to the subject. Titled "Reflections on Atrocities," the account printed the reactions of three editors, one of whom recalled "with horror" the strangling rooms and "medical experiment building" at Buchenwald.[43] The briefest of three statements was titled "Words Cannot Describe Horrors." Its opening sentence attended less to the atrocities and more to their inscription as public record. "American reporters," it began, "had accurately and fully reported the atrocities of Buchenwald and Dachau." They

> went in with the liberating troops and had an opportunity to see at first hand much more than was left for our observation. . . . What we saw, however, was enough to convince anyone of the Nazi's systematic program of starvation, torture and debasement. If our reporters erred at all it was on the side of under-

146

statement, because words are inadequate to describe the utter horror and degradation of those establishments.[44]

These accounts did not include pictures or other visual images, and they provided what appeared to be a metadiscourse on the events in war-torn Europe. This implied that the primary authority for documenting the atrocities still rested with journalists on assignment in the region.

Significantly, each of these categories of witnesses did not fill its quota. The more witnesses who could corroborate a given story, the stronger the evidence. Thus, congressional committees were depicted as having fallen "into the pattern already described in appalling detail by newsreels and correspondents."[45] There appeared to be a curious strength in the numbers of people validating the same details, curious because it worked against journalistic objectives of "scooping" the opposition. Reporters appeared to find solace in producing additional reports to confirm earlier ones. This was perhaps because witnesses helped establish an authoritative voice in this particular story, so that it mattered little whether usual modes of news presentation were followed. It was also interesting that, in each of these cases, words were used as an index of referentiality, the same referentiality that images were expected to fulfill.

Yet the eyewitness report was problematic. It was an insufficient means of documenting what reporters saw. Often unable to provide the identity, name, or nationality of the camp's victims, reporters began to sprinkle their narratives with comments that admitted their own insufficiencies— insufficiencies of language, genre, and of words themselves.[46] Much of the unbelievable character of what they saw necessitated displacement, reversal, or even denial of earlier coverage, and forced them to work against their own carefully crafted standards of credibility in order to establish an authoritative voice. This created a professional quandary: recognizing that existing standards of news-telling fell short when reporting the camps, reporters similarly recognized their inability to process what they saw into a plausible narrative.

Reporters thereby had to admit the insufficiency of their narratives. One insufficiency had to do with words themselves, seen as inadequate carriers of the information they

147

were expected to bear. "Anything you hear . . . will be under-statement," said one observer.[47] "Buchenwald," said another, "is beyond all comprehension. You just can't understand it even when you've seen it."[48] Perhaps the most famous re-counting of Buchenwald's liberation came neither from writ-ten word nor photographic image but from sound. CBS Radio correspondent Edward R. Murrow observed that "the stink was beyond description. As we walked out into the courtyard, a man fell dead. Two others, they must have been over 60, were crawling on the ground."[49] Yet he "begged his audience to believe him," saying that "I have reported what I saw and heard. But only part of it. For most of it, I have no words."[50] Other reporters emphasized the generic inadequacy of the eyewitness report. One *New York Times* reporter contended that "it is impossible to tell a connected story of the horrors of Buchenwald."[51] Another reporter admitted that "in this war we have had more than our share of atrocity stories, but Buchenwald is not a story."[52] Still other reporters ad-dressed the inadequacy of news language in general, claiming that the atrocities challenged existing standards of language appropriateness. "If you tried to tell the actual facts of the Buchenwald horrors, you would get a story of obscenity and filth that would be unprintable."[53] One *New York Times* re-porter, admitting that "even a hint of the present hygienic conditions would be unprintable," said that "writers have tried to describe these things, but words cannot describe them, and even if they could, there are details too filthy to be printed anywhere."[54]

In each case, reporters faced difficulties in recording the camps. The eyewitness report, as a representational strat-egy, was insufficient to document what they saw. Standards of appropriate language, genre, and words themselves were all unable to capture the scenes of Buchenwald. In short, reporters needed better devices through which to establish their authority.

Buchenwald in Image

Images offered one such device. For those who did not experience the camps firsthand, the photographic record pro-vided on liberation offered visual documentary proof of what had happened inside their boundaries. Images were used as confirmatory tools that upheld the veracity of what news organizations needed to report.

As with words, photographs represented scenes that pushed the boundaries of representation. As with words, pictures did not convey the enormity or extent of what had happened. "I have written [this] only because I thought I ought to," said one observer in an author's note to an editor, three months after visiting Buchenwald. "*Au fond* I don't like horrors any more than you do. It probably won't be believed—even with the dozens of photographs I have taken."[55] But pictures offered graphic representations of the atrocities. Photographers, one reporter claimed, "sent pictures so horrible that no newspaper normally would use them, but they were less horrible than the reality."[56] For news organizations, photographs captured the atrocities in a far more graphic, and therefore communicative, manner than did words. And unlike the emphasis on witnesses and territory that served as internal authenticating devices of eyewitness reports, images offered a device of authentication that was external, even preferable, to words.

Foremost among the American photographers who documented the camps was Margaret Bourke-White. Her pictures, in one view, "made Americans believe in the Nazi atrocities for the first time."[57] Not only was she credited with developing the natural photographic style that came to be associated with the visual documentation of the camps,[58] but, together with *Time* writer Percival Knauth, she followed Patton's troops into Buchenwald. Once there, said one biographer, she

> set to work immediately. A crowd of men in prison clothes stood silently behind barbed wire. She stood in front of them with a flash to take their picture; not one of them reacted. The camera, which automatically forces self-consciousness on its subjects, could not do so here; Buchenwald had stripped away self-consciousness and ordinary response. Liberated, the skeletal figures stare from her photograph with the eyes of men who have seen too much, their faced framed by wire, their lives by an unbearable past and an unimaginable future. No one registers joy, relief, or even recognition; it is as if they have died and yet are keeping watch. The frame cuts off the lineup on either side, making it seem like a fragment of a group that goes on forever.[59]

149

5.1 Margaret Bourke-White, "Victims of the Buchenwald Concentration Camp." National Archives, courtesy of USHMM Photo Archives.

Bourke-White photographed all that she saw—the bodies, the charred skulls, the weeping German civilians, the gallows, the ovens full of ashes.[60]

Bourke-White's most famous shot was titled simply "Victims of the Buchenwald Concentration Camp." She portrayed piles of human feet and heads situated at an angle from the camera (fig. 5.1). The pile gave viewers the impression that it was about to spill over onto the photographer, and that it was barred from doing so only by a thin steel rod at the bottom of the picture. Other photographs, less renowned than Bourke-White's, showed the same pile of bodies from a long shot, a perspective that revealed them to be stacked atop a wagon in the camp's courtyard. The long shot, and all that it symbolized, was frequently used by photographers to depict visually the witnessing activities of different groups, such as Weimar civilians facing Allied troops or official delegations inspecting the bodies.[61]

Techniques of Universalization

From the beginning, images of Buchenwald served as universal markers more effectively than referential ones. Again, this was the inverse of what images were expected to do.

While many images offered few identifiers of a story's specific locale, they fit well within more general discourse about the German war machinery. Often, they lacked subject name, place, photographer, and photographic agency. One 1945 column on foreign news appended a photograph of three near-naked men under the title "Buchenwald Survivors: Were They Germany's Hope?" (fig. 5.2).[62] While the caption explained that the men were survivors, the accompanying text told of an underground movement at the camp that had planned to build an antifascist Reich. Yet that text was nowhere recognizable in the by-then familiar image of broken and despairing bodies.[63]

Captions succeeded in large part to universalize the images they described. One five-page article on the camps, published in April 1945, brought together reports by *Life* and *Time* correspondents who had been at Buchenwald and other camps. Their vignettes were illustrated by images that were presented as being representative of atrocities at all the camps—a commandant, a mass burial, a common grave, a charred body, *human* cordwood. While the images themselves oscillated between pictures of the many and pictures of the few, portraying both individual agony and the far-reaching repetitiveness of mass atrocity, the captions to the images were particularly instrumental in negotiating a leap from referentiality to universality.

Each picture was anchored in a precise location via a parenthesis. A depiction of a stack of bodies, accredited to International Pictures, bore the rather curious caption: "Human Cordwood (Buchenwald)." A secondary caption added little detail: "Once they had minds and lives and destinies."[64] Setting off the word "Buchenwald" in parentheses (and marking the names of other camps in a similar fashion) narratively signaled to readers that the locale of the atrocities was secondary, almost an afterthought. Where events took place was not only noninstrumental but possibly irrelevant to the image's more universal meaning. When they took place was not noted at all. The captions seemed to suggest that the events depicted in the photographs could have taken place anywhere

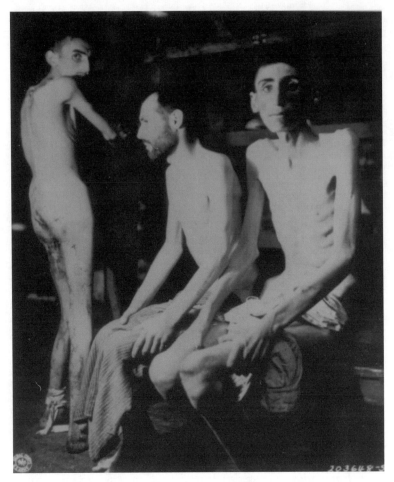

5.2 National Archives, courtesy of USHMM Photo Archives.

in the Third Reich and anytime under its reign. Thus, through the very captions that could have anchored photographs as precise referential documents, news organizations deprived the images of their referentiality and enhanced their universal quality. Images became less useful as identifiable markers of specific activities and more as representative indices of general wartime circumstance.

The secondary captions to many of the photographs achieved the same aim. One caption observed that the cor-

152

responding image of a mass burial was "as irrefutable as death." This was odd, in that the photograph showed scores of dead bodies lined up in one long grave, leaving readers to ponder precisely what was irrefutable about the image. In the text of the article, however, readers learned that the phrase referred to *reporters finding* "the evidence of the camps . . . as irrefutable as death."[65] Comments like these positioned the photograph in an uneven balance with the text, a balance that worked against the image's referentiality.

Another way of universalizing images was by credits. At times, the photographic credit lines were presented elsewhere in the journal, as when the *New York Times* presented an image of Buchenwald's crowded bunks with little detail about where, how, or by whom it was taken; readers skimming through the newspaper, however, learned on another page that it had been taken by the Associated Press.[66] Other times, photographs were printed without the credits of a specific photographer or photographic agency. A highly referenced and carefully attributed eyewitness report discussing the Allied War Department's official report on Buchenwald was presented alongside an unattributed, uncredited photograph of three ravaged men. The different degree of attribution accorded word and image was striking, in that one was carefully accounted for while the other was accounted for not at all.[67] Still another photograph—Bourke-White's renowned shot of bodies heaped across a wagon—was frequently included without attribution.[68]

Yet another way of universalizing images was achieved by photographic spreads, a presentational format made familiar by the widely read picture magazines. In newspapers, spreads were often delegated to the so-called pictorial pages, where they presented usually four to eight images that were separated from the text. The *Philadelphia Inquirer,* for instance, included photographic shots of Buchenwald, Nordhausen, and other locales on its pictorial page.[69] But photographic spreads were far more common in picture magazines. In May 1945, a few weeks after the first photographs of the liberation had been distributed, *Life* magazine published a five-page photographic spread called simply "Atrocities." The photographs displayed a range of Nazi-inflicted horrors, including dazed prisoners at Buchenwald, dying women at Belsen, and burning bodies at Gardelegen.[70] At about the same time, *Look,*

Picture Post, and the *Illustrated London News* all published photographic spreads on the atrocities.[71] The *Illustrated London News* published a detachable four-page supplement with pictures of the camps. The images, said the journal, are "given as a record for all time of German crimes."[72] Interestingly, *Life* offered justification as to why it had elected to print the photographs:

> Last week Americans could no longer doubt stories of Nazi cruelty. For the first time there was irrefutable evidence as the advancing Allied armies captured camps. . . . With the armies in Germany were four *Life* photographers whose pictures are presented on these pages. The things they show are horrible. They are printed for the reason stated seven years ago when, in publishing early pictures of war's death and destruction in Spain and China, *Life* stated, "Dead men have indeed died in vain if live men refuse to look at them."[73]

Such a rationale suggested a certain ambivalence surrounding the publication of the images.[74] Audiences were not consensual about the need to regard them.

Yet in each case, images served news organizations well. Acting as markers of universality, alongside the text's referentiality, they helped position discourse about Nazism within the broad parameters against which it needed to be judged. More than other tools of documentation, images made the discourse simultaneously comprehensible and beyond comprehension. Referentiality, in such a scenario, would have made images fall short of such an achievement.

Visualizing Territory and Witnesses

Interestingly, the movement from referentiality to universality was achieved primarily by universalizing the two elements central to the eyewitness report—eyewitnesses and territory. Through both features, discourse about the camps was pushed from a specific reference to one camp or victim into a general discussion of the atrocities in all the camps.

Thus, images provided a prolonged moment of witnessing. Photographs were displayed that showed "Germans viewing the atrocities" or "officials looking with horror." Sometimes shots were presented with just witnesses and no atrocities. This made the act of witnessing central in a way that was lost in reporters' accounts, where witnessing was rendered part of a larger, more coherent narrative.

As with words, witnesses helped authenticate the visual message of the atrocities, a point confirmed by the SS and Wehrmacht soldiers' own tendency to pose beneath people they had just hung.[75] As suggested earlier, reporters tried to authenticate their reports of what had happened by using soldiers, officials, and politicians as agents of confirmation. Here, too, authenticity was established by photographing soldiers and officials in front of heaps of bodies. Yet often authenticity was problematic, simply because the details were wrong. One such photograph in *Time* magazine labeled an army major staring from behind a heap of bodies as being at Buchenwald (fig. 5.3). The same photo, however, had been used a week earlier both by *Newsweek,* in an article about Nordhausen that identified the bodies as being at Ohrdruf, and in the *Stars and Stripes,* where the bodies were also described as being at Ohrdruf.[76] Yet at the more generalized level, the details were valid. In convincing a skeptical world of the atrocities, it mattered little whether a stack of bodies was at Ohrdruf or Buchenwald. What mattered was that it had happened.[77]

The prisoners and victims of the camps were, again, the primary index of witnessing activity. In most cases, the prisoners were voiceless and anonymous, a point that underscored their generalized status. One famous photograph of Buchenwald portrayed an angled shot of worn, half-crazed faces staring out from crowded bunks. The photograph, originally taken by the Associated Press, appeared in the *New York Times Magazine* three weeks after the first reports, where its caption read "Crowded Bunks in the Prison Camp at Buchenwald."[78] This particular photographic shot also achieved some degree of notoriety when two of its portrayed individuals took on public identities in later years—noted author Elie Wiesel and Los Angeles businessman Mel Mermelstein, who in the eighties challenged the claims of the revisionist Institute for Historical Review in court and won.[79]

Both the German civilian and the Western official were frequently visualized witnesses. Pictures showed groups of German civilians "forced by Yank military police to look at a truckload of dead prisoners at the nearby Buchenwald camp"

155

5.3 National Archives, courtesy of CORBIS.

(fig. 5.4). One photograph, entitled "Nazi Barbarism" and attributed to AP Wirephoto, showed the civilians with their backs to the camera as they faced both a group of Allied soldiers and a stack of dead bodies.[80] Many news organizations prominently featured photographs of the official delegations as they were about to depart for Germany.[81] One such photograph accompanied a *Newsweek* article about another congressional delegation to Buchenwald and Dachau. The photograph portrayed three congressional representatives in a somewhat stupefied posture, looking beyond the photographer at some unknown horror. Nowhere were the atrocities to be seen. The picture, attributed to British Combine, was not identified by place or date, and the caption conveyed in only the most general terms that "Congress Views the Atrocities." No more definitive detail was provided.[82]

Images similarly generalized the territory of the camps. Unlike the narratives of reporters, where concrete word-tours took readers on the routes to the crematorium, images served to generalize the same territory by allowing the locale of the camp to become representative of the larger terrain suffering

5.4 National Archives, courtesy of USHMM Photo Archives.

under the Nazis. News organizations achieved this in three ways: First, they augmented stories about certain locales and atrocities by providing images of other locales and atrocities. For instance, a picture about Nordhausen was used to help illustrate an article about Buchenwald, Erla, and Belsen.[83] Second, news organizations used specific visual markers—such as one picture each from Buchenwald, Nordhausen, Ohrdruf, and Gotha—to illustrate a general story about atrocities, even if the photographs had little to do with the discussion in the text.[84] Sometimes news organizations did not even bother to identify the location of the photographs, and sometimes the locations were misidentified.[85] And third, images of Buchenwald were simply left out of chronicles about Buchenwald; instead, word-stories were visually depicted by images that showed emaciated American soldiers at Marktreidweitz, carnage at Gardelegen, or Soviet infantrymen storming a German position.[86] None of these images bore any particular connection

157

to Buchenwald, but they fit within a more general discourse about the German war machinery.

In all cases, the photographs lacked identifying attributes. Often, they bore no subject name, place, photographer or photographic agency. This helped to underscore the image's universal status. *P.M.* magazine pictorially presented its discussion of the highly referenced and carefully documented official report on Buchenwald with one lone, unattributed image—a few near-naked men staring with dazed eyes into the camera. The caption read, "At the Nazis' 'extermination camp' of Buchenwald, these men were starved. The one in foreground is a Hungarian Jew."[87] No attribution accompanied the photograph, no date on which it was taken, no identification of the individuals it portrayed. Like many other photographs, the only identifying attribute was the specific place in which it was photographed.

Thus, photographs universalized visual depictions of the atrocities at the same time as they generalized two attributes of the reporters' own eyewitness reports—witnesses and territory. Photographs offered images that were constructed around a prolonged moment of witnessing, a moment lost in the reporters' attempts to make witnesses' words and activities part of a narrative. Similarly, images of territory created strong links between many locales suffering under Nazi control, links that were lost in the concrete word-tours that grounded the eyewitness reports of reporters.

Visual representations of both witnesses and territory underscored links with broader interpretive schema by which it was possible to universalize what had happened; the same features in the hands of reporters closed off interpretation by grounding the narratives in the here and now. In one case, interpretation was closed off; in the other, it was opened up. The opening up of narratives challenged journalistic modes of representation, however, which had traditionally posited that the more horrific the image, the more detailed the image's anchoring needed to be. Instead, journalists here provided less information when it was most needed. In this way images almost seemed to take over from words the capacity to tell the story of the liberation. Visual representation also directly affected the shape of the recollection that resulted from this record. In many cases, the images remained so devoid of identifiable detail that it was difficult to anchor them in a given physical or geographic place. Yet the more universal the place they were accorded, the more effective carriers of the collective memory they would be.

Particular Knowledges, Particular Memories

The liberation underscored the potency of the photographic image as a documentary tool. In contrast to the earlier muted word-stories of the camps, the image-making apparatus in all its forms helped turn collective disbelief into the shock and horror of recognition. Photographic evidence meant that the atrocities of the camps "could not be denied. . . . Buchenwald, Belsen, Dachau—their images were etched in memory forever."[88] Citing "distance, suspicion, what you will," the London-based *World's Press News* said that "something held back full appreciation on the part of the British and American peoples. But these pictures————."[89] Photographs were thereby presented across the Allied front with an authority and surefootedness that underscored their central role in muting public skepticism. On some level, news organizations recognized that images were capable of conveying the very horror that had incapacitated words. Such was the reigning assumption of the time—that the photograph had helped freeze the camps within a space of undeniability, a space that would be largely unchallenged in the years to come.

So it was that journals, newspapers, and newsmagazines, already at the time of the liberation, began their accounts of the camps by hailing the "newspictures, a crop of unforgettable first-hand accounts of conditions in German concentration camps, [that] have set Europe and the world asking one question: How is it possible . . . ?"[90] Embedded within the ongoing attempt to convince the American public that what had happened was real were references to pictures and first-hand accounts. "Through pictures the impact of the war was brought home to the people."[91] For those who could not witness the atrocities firsthand, the military made available photographic exhibitions and atrocity newsreels, and the London *Daily Mail* published atrocity photographs in pamphlet form.[92] Through it all, news organizations applauded and facilitated the need to bear witness, though some questioned

the change in censorship policy implied by the officially sanc-
tioned displays of the atrocities.[93]

Shortly after the photographic spreads on the atrocities
were published in the United States and Britain in the spring
of 1945, letters to the editor arrived in droves.[94] The majority
came from readers who claimed that the images should be
used to fill a historical function. One reader argued that "these
things have got to be shown. The world has to know that they
were not dreamed up by newsmen but actually happened."
Another suggested that *Life* "have its atrocity photographs
blown up to mural size" to adorn the room where the peace
conference would be held. The press, said another, should
never forget that "seeing is believing." A minority of readers
felt that the images would be "detrimental to clear thinking
about peace." But in both cases, the image's centrality was
underscored. As one reader opined, "Maybe it would be well
to . . . rerun those pictures in 1965 . . . on the 20th anniversary of V-E Day. We are such forgetful people."[95]

In response to the centrality of images, two discourses
about the photograph emerged. One tackled the image's failure to adequately reproduce reality. People recognized that
images were not quite up to the task of complete documentation. One military newspaper admitted that there "has been
no picture story since the invention of photography to match
the impact of the layouts now being run on the Nazi atrocities." Soldiers everywhere, it said, could know "that within
the limits of the printed word and the engraver's art a serious effort is being made to bring home to decent humans
the truth of what they found."[96] Yet the photographs of the
camps were "infinitely less terrible than the reality we saw. . . .
No appreciation of the full horror is conveyed even by [the
pictures]."[97] News organizations responded by readily publishing many photographs that came their way. "Even the most
staid of British newspapers are carrying full pages of the
brutally grim pictures which came out of the camps," said
one.[98] The apparent abandonment of selectivity criteria was
odd, in that it contrasted starkly with the caution of certain
reporters when reporting the atrocities in words. It was as if
once photographic images became available to buttress the
verbal accounts of the camps, reporters felt freer (or perhaps
on more solid ground) about giving such accounts coverage.
At the same time, it almost appeared as if public belief in the

photographs was enhanced when soldiers, not professional photographers, took the images. In one view, the public appreciated the amateur shots "in which there could be no doctoring of scenes and no faking of film."[99]

The other discourse accompanying recognition of the image's limitations concerned suggestions that the photographs had been faked or forged. Certain soldiers, on coming home, were told that their personal photographs were propaganda, and one claimed that his wife, unable to contain her disbelief, tore up the snapshots he had taken of the camps.[100] Writing in the *Progressive* of May 1945, Milton Mayer argued against the authenticity of the photographic evidence. Discussing the worthlessness of venting vengeance against Germany, he questioned the stories and photographs then permeating the newspapers:

> Let us assume that the stories are all true. There are, to be sure, fantastic discrepancies in the reports. And the character of the evidence—including photographs of gas chambers and piles of emaciated bodies, the testimony of liberated prisoners, and the inspections of the scene after the fact—would not be held under ordinary American judicial practice to be sufficient for conviction in a capital crime.[101]

As one British MP said in May 1945, "There still appears to be a considerable number of people who wish to believe that photographs are fakes . . . [but] it would be impossible to persuade large numbers of British and American soldiers, and ten Members of Parliament, to permit their photographs to be super-imposed on fake pictures."[102] Suspicions about the image motivated the *Stars and Stripes* to run an editorial in April 1945 entitled "The Pictures Don't Lie." The piece began by admitting that Allied soldiers would be "reassured to know that the world press is publishing the photographic evidence with unprecedented candor." The article cautioned that the pictures brought home "as no other medium possibly could" what was happening in Germany. Both "those who shrugged off the reports of German atrocities as professionally clever repetitions of the amateurish stories of World War I" and "those who could not visualize from word pictures the ghastly realities" were convinced, in one newspaper's view, by the pictures. They were "seeing the pay-off on history's most inhuman barbarity": "Few of the pictures are for feeble stomachs. Few are of the type that any considerate editor would publish in normal times in a newspaper of general circulation. But in the belief that the public must know, and must see to believe, even conservative publications are opening their pages to unretouched photographs of Belsen, Ohrdruf and Buchenwald."[103] Both discourses suggest the degree to which the photographic image had been set up as conclusive evidence of atrocities in the camps. Public belief, for those who had not experienced the Holocaust personally, hinged on the photograph, and this linkage would persist into collective memory.

Yet there was surprisingly little discourse about the sloppy or inefficient use of photographs to recount the horrors of the Nazi camps. The fact that images appeared with no accreditation, with wrong or misleading captions, or with a questionable relationship to the words they were used to visually depict mattered little in the face of an urgent need to document the atrocities of the camps. Such circumstances allowed the image to emerge as a universal marker of the atrocities, a status that all but displaced its referential qualities.

Conclusion

Today, more than fifty years after the liberation of the European concentration camps, we are still presented with grim reminders of the documented horror of the Nazi regime. From the opening of the United States Holocaust Memorial Museum to the release of *Schindler's List,* debates over Holocaust denial in campus newspapers, or contemporary instances of genocide, photographic images of the camps continue to occupy our public domain, reminding us of the evil and horror witnessed but half a century ago. Images taken during the liberation are continuously recycled in newsmagazines, books, and televisual retrospectives, and are plastered across the walls and corridors of Holocaust museums and memorials. As one observer recently said, "They sit in our consciousness as half-repressed photographs and newsreels, the first images—always present reminders of what is now called the Holocaust."[104] They are one bearing wall, among many, of the house that contains Holocaust memory.

Yet the problem with Holocaust imagery, as Andreas Huyssen recently claimed, is "not forgetting, but rather [its] ubiquitousness, the excess."[105] By way of excess, images of the Holocaust have undergone a transformation of sorts: They have gone from providing knowledge and serving as archival documentation to keeping events before our eyes so that they may be transmitted to future generations.[106] They have become tools not only of evidence but for creating another generation that can continue to bear witness. As Margaret Bourke-White said long ago, "Difficult as these things may be to report or to photograph, it is something we must do. . . . Our obligation is to pass it on to others."[107]

If that is so, we need to be more vigilant about the modes we have now and had then for documenting the events of our real life. The pattern of universalizing images, evident already at the time of the camps' liberation, remains today one of the major points of contention surrounding contemporary visual representations of the Holocaust.[108] In recognizing the limits of Holocaust images at the same time as we continue to applaud their function as documentary tools, we may thereby be able to fashion the instantiation of memory in a way that addresses not only those who uphold it but those who deny it as well. In short, in allowing for what Huyssen called "the unchecked proliferation of the trope," we may also recognize its ossification.[109]

Hayden White recently argued that "the kind of anomalies, enigmas, and dead ends met with in discussions of the representation of the Holocaust are the result of a conception of discourse that owes too much to a realism that is inadequate to the representation of events."[110] This may be part of the problem with journalism, in that we have traditionally considered it too much an indexing agent of reality. Journalism has long attempted to maintain its privileged status as the "true and accurate recorder."[111] That view, however, may in fact have clouded our ability to regard it not as the first draft of history but as yet another form—among many—of collective remembering. It is within such a perspective that the many complementary modes of documenting *within* journalism may come to light. And given the incongruities across different kinds of journalistic representation suggested by this contained exploration of the press during the spring and summer of 1945, that may be no small aim.

One reporter said not long ago that it is only when "literal memory ends that cultural memory can begin."[112] This chapter has attempted to explore some of the pathways by which one small but important dimension of the cultural memory of the Holocaust was first instantiated. It suggests that cultural memory often begins when it is least expected, in the establishment of the original record from which memory springs.

Notes

Many thanks to the Annenberg School for Communication at the University of Pennsylvania, members of the PARSS Cultural Studies Group at the University of Pennsylvania, the Shelby Cullom Davis Center for Historical Study at Princeton University, and the Department of Rhetoric and Communication at Temple University for commenting on early versions of this essay. Thanks are also due Temple University for a Grant-in-Aid-of-Research, the Freedom Forum Center for Media Studies at Columbia University for a Research Fellowship, the John H. Simon Guggenheim Memorial Foundation for a Fellowship, and the Joan Shorenstein Center on the Press, Politics and Public Policy at the John F. Kennedy School of Government at Harvard University for a Goldsmith Research Award that all enabled me to complete the *Remembering to Forget* project.

1. Janet Maslin, "Imagining the Holocaust to Remember It," *New York Times,* December 15, 1993, C19.

2. The project is entitled *Remembering to Forget: Holocaust Memory through the Camera's Eye* (University of Chicago Press, 1998).

   It is important to mention that there are no uninvolved terms in a project about the Holocaust, and for that reason I have elected to be as definitive as possible about its parameters. This project is *not* about Holocaust remembrance per se, but about one part of its memory, seen here as a particularistic filter through which we appropriate its events. It is *not* about all that we have come to know about the atrocities of the camps, but about what we were told on their initial representation as news at the time of the camps' liberation. It is *not* about a range of mediated modes of representing the Holocaust— such as newsreels, radio, books, or other occupants of its field of public representations—but about what might be called its ground floor of public memory, its representation in newspapers, newsmagazines, and picture magazines during the spring and summer of 1945. It is *not* about the memory of many nations and nationals involved in the camps' liberation, such as Soviet journalists and photographers, but focuses primarily on their American and British counterparts. It is *not* about all accounts of the atrocities, but adopts a synecdochic mode of representing Holocaust memory by addressing one event—the liberation of the European concentration camps. Yet in attempting to address the topic of this project—American and British photojournalism and the liberation of the European concentration camps of World War II—the essay of necessity considers many of these same issues that appear initially to be out of bounds.

This chapter is based on an analysis of the popular, trade, and military press during the summer and spring of 1945. I paid equal attention to American and British daily newspapers, newsmagazines, and picture magazines, as well as trade publications that circulated at the time among both reporters and photographers in the United States and Britain.

3. Pierre Nora, "Between Memory and History: *Les Lieux de mémoire*," *Representations* 26 (1989): 13.

4. Maurice Halbwachs, *The Collective Memory* (New York: Harper and Row, 1980 [1950]).

5. James Young, *The Texture of Memory: Holocaust Memorials and Meaning* (New Haven, Conn.: Yale University Press, 1993), 6. For an elaboration of how this occurs in retellings of the Kennedy assassination, see Barbie Zelizer, *Covering the Body: The Kennedy Assassination, the Media, and the Shaping of Collective Memory* (Chicago: University of Chicago Press, 1992).

6. Geoffrey Hartman, ed., *Holocaust Remembrance* (Cambridge, Mass.: Blackwell, 1994), 4.

7. Saul Friedlander, "Introduction," in *Probing the Limits of Representation*, ed. S. Friedlander (Cambridge, Mass.: Harvard University Press, 1992), 3. Berel Lang has characterized the atrocities as being inherently "anti-representational," in that they work against the kind of event depictable in a factual or literal manner. See Berel Lang, *Act and Idea in the Nazi Genocide* (Chicago: University of Chicago Press, 1990), 160.

8. For more on this, see Barbie Zelizer, "Wirephoto and the Discourse of Resistance," *Journal of Communication* 45.2 (Spring 1995): 78–92. Also see Barbie Zelizer, "Words Against Images: Newswork in the Age of Photography," in *Newsworkers: Towards a History of the Rank and File*, ed. Hanno Hardt and Bonnie Brennen (Minneapolis: University of Minnesota Press, 1995), 135–59.

9. Hartman, ed., *Holocaust Remembrance*, 269, n. 23. Hartman is paraphrasing Anton Kaes's views on film and the Holocaust,

in which Kaes claims that a stock of visual images has impregnated its filmic representations. See Anton Kaes, *From "Hitler" to "Heimat": The Return of History as Film* (Cambridge, Mass.: Harvard University Press, 1989).

10. See Fred Ritchin, *In Our Own Image* (New York: Aperture, 1990), 7. This was particularly relevant to word reporters, whose credibility with the public on the eve of the war had dipped to new lows. Polls recorded that one in three persons disbelieved what they read in the press. Cited in William Stott, *Documentary Expression and Thirties America* (Chicago: University of Chicago Press, 1973), 79.

11. See Ritchin, *In Our Own Image*, 1.

12. There is a vast literature distinguishing between the photograph's functions of denotation and connotation, between referentiality and universality. See, in particular, Roland Barthes, "The Rhetoric of the Image," in *Image, Music, Text* (New York: Hill and Wang, 1977); Roland Barthes, *Camera Lucida* (London: Jonathan Cape, 1981); Allan Sekula, "On the Invention of Photographic Meaning," *Photography Against the Grain* (Halifax: Press of the Nova Scotia College of Art and Design, 1984 [1974]); Rudolf Arnheim, "The Images of Pictures and Words," *Word and Image* 2.4 (October–December 1986): 306–10; and Stuart Hall, "The Determinations of News Photographs," *The Manufacture of News*, ed. Stanley Cohen and Jock Young (London: Sage, 1974). Also see Susan Sontag, *On Photography* (New York: Anchor Books, 1977), whose recollection of Holocaust photographs has been extensively quoted. "Nothing I have seen," she said, "in photographs or in real life ever cut me as sharply, deeply, instantaneously. Indeed, it seems plausible to me to divide my life into two parts, before I saw those photographs (I was twelve) and after" (20).

13. David D. Cooke, "News Pictures," *Photo-Era Magazine* (June 1931): 315.

14. Recording the war was, in one view, "a twilight of the gods. No time to think about it or interpret it. Just rush to photograph it; write it; cable it. Record it now—think about it later. History will form the judgments." See Margaret Bourke-White, *Portrait of Myself* (New York: Simon and Schuster, 1963), 258.

15. For a forceful discussion of the way in which practices of use determine the power invested in the photograph, see John Tagg, *The Burden of Representation* (Minneapolis: University of Minnesota Press, 1988). He claims that "photography as such has no identity. Its status as a technology varies with the power relations which invest it. Its nature as a practice depends on the institutions and agents which define it and set it to work" (63).

166

16. This was, of course, a matter of degree. When compared with the photographs of World War I—most of whose headlines and captions "rarely identified the precise battle or location pictured in the images" (Susan Moeller, *Shooting War* [New York: Basic Books, 1989], 135), the images of World War II appeared highly documented. But when compared with their contemporaneous competitor, words, they were highly lacking.

17. That year, one photographic trade journal advised photographers who wanted to submit their photographs to newspapers against using "only general terms as caption material." A "photograph can be sold to a newspaper editor only if it carries his kind of caption," one that "should have all the pertinent facts" and should never be faked, "for you can almost be hanged for it" (M. W. MacPherson, "Newspaper Picture Captions," *American Photography* [September 1946]: 46).

18. Images tended to receive credits only when they were truly exceptional, and cameramen pleaded to be recognized by name. As one photographer complained in 1944, "The war cameramen expose themselves to all the dangers of enemy fire [that correspondents do] yet receive little of the glory" (cited in Jack Price, "Credit Line Asked for War Photographers," *Editor and Publisher,* October 28, 1944, 64).

19. While recognizing debates as to whether or not the liberation was in fact an action of emancipation for those confined in the camps, this chapter subscribes to the view that certain activities of liberation did take place, even if they were not as widespread as the liberating forces claimed. For a discussion of how the liberation of Belsen was accompanied by days of shooting inmates, continued hunger, and lack of sanitation, see Hagit Lavsky, "The Day After: Bergen-Belsen from Concentration Camp to the Centre of the Jewish Survivors in Germany," *German History* 11.1 (1993): 36–59.

20. Templeton Peck, "Evening Editorial, American Broadcasting Station in Europe," April 19, 1944. Taken from papers of Templeton Peck, Box no. 1, Hoover Institution Archives, Stanford University.

21. "Nazi Atrocities," *New Republic,* April 30, 1945, 572.

22. This is discussed extensively in Deborah E. Lipstadt, *Beyond Belief: The American Press and the Coming of the Holocaust, 1933–1945* (New York: Free Press, 1986).

23. Lipstadt, *Beyond Belief,* 20.

24. Patrick G. Walker, "The Terror in Europe," *Picture Post,* October 11, 1941, 8. No credit was given for the photograph.

25. It appears that the writer of that letter photographed the camp's liberation by accident: "The morning Ohrdruf was liberated,"

167

he wrote, "I was there. Several days before I had picked up a camera that had about ten pictures left on the film, and I took them there" (letter from Raymond J. Young to John B. Coulston, from file "Jews in the American Army Liberation of Ohrdruf," Document B/60; K/15/82, Yad Vashem Archive, Jerusalem, Israel). It is fair to assume that such circumstances for documenting the camps were fairly common.

26. *Atrocities and Other Conditions in Concentration Camps in Germany (Report to U.S. Congress)* (Washington, D.C.: United States Government Printing Office, 1945). Also see "Official Report on Buchenwald Camp," *P.M.*, April 30, 1945, 9.

27. Cited in Vicki Goldberg, *Margaret Bourke-White: A Biography* (Reading, Mass.: Addison-Wesley, Inc., 1987), 290.

28. Harold Denny, "Despair Blankets Buchenwald Camp," *New York Times*, April 20, 1945, 3.

29. Denny, "Despair Blankets Buchenwald Camp," 3.

30. This derived in part from language and cultural barriers.

31. These categories of witness differ somewhat from those more generally invoked in Holocaust literature—that is, perpetrators, victims, and bystanders (see Raul Hilberg, *The Destruction of the European Jews* [New York: Holmes and Meier, 1985]). Journalistic accounts did not so much attempt to offer *different* performances of the act of seeing but were instead situated against the seemingly omniscient authority of the journalist and contrasted against it. They do, however, somewhat correspond to what Dori Laub has suggested concerning the levels of witnessing activity: There exist "the level of being a witness to oneself within the experience; the level of being a witness to the testimonies of others; and the level of being a witness to the process of witnessing itself" (Dori Laub, "An Event Without a Witness," in Shoshana Felman and Dori Laub, *Testimony: Crises of Witnessing in Literature, Psychoanalysis, and History* [New York: Routledge, 1992], 75).

32. Denny, "Despair Blankets Buchenwald Camp," 3.

33. The liberation of other camps generated similar accounts. For instance, British newspapers recorded in detail the reactions of German nationals to the atrocities at Belsen, a camp liberated by the British. One paper recounted that when members of the German SS were forced to bury the dead, the SS women were "unmoved by the grisliness of their task" and "one even smiled as she helped bundle the corpses into the pit" (Edwin Tetlow, "Belsen: The Final Horror," *Daily Mail*, April 20, 1945).

34. Percival Knauth, "Buchenwald," *Time*, April 30, 1945, 44.

35. Denny, "Despair Blankets Buchenwald Camp," 3.

36. Knauth, "Buchenwald," 42.

37. Knauth, "Buchenwald," 41.
38. "To Look at Horror," *Newsweek*, May 28, 1945, 34. Also see "Congress, Press to View Horrors," *New York Times*, April 22, 1945, 13.
39. "Buchenwald Tour Shocking to M.P.s," *New York Times*, April 23, 1945, 5.
40. "Congressmen Plan to See More Camps," *New York Times*, April 27, 1945, 3.
41. "Buchenwald Tour Shocking to M.P.s," 5. Also see "Congressmen See Buchenwald," *New York Times*, April 22, 1945, 13; "War Crimes Group to Inspect Camps," *New York Times*, April 25, 1945, 3.
42. For example, see "Editors Inspect Buchenwald," *New York Times*, April 26, 1945, 12.
43. Robert Chandler, "Horrors Recalled," *ASNE Bulletin* 1 (June 1945): n.p. The editors were from the *Minneapolis Star-Journal and Tribune*, the *Los Angeles Times*, and the Scripps-Howard Newspaper Alliance.
44. Walker Stone, "Words Cannot Describe Horrors," *ASNE Bulletin* 1 (June 1945): n.p.
45. "To Look at Horror," *Newsweek*, May 28, 1945, 35.
46. The anonymity of victims was slightly offset in coverage of the liberation of Maidanek, where word reporters recounted seeing piles of passports and documents (Richard Lauterbach, "Murder, Inc.," *Time*, September 11, 1944, 36). Early attempts to assign identities to dead victims generated speculative stories alleging that France's ex-premier Leon Blum had perished either at Maidanek ("Foreign News: Poland," *Time*, August 21, 1944, 36) or at Buchenwald (Ivan H. Peterman, "51,000 Prisoners Killed By Nazis in One Camp," *Philadelphia Inquirer*, April 22, 1945, 4). Most word reporters, however, did not at the time attempt identification of the victims who perished in the camps. This may have ultimately worked against a recognition of Jewish victimization in the Holocaust.
47. "Kunkel Appalled by Horror Camp," *Philadelphia Inquirer*, April 29, 1945, 1.
48. Knauth, "Buchenwald," 41.
49. Edward R. Murrow, "Buchenwald Was a Living Death," *Stars and Stripes*, April 17, 1945, 4. CBS veteran Fred Friendly later called Murrow's radio broadcast "the best piece of television journalism ever done and obviously there are no pictures. . . . Your mind's eye [transports] you to Buchenwald swifter and with more accuracy than any television camera, electronic or film could ever do" (Fred Friendly/Edward R. Murrow Tape, 1961, Yad Vashem Archives, No. 0315264, Jerusalem, Israel).

50. Cited in Philip Knightley, *The First Casualty: From the Crimea to Vietnam: The War Correspondent as Hero, Propagandist, and Myth Maker* (New York and London: Harcourt Brace Jovanovich, 1975), 329.
51. Julius Ochs Adler, "Buchenwald Worse Than Battlefield," *New York Times,* April 28, 1945, 6.
52. Knauth, "Buchenwald," 40.
53. "Real Horror of Nazi Camps 'Unprintable,'" *Stars and Stripes,* April 30, 1945, 3.
54. Denny, "Despair Blankets Buchenwald Camp," 3; Harold Denny, "'The World Must Not Forget,'" *New York Times,* May 5, 1945, 9.
55. Charles R Codman, "For the Record: Buchenwald," *Atlantic* (July 1945): 54.
56. Denny, "'The World Must Not Forget,'" 9. He went on to say that images were incomplete because they did not capture the stench of the camps, a sentiment echoed by many who experienced the liberation firsthand. In fact, those responsible for recording the liberation ran a continuous comparison of the role of the different senses in helping to remember. The visual image was contrasted to the word image, and both were contrasted to the sense of smell, which, of course, was beyond the limits of representation of any medium at the time. Also see Edward R. Murrow, "Despatch by Ed Murrow—CBS," transcription, April 15, 1945, 2 (Templeton Peck Papers, box no. 1, Hoover Institution Archives, Stanford University).
57. Goldberg, *Margaret Bourke-White,* 290.
58. Petr Tausk, *Photography in the 20th Century* (London: Focal Press, 1980): 110.
59. Goldberg, *Margaret Bourke-White,* 290.
60. Bourke-White was so changed by her experience at Buchenwald that it prompted her to write an entire book about Germany. She wrote that photographing the camps involved working from within a "self-imposed stupor." The camera almost provided "a relief. It interposed a slight barrier between myself and the horror in front of me. . . . I have to work with a veil over my mind. In photographing the murder camps, the protective veil was so tightly drawn that I hardly knew what I had taken until I saw prints of my own photographs. It was as though I was seeing these horrors for the first time" (Margaret Bourke-White, *"Dear Fatherland, Rest Quietly"* (New York: Simon and Schuster, 1946), 73; also see Margaret Bourke-White, *Portrait of Myself,* 259.
61. Photograph entitled "Nazi Barbarism," *Philadelphia Inquirer,* April 26, 1945, 14. Also see "Penna. Congressman Sees Evi-

dence of Foe's Cruelty," *Philadelphia Inquirer,* April 26, 1945, 14. Bourke-White's close-up shot also has been widely recycled in retrospectives about World War II (e.g., "WWII: 40 Years Later," *Life* [Spring–Summer 1985]: 80–81).

62. Picture appended to "Foreign News: Germany," *Time,* May 14, 1945, 43.

63. This pattern would hold up over the years. A picture of Buchenwald that showed scores of male prisoners behind a barbed-wire fence, photographed by Margaret Bourke-White and entitled "Survivors Behind Barbed Wire, Buchenwald 1945," would later become a visual marker of the Holocaust, recycled in dozens of retrospectives on the Holocaust and overviews of photojournalism (e.g., "Life: 50 Years," *Life* [Special Anniversary Issue, Fall 1986]: 192; Wilson Hicks, *Words and Pictures* [New York: Harper and Brothers Publishing, 1952]). Ironically, at the time of the liberation, the photograph itself was not published. See Vicki Goldberg, *The Power of Photography* (New York: Abbeville Publishing Group, 1991), 37.

64. Picture appended to article by Knauth, "Buchenwald," 42. In fact, such an approach to pictures and captions appears to have characterized the newsmagazine. In *Time,* "the caption, consisting of the subject's name and a few short provocative words, served as a teaser to draw the reader into the story nearby." Only in the late forties did the magazine make "use with some frequency of the single news picture with a definitive caption as a self-contained entity." See Wilson Hicks, *Words and Pictures,* 37–38.

65. This picture was appended to a series of eyewitness reports from Erla, Belsen, and Buchenwald, but there was no such report from Nordhausen. The photograph thus served as the *only* marker of Nordhausen in the *Time* account. See "Foreign News: Germany," *Time,* April 30, 1945, 38.

66. Picture appended to Denny, " 'The World Must Not Forget,' " 42. We need only consider how unusual it would be to find a word reporter's byline situated elsewhere in a newspaper. I might add that this same photograph has since become a visual marker of Holocaust remembrance, where it has been actively circulated in books (Martin Gilbert, *Atlas of the Holocaust* [London: Pergamon Press, 1988], 239), articles about Holocaust deniers (Kenneth L. Woodward, "Hitler and the Holocaust," *Newsweek,* July 11, 1977, 77), and articles about so-called Holocaust politics (Walter Goodman, "The Politics of the Holocaust," *Newsweek,* September 27, 1982, 33). It is telling that two articles appeared in the same journal, which suggests that the photograph is part of that particular news organization's

photographic archive. This is a significant pattern behind the recycling of visual images in memory about the Holocaust.

67. Picture appended to "Official Report on Buchenwald Camp," *P.M.*, April 30, 1945, 9.

68. See "This Was Nazi Germany—Blood, Starvation, the Stench of Death," *Stars and Stripes*, April 23, 1945, 4–5; and "German Atrocities View Camps," *Illustrated London News*, April 28, 1945, iv (supplement).

69. "Daily Feature and Pictorial Page," *Philadelphia Inquirer*, April 26, 1945, 14.

70. "Atrocities," *Life*, May 5, 1945, 32–37.

71. "Lest We Forget," *Look*, May 15, 1945, 51–55; "The Problem That Makes All Europe Wonder," *Picture Post*, May 5, 1945, 7–11, 26; "German Atrocities in British Camps," *Illustrated London News*, April 28, 1945, i (supplement).

72. "German Atrocities in British Camps," i (supplement). Interestingly, the following week the journal's editorial board was still not convinced that the photographs had done their job, for it printed a series of drawings depicting many of the same camp scenes that had already been shown in photographs. Unlike the photographs, however, the drawings bore the name and signature of the artist who drew them (Bryan de Grineau, "As Dore Might Have Conceived It: Belsen Death Camp," *Illustrated London News*, May 5, 1945, 471–73).

73. "Atrocities," *Life*, May 7, 1945, 33.

74. Such was also the case with the so-called atrocity newsreels. While the Signal Corps released footage to the major newsreel companies, many questioned the wisdom of showing scenes of the camps. They argued that it would increase the difficulties of making peace with the Germans. This seemed "inspired, at least in part, by an unwillingness to confront the scenes themselves" (Robert H. Abzug, *Inside the Vicious Heart* [New York: Oxford University Press, 1985], 135).

75. See, for example, Istvan Deak, "Strategies of Hell," *New York Review of Books*, October 8, 1992, 10.

76. The three articles using the same photograph included Knauth, "Buchenwald," 42; Al Newman, "Nordhausen: A Hell Factory Worked by the Living Dead," *Newsweek*, April 23, 1945, 52; and "This Was Nazi Germany—Blood, Starvation, the Stench of Death," 4–5. In fact, the bodies were at Ohrdruf, and the photograph was a war pool photo, jointly attributed to British Combine and Acme Photo. It was taken somewhere between April 4 and 8, 1945 (Photo 1460/41, F 15476, Yad Vashem Pictorial Archive, Jerusalem, Israel).

77. Compare Katriel, "Sites of Memory: Discourses of the Past in Israeli Pioneering Settlement Museums," 116–18 (Eds.).

78. Picture appended to Denny, "'We Must Not Forget,'" 42.
79. Melinda Beck, "Footnote to the Holocaust," *Newsweek*, October 19, 1981, 73. The article portrayed a photographic shot of Mermelstein holding a framed copy of the original Associated Press photograph. Interestingly, in the more recent image, the attribution of the original photograph was displaced to accommodate the attribution of the more recent shot of Mermelstein holding the Buchenwald photo.
80. "Nazi Barbarism," picture appended to "Daily Feature and Pictorial Page," *Philadelphia Inquirer*, April 26, 1945, 14.
81. See, for example, picture appended to "American Legislators in Europe to Investigate Atrocities," *New York Times*, April 25, 1945, 3. Also see picture appended to Ben Hibbs, "Journey to a Shattered World," *Saturday Evening Post*, June 9, 1945, 20, where a photograph of Eisenhower talking with a group of editors and publishers topped the story of atrocities in the camps.
82. Picture appended to "To Look at Horror," *Newsweek*, May 28, 1945, 35.
83. Picture appended to "Germany: Foreign News," *Time*, April 30, 1945, 38–45.
84. Pictures appended to "This Was Nazi Germany—Blood, Starvation, the Stench of Death," 4–5. Ohrdruf was mistakenly identified as Buchenwald and Gotha.
85. Pictures appended to "The Problem That Makes All Europe Wonder," *Picture Post*, May 5, 1945, 7–11. Of eleven images, only two (from Nordhausen) were identified by location.
86. Pictures appended to "Congressmen Plan to See More Camps," *New York Times*, April 27, 1945, 3; Ivan H. Peterman, "Nazis Kill 51,000 in Single Camp," *Philadelphia Inquirer*, April 22, 1945, 4; Gene Currivan, "Germans Murder 5,000 Prisoners Removed From Buchenwald Camp," *New York Times*, April 30, 1945, 5.
87. Picture appended to "Official Report on Buchenwald Camp," *P.M.*, April 30, 1945, 9. This was one of the few times Jews were even mentioned in captions, a point which may have facilitated a suppression of Jewish victimization of the Holocaust.
88. Goldberg, *Margaret Bourke-White*, 290.
89. "Public Crowd for Pictures of Atrocities," *World's Press News*, April 26, 1945, 1.
90. "The Problem That Makes All Europe Wonder," *Picture Post*, May 5, 1945, 7.
91. Jorge Lewinski, *The Camera at War* (New York: Simon and Schuster, 1978), 136.
92. *Lest We Forget* (London: Associated Press, 1945).
93. See, for instance, John M. McCullough, "Publicity Given

Atrocities in Reich Stirs Speculation," *Philadelphia Inquirer,* April 24, 1945, 16.

94. E.g., "Atrocities: Letters to Editor," *Life,* May 28, 1945, 2–4; "Supplement to Committee, Letters to the Times," *New York Times,* May 7, 1945, 16.

95. All citations in "Atrocities: Letters to Editor," 4.

96. "The Pictures Don't Lie," *Stars and Stripes,* April 26, 1945, 2. Interestingly, the paper used an unattributed and uncaptioned photograph of a burnt body to illustrate its point about the image's authenticity. The picture, in fact, was a Signal Corps photograph of the body of a slave laborer burned and machine-gunned to death by the German troops at Leipzig, Germany, on April 13, 1945, but it was not identified as such by the *Stars and Stripes,* despite the fact that the newspaper apparently received such documentation with the photograph (see "Massacre at Leipzig," Document no. 14581/166, SC 203743–S, Yad Vashem Pictorial Archive, Jerusalem, Israel).

97. "Europe's Problem: What M.P.'s Say of the Nazi Horror Camps," *Picture Post,* May 12, 1945, 25.

98. "The Pictures Don't Lie," *Stars and Stripes,* April 26, 1945, 2.

99. Abzug, *Inside the Vicious Heart,* 138.

100. Abzug, *Inside the Vicious Heart,* 138.

101. Milton Mayer, "Let the Swiss Do It!" *Progressive,* May 14, 1945.

102. "Europe's Problem: What M.P.'s Say of the Nazi Horror Camps," *Picture Post,* May 12, 1945, 25.

103. "The Pictures Don't Lie," 2.

104. Abzug, *Inside the Vicious Heart,* ix.

105. Andreas Huyssen, "Monument and Memory in a Post-Modern Eye," *Yale Journal of Criticism* (Fall 1993): 256.

106. Annette Wieviorka, "On Testimony," in *Holocaust Remembrance,* ed. Hartman, 24.

107. Bourke-White, *Portrait of Myself,* 160.

108. This issue surfaced surrounding Alain Resnais' film *Night and Fog,* but it has continued to be a major critical theme of Holocaust representations.

109. Huyssen, "Monument and Memory," 256.

110. Hayden White, "Historical Emplotment and the Problem of Truth," in *Probing the Limits of Representation,* ed. Friedlander, 50.

111. The status of journalistic veracity has been consistently encroached upon by other kinds of recorders. In making *Schindler's List,* for instance, Steven Spielberg admitted that he "wanted to do more CNN reporting with a camera I could hold in my hand," and he reportedly told his cast "we're not making a film, we're making a document" (cited in Richard Schickel,

"Heart of Darkness," *Time*, December 13, 1993, 75). Likewise, he was elsewhere hailed for having become "an unblinking reporter" (David Ansen, "Spielberg's Obsession," *Newsweek*, December 20, 1993, 114).

112. Jonathan Alter, "After the Survivors," *Newsweek*, December 20, 1993, 117.

6

Custer Loses Again: The Contestation over Commodified Public Memory

Roberta Pearson

In 1874, the commander of a cavalry regiment serving on the American frontier wrote a series of articles for the *Galaxy* magazine chronicling his adventures. This officer had enjoyed a very successful Civil War, his military exploits and flamboyant persona endearing him to Union journalists and their readers, but killing Indians proved a more thankless task than killing Confederates.

> How many military men have reaped laurels from their Indian campaigns? Does he strive to win the approving smile of his countrymen? . . . If he survives the campaign he can feel assured of this fact, that one half of his fellow-citizens at home will revile him for his zeal and pronounce his success . . . a massacre of poor, defenseless, harmless Indians; while the other half, if his efforts . . . are not crowned with satisfactory results, will cry, "Down with him."[1]

George Armstrong Custer, whose writing reveals him to be rather more complicated than the one-dimensional character of much popular culture, knew that he made history but that others determined its meaning. Since Custer's death at the Little Bighorn in 1876, his career as a popular hero/villain serves as a prime example of the fluidity of the representation of historical events and figures. The Native American military triumph annihilated more than two hundred members of the 7th Cavalry along with its colonel, but also transformed Custer from a controversial commander, who was indeed accused of killing "poor, defenseless, harmless Indians," to a martyred hero on the shining altar of Manifest Destiny—an image maintained by his wife, Elizabeth, and hagiographic biographers for the subsequent half-century plus. The year 1934 marked a clear turning point for Custer's reputation, as Frederick Van de Water published his influential biography, *Glory Hunter,* which portrayed Custer as ambitious, selfish, reckless, and a rather bad tactician. Custer continued to figure as the hero of some popular texts, but *Glory Hunter*'s interpretation shaped many subsequent representations, and by the 1960s much popular culture portrayed him as an outright villain.[2]

Diverse representations continue even today. In May 1995, both the CBS series *Dr. Quinn, Medicine Woman* and the United Paramount Network series *Legend* featured "guest appearances" by George Armstrong Custer. *Legend*'s fairly sympathetic Custer exposed corrupt officials profiteering from army supplies. *Dr. Quinn*'s monstrous Custer believed that "the only good Indian is a dead Indian" and massacred helpless women and children. As these examples show, popular culture is still contradictory, but until recently the U.S. government, the keeper of official memory, had presented Custer and his troopers as the heroes of the Little Bighorn. Native American novelist James Welch describes a battlefield tour that was

> designed to show the battle from the white point of view. [Being placed in] Custer's shoes, in Reno's and Benteen's shoes . . . is the perspective that the tourist gets. The road follows the various positions of the 7th Cavalry. The manifold literature tells the story from these positions. The tourist is encouraged to look down from these rolling hills, these ridges, and imagine what it must have been like for the soldiers to be completely overwhelmed by half-naked, yipping savages.[3]

Custer's greatest public relations disaster occurred in 1991, when the U.S. Congress, after considerable lobbying by the American Indian Movement, changed the name of the Custer Battlefield National Monument to the Little Bighorn Battlefield National Monument. The name change that metaphorically annihilated Custer a hundred and sixteen years after his death constituted a lasting victory for Native Americans on the battleground of historical representation. Journalists viewed the congressional action as a significant defeat for a figure who had retained a prominent position in the national consciousness despite having died over a century ago. "Custer Loses Again," said the headline in the *Progressive*.[4] "Custer Loses Again at Little Bighorn in Montana," said the headline in *Sunset Magazine*.[5] In 1990, *People* magazine had employed the same metaphor when reporting on the appointment of a Native American, Barbara Booher, as the new superintendent of the Custer Battlefield National Monument. "General Custer Loses at Little Big Horn Again as an Indian Activist Becomes Keeper of His Legend." Custer fans reacted as negatively to this appointment as they did a year later to the battlefield name change. "'I don't want to sound racist and chauvinist,' says Jerry Russell, . . . member of the Little Big Horn Associates, a national group that guards the old warrior's memory, 'But I want the lady out of there. She's not qualified.'"[6]

Booher's comments in the *People* article must have confirmed Mr. Russell's worst fears. "The story is out of balance. . . . It doesn't take much to look at the exhibits and see that everything is tilted toward Custer, who was the loser in that battle. . . . The Battle of the Little Big Horn is really an Indian story." Renaming the battle site the Little Bighorn Battlefield National Monument meant that the Custer and his 7th Cavalry were no longer to be cast as the heroes, with their Indian foes playing the supporting and often uncredited roles. Congress's authorization of the construction of a monument to the fallen Native Americans to counterbalance the one to the fallen soldiers was one of many shifts in narrative perspective that would take place at the site under Barbara Booher's leadership.

Commodified Public Memory

The struggle over the narrative representation of the Little Bighorn battle was a struggle over memory: Whose memories, white or Native American, would the battle site legitimate, and how would this selective legitimation shape the memories of subsequent generations? In an oft-referenced passage, Michel Foucault spoke of the connection between memory and popular resistance.

People . . . barred from writing, from producing their books themselves, from drawing up their own historical accounts . . . nevertheless do have a way of recording history, or remembering it, of keeping it fresh and using it. This popular history was . . . even more alive, more clearly formulated in the 19th century, where, for instance, there was a whole tradition of struggles which were transmitted orally, or in writing or songs, etc. Now, a whole number of apparatuses have been set up ("popular literature," cheap books and the stuff that's taught in school as well) to obstruct the flow of this popular memory. . . . Today, cheap books aren't enough. There are much more effective means like television and the cinema. This was one way of reprogramming popular memory. . . . Since memory is actually a very important factor in struggle, if one controls people's memory, one controls their dynamism.[7]

The phrase "a whole tradition of struggles which were transmitted orally, or in writing or songs" aptly describes the transmission of "traditional" Native American history that contributed to the reconfiguration of the historical representation of the Little Bighorn in 1991. From generation to generation, the descendants of the Lakota and Cheyenne warriors who fought Custer, as well as of the Crow scouts who guided him, have passed down their ancestors' accounts of the battle to construct an alternative representation that differs crucially from the image of the gallant "last stand" maintained by the U.S. government. For example, a song written in the 1960s presents the Native American leaders as the battle's heroes: "With victories he [Custer] was swimming / He killed children, dogs and women / But the general he don't ride well anymore. / Crazy Horse sent out the Call / To Sitting Bull and Gall / And the general he don't ride well anymore."[8]

Foucault correctly points to the importance of such memories, yet the persistence of Native American oral tradition into the media-saturated twentieth century might have surprised him. His conception of the "popular" and of the "control" of the popular as separate entities causes him to be too optimistic about the past and too pessimistic about the present. Michael Bommes and Patrick Wright criticized Foucault's failure to account for the dialectical interaction between the "popular" and the "dominant."

To think in terms of "popular memory" is to risk treating "the popular" as if it were wholly unified, fully achieved and therefore

179

capable of sustaining a memory wholly apart from the dominant constructions of the past. It is also to risk isolating these dominant constructions from any "popular" response which may be made to them. Questions of acquiescence, deference and resistance cannot be dealt with adequately if the constructions in question are considered apart from "popular memory"—as if they were entirely programmatic and defined only in the motions with which they are laid on from above.[9]

The Popular Memory Group is here conceiving of the functioning of memory within a hegemonic order, which British cultural studies has conceived of as a fluid and unstable site of contestation between the dominant social formations in the ruling power bloc and those marginalized social formations seeking concessions from the dominant, and whom the dominant constantly strives to incorporate. A hegemonic order is not monolithic or totalizing; the dominant tolerate alternative world views and, even more important, the dominated have a potential for resistance that might produce change, perhaps even a different hegemonic order. As Raymond Williams says, "Hegemony is not singular. Its own internal structures are highly complex, and have continually to be renewed, recreated and defended; and by the same token . . . they can be continually challenged and in certain respects modified."[10] Conceptualizing the hegemonic order as dynamic and conflictual means interrogating Foucault's assumption that mass media reprogram memory by representing the values of the dominant social formations. Rather, as a component of the hegemonic order, historical representation becomes a site of struggle between different voices seeking to construct versions of the past that accord with their memories.

Illuminating the connections between memory and the hegemonic order requires pausing for a moment to specify what kind of memory is at issue, since, as the chapters in this volume and a rapidly growing literature will attest, scholars have used the word to refer to many different and sometimes contradictory concepts. Some historians have distinguished between individual, group, or collective memory as an attribute of individuals or collections of individuals, and official memory as an attribute of state or civil institutions. Others have contrasted memory, associated with the people, with history, associated with the dominant, arguing that the former is continuous and the latter disjunctive. For example, Pierre Nora asserts that "memory is life, borne by living societies founded in its name. . . . History . . . is the reconstruction, always problematic and incomplete, of what is no longer. Memory is a perpetually actual phenomenon, a bond tying us to the eternal present; history is a representation of the past."[11]

In this essay, I shall be discussing representations of historical events that together constitute what I term "commodified public memory." "Commodified" refers to the economic incentives—either direct in terms of sales profits or advertising revenues, or indirect in terms of private grants, membership rolls, and government funding—that structure these representations. "Public" deliberately resonates with the concept of the public sphere, for the historical representations comprising commodified public memory usually originate from state or civic institutions. The use of "public" rather than "popular" indicates that commodified public memory emanates from above, from such central institutions of the hegemonic order as the government and private corporations. While individuals and groups of individuals retain separate memories that often form the basis for contestation, the powerful institutions producing and circulating commodified public memory ensure that certain historical representations become both ubiquitous and dominant.

Commodified public memory, a subset of the hegemonic order, exhibits the same simultaneous fluidity and stability: the representations that have achieved dominance at one particular historical moment are constantly challenged from below. Yet the dominance by a specific set of representations temporarily ends, and, in the process, erases the signs of, contestation. The naturalized and widely accepted dominant representations temporarily halt history, establishing a set of unquestioned, frozen, and abstracted "facts" that play a crucial role in the construction of a dominant national identity. Bommes and Wright argue that the activities of the British National Heritage organization produce the effect "as if a strange and obliterating glaciation is being drawn across the entire surface of social life, as if history is being frozen over, arrested and in this sense 'stopped.' National Heritage appears to involve nothing less than the abolition of all contradiction in the name of a national culture. . . . History appears

181

not as necessity, struggle or transformation but as 'our' National 'Heritage."[12]

The reduction of a processual and conflictual history to a limited set of representations of a limited set of events, figures, and sites lends itself to further commodification: Commodified public memory continually reinforces itself. As Michel-Rolph Trouillot said about Columbus and "the discovery,"

> discovery has lost its processual character. It has become a single and simple moment, cut from its antecedents . . . and its context. . . . It is not a process anymore, but a "fact": on *this* day, in 1492, Christopher Columbus discovered the Bahamas. As a set event, void of context, it befits travel agents, airlines, politicians, the media, or the states who sell it in the prepackaged forms under which "the public" has come to expect history to present itself. It is a product of power whose label has been cleansed of traces of power.[13]

We now live in the age of commodified public memory, a commodification driven by the state and increasingly by giant corporations. Michael Kammen observes that "the United States had begun moving toward the commercial management of public memory," referring to the fact that "particular brands of cola, wine, sausage, hotel chains, and other products or industries bought into and 'brought you' the centennial of the Statue of Liberty in 1986, and less flagrantly the bicentennial of the U.S. Constitution a year later."[14] These same colas, hotel chains, and sausages sponsor the plethora of media specials that mark the anniversaries of significant historical events, such as the thirtieth anniversary of the Kennedy assassination or the fiftieth anniversaries of Pearl Harbor and of V-E Day.

Not confined to particular commemorations, commodified public memory functions year-round. The Disney empire, already offering a sanitized and celebratory version of the Pax Americana at Disneyland and Disney World and in *Pocahontas* and other films, proposed building an American history theme park on the site of a Civil War battlefield. The eleven-hour PBS documentary *The Civil War* achieved unprecedented critical acclaim and ratings success, and importunate affiliates regularly rebroadcast the series during their pledge drives. The Arts and Entertainment Network recently launched an entire cable channel, the History TV Network, which features historical documentaries, fiction movies, and mini-series and is carried by cable companies in the United Kingdom. Advertisements in middle-brow publications continually push historical memorabilia such as the Franklin Mint's "Indian Heritage" Plate Collection. Exhibiting the historical effacement typical of commodified public memory, the collection consists of six "magnificent portraits of Native American braves" posed on horseback against the background of majestic landscapes, and forever abstracted from the historical process of the Westward expansion that destroyed their lifestyle.

The Battle over the Battlefield

A CBS Evening News story of May 25, 1991, that reported on the debates between Native Americans seeking to have their collective memories acknowledged and whites defending the status quo illustrates the process by which commodified public memory suppresses controversy and freezes history.[15] Filmed at the Little Bighorn battlefield, the report begins with invocations of the commodified public memory of the gallant, but ultimately tragic, Last Stand. A long shot of the sky is followed by a tilt down to the 7th Cavalry headstones. In a standup, the reporter says, "In the place where George Armstrong Custer and the Army's 7th cavalry fell in the most famous battle of the American west, there's a skirmish now about honor and memory and the meaning of a name." After explaining that Representative Ben Nighthorse Campbell has introduced a bill to change the battlefield's name, the reporter continues, "Custer's Last Stand has long been officially remembered from the cavalry's point of view—an heroic struggle against overwhelming forces that ended in the death of almost three hundred soldiers." Shots of twentieth-century paintings according with commodified public memory's image of the battle's final moments accompany the voice-over.

The reporter then shifts narrative perspective. "No marker honors the Indian dead. The proposal to rename the national park Little Bighorn National Battlefield would also erect a memorial to the Indians who died defending their camp against Custer's troops." In a standup, Tony Prairie Bear, of the Cheyenne National Council, explains, "We want

183

to be recognized for our efforts too." The report then cuts to shots of the annual reenactment of the battle, as the reporter points to the motivation that often serves to protect commodified public memory from contestation. "It's a conflict too over profit. A tourist pageant each year plays out the past in a dusty reenactment of Custer's Last Stand. Some worry changing the name could hurt the business that draws a quarter of a million visitors each year to this quarter of Montana." Shots of Custer memorabilia and an interview with Custer buff Bill Wells follow. Wells asserts, "Like it or not, the name Custer is what draws people to that battlefield."

While the report alludes to the profit motive sustaining dominant historical representations, and while it seemingly gives both sides of the story to accord with journalistic notions of "balance" and objectivity, the reduction of the debate to two clearly opposed positions, whites versus Native Americans, suppresses contradiction and contestation. Some whites supported the name change and the Indian memorial as a means of augmenting the site's commercial appeal. Representative Ron Marlenee of Montana said in the congressional debate, "I wish to note that the entire state of Montana stands to benefit from erection of this memorial. Its establishment will further enhance the already worldwide and national significance of Custer Battlefield National Monument, increasing its drawing power as a major historical site in the United States."[16]

The report also fails to mention that Montana's Native Americans have a large financial stake in the reenactment. Since 1964, the centennial of Montana's statehood, members of the Crow tribe, which owns much of the land surrounding the federal park, have staged a yearly reenactment of the battle that draws thousands of tourists who pay eight dollars a head.[17] While the reenactment presents the Indians as the heroes, some Native American activists have seen it as demeaning. *Indian Country Today* reported in 1993 that

> ancestors [sic] of the original tribes that participated in the Battle . . . are protesting on grounds the reenactment exploits the battle by chasing the tourist dollar. . . . The Executive Board of the Fort Peck Assiniboine and Sioux tribes . . . voted unanimously to oppose the annual re-enactment. . . . "The battle re-enactment does not provide a message of hope for a better tomorrow for the thousands of Indian and non-Indian children

who visit the battlefield every year. What are we teaching our children?" Caleb Shields [chairman of the Fort Peck Tribes] asked. . . . Russell Means, co-founder of the American Indian Movement [said], "It perpetuates all kinds of stereotypes."[18]

The report also hints at the manner in which commodified public memory may eventually efface the clash of memories of the present-day battle and the clash of cultures of its bloodier antecedent to contribute to a cohesive sense of national identity. The first and last lines of the reporter's narration echo each other. The report begins: "Some Montana residents are wrestling with a difficult question. How best to remember their fallen heroes on both sides of a bitter struggle." The report ends: "The national park service favors the change as a step toward better understanding between Indians and whites." In *The Conquest of America,* Tzvetan Todorov argues that one can consider the other as unequal, and thereby clearly inferior, or project one's own values onto the other, in the process eradicating difference. "Difference is corrupted into inequality, equality into identity."[19] As a result, "What is denied is the existence of a human substance truly other, something capable of being not merely an imperfect state of oneself."[20]

Examination of the congressional debates over the name change and memorial to the Indian dead reveals how commodified public memory incorporates alternative collective memories and corrupts equality into identity. Representative John Rhodes of Arizona (R), asserted that the legislation was intended to "honor the Cheyenne, Sioux and other Indian Nations who gave their lives to defend their families, life-style, culture and their lands,"[21] the implication being, of course, that any right-thinking individual would have behaved in precisely the same manner. Representative Burns made this sentiment more explicit. "These people fought to save what they believed was theirs and rightfully theirs. They did what any of us would have done to save and protect our own families and homeland."[22] These statements cast the Indians as the heroes, but, at least as far as the U.S. Congress is concerned, this does not necessitate casting their white opponents as the villains. For the commodified public memory of the Little Bighorn to function in the service of national identity, both sides must be represented as equally valorous. Representative

Ben Nighthorse Campbell, the Native American who originally introduced the legislation, said, "The Indians fought valiantly for their way of life, their families, as they knew their very survival was at stake. . . . The soldiers fought bravely, too, believing that their battles would make the West safe for settlers, miners, trappers, and others who sought fortunes and their futures during our Nation's westward expansion."[23] As we shall see later, Native American eyewitness accounts, substantiated by archaeological evidence, cast doubt on the 7th's heroism, but politicians do not permit alternative representations to intrude upon their contributions to commodified public memory. Senator Max Baucus reached the heights of hackneyed political oratory as he lent his support to Nighthorse's legislation:

> Let us continue to reflect upon lessons that the events of the Little Big Horn continue to urge upon us. Both victory and defeat are usually transitory but the human values of struggle and sacrifice endure throughout history. . . . Let us all one day stand on the slope of "Last Stand Hill" and looking out remember that the sacrifice of all Americans of many colors and cultures make this great country what it is.[24]

The debate over the battlefield constituted the height of contestation over the commodified public memory of Custer and the Little Bighorn, yet also contained the seeds of a new orthodoxy that may efface controversy and freeze history: This particular historical incident can be seen as a microcosm of hegemonic reconfiguration. Raymond Williams has argued that at a specific historical moment there is a dominant culture that is "always passed off as 'the tradition,' 'the significant past.'" Existing simultaneously, however, are "alternative meanings and values, the alternative opinions and attitudes, even some alternative senses of the world, which can be accommodated and tolerated within a particular effective and dominant culture."[25] Williams explains that some of these alternative meanings and values are associated with residual social formations. "By 'residual' I mean that some experiences, meanings and values, which cannot be verified or cannot be expressed in terms of the dominant culture, are nevertheless lived and practised on the basis of the residue . . . of some previous social formation."[26]

186

Distinguishing clearly the alternative residual position with regard to Custer and the Little Bighorn in the 1990s might be more easily accomplished in the twenty-first century, since lack of hindsight handicaps the analyst of contemporary hegemonic configurations. Williams's characterization of the residual as "the residue . . . of some previous social formations," however, points to Custer buffs, a subset of those supposedly beleaguered white males now threatened by previously marginalized social formations, and to activist Native Americans, one of those previously marginalized formations, who had maintained a strong connection to their ancestors and the past through oral traditions.

The Custer buffs defended an image of the gallant and heroic last stand that had been "passed off as *'the* tradition,' *'the* significant past' " for a half-century—until Van de Water's *Glory Hunter* challenged its dominance—and that still maintained a strong presence in certain commodified public memory texts. Jerry Russell, the same gentleman who objected to Booher's appointment as superintendent of the battlefield, also opposed changing the site's name. To Russell, the Indians who fought and died at the Little Bighorn were not freedom fighters defending their homeland, but simply "the enemy."[27] In the congressional debates, the sole representative who opposed renaming the battlefield, Representative John Dingell, from the Michigan district that includes Custer's hometown of Monroe, echoed Russell's sentiments. Dingell saw the proposal as a betrayal of the U.S. troops who had died at the Little Bighorn.

> Those who died in the uniform of the United States . . . did so as persons serving their Nation, honestly believing in the justice and rightness of their cause. . . . To now rewrite history and say . . . that it is improper that we should name that battlefield after General Custer, or that . . . he or the men who served there and died there were behaving improperly, is indeed to distort history in a curious and . . . seriously improper way.[28]

On the other side, Hugh White Clay, a Crow Indian interviewed for a CBS *Eye on America* segment on December 28, 1992, stood by the grave markers of the fallen cavalry troopers and asserted, "These headstones represent a race of people that came into our land with one thing in mind—to genocide native

187

Americans."[29] As opposed to these alternative residual positions, Congress's authorization of the name change and the monument to the Indian dead constitutes the first official acknowledgment of what may be a newly emerging commodified public memory that blurs the differences between whites and Indians in the service of a national identity that is predicated on the heroism and sacrifice of both sides.

The Television Documentaries

The above analysis of the battle over the battlefield suggests that a refinement of the concept of commodified public memory might be in order; it is necessary to distinguish between the official commodified public memory issuing from state institutions and the popular commodified public memory issuing from the culture industries, since they seem to follow different temporal trajectories.[30] As Tony Bennett and Janet Woollacott suggest, the latter may be more mobile than the former.

> Periods of generic change and innovation in popular fiction often coincide with those in which the ideological articulations through which hegemony was previously secured are no longer working to produce popular consent. In such moments, popular fictional forms may often prove more mobile and adaptable than more "organic," deeply implanted and institutionally solidified political ideologies. . . . Its particular sensitivity in this regard may be attributable to the fact that, through the market, it is more closely in touch with popular sentiment, quicker to register when specific ideological combinations are losing their "pulling power" and able to act as a testing ground for new ideological combinations.[31]

The same may hold true for the culture industries' supposedly "factual" representations of "real" popular heroes, such as George Armstrong Custer. Yet we should not conceive of the culture industries and the popular as totalities but rather as fields of contradictions in which the residual traces of previously dominant commodified public memory, such as the image of the "gallant last stand," retain a strong presence. At the same moment, a newly emerging dominant may be incorporating the residual values of marginalized social formations never acknowledged by the previously dominant. Some texts originating with the culture industries will accord entirely with a commodified public memory once dominant but now rapidly transforming to the residual. Others alternate between the residual and the newly emerging dominant in a contradictory fashion. Yet others must acknowledge the residual even as they contest it. With regard to Custer then, the residual image of the "gallant last stand," the residual image of the troopers as wanton murderers, and the newly emerging dominant that blurs differences may all exist simultaneously in different texts and occasionally even in the same text.

This section examines five television documentaries that deal wholly or in part with George Armstrong Custer and the Battle of the Little Bighorn. They all were shown during 1992 and 1993, immediately following the reconfiguring of the official commodified public memory of the man and the event: *Crossed Sabers* (a history of the U.S. Cavalry), Arts and Entertainment Network; "Last Stand at Little Big Horn," an episode of the PBS *American Experience* series; "Indians" and "Soldiers," two episodes of the ten-hour mini-series *The Wild West*, distributed by Warner Bros. Domestic Television; "Custer and the Seventh Cavalry," an episode of the Arts and Entertainment Network's *Real West* series; and "A Good Day to Die," an episode of the Discovery Channel's *How the West Was Lost* series about Native Americans.

This essay focuses on the five documentaries' narrative perspectives to determine their relationship to residual collective memories and to residual and newly emerging commodified public memories. Some of the documentaries under consideration seek to include, or perhaps more correctly incorporate, a residual alternative Native American perspective in questioning dominant hegemonic values such as progress, anthropocentrism, and capitalism by contrasting our (Euro-Americans') "ordinary understanding of the nature of man and his world," to use Williams's phrase, with the traditional Native American understanding. Rather than simply bewailing the fate of the native peoples, which has become almost mandatory in an age that demands obeisance to the principle if not the practice of racial equality, this residual alternative perspective details the central elements of Lakota and Cheyenne cultures, suggests that these peoples possess coherent world

views different from but at least equal to the Euro-Americans',
and sometimes proposes that westward expansion was not the
inevitable triumph of a superior civilization. As we shall see,
this alternative residual is in some cases incorporated into the
newly emerging dominant commodified public memory, while
in other cases it still seems to represent an as-yet unincorpo-
rated opposition to the dominant. The opposing residual alternative perspective, above associated with the Custer buffs,
continues to portray the cavalry as the heroes in the drama
of the expansion of "Western civilization" across the savage
wilderness of the American plains.

As one might predict from its subject matter, *Crossed
Sabers*, the history of the U.S. Cavalry, laments the passing of
a proud people, but at the same time justifies the government's
expansionist and exterminationist policies. Let us consider a
few key sentences from the voice-over narration. "In the late
1800s there were nearly one hundred Indian tribes totalling
some three hundred thousand people spread over a million
square miles of *US territory*" (my emphasis).[32] During the
period of westward expansion, the native peoples living in
these millions of square miles were quite surprised to discover
that they inhabited *US territory* and not the land that their
ancestors had occupied for hundreds of years. But the narrator, echoing a well-worn argument, implies that the Native
Americans had essentially ceded their rights by not properly
exploiting the land in accordance with Euro-American economic practices. "Most Indians were not farmers or builders
and many made a practice of raiding other tribes." They may
not have farmed or built in the European sense, but the Plains
tribes did change the land to suit their lifestyles.

> Indians . . . set prairie fires to get earlier growth of grasses in the
> spring. . . . Trees either died in the fires or were cut down by the
> Indians to get food for their horses. The horses themselves were
> representatives of one ecosystem that had made themselves at
> home in another. To make horses more comfortable, the Indi-
> ans were busy modifying their environment, changing patterns
> of warfare and subsistence, and doing all kinds of interesting
> things supposedly reserved for whites.[33]

And while the Cheyenne, the Lakota, and the other Plains
tribes regularly raided their neighbors, the narrator neglects

to mention that these raiders had as their principle goals the acquisition of material goods and martial glory, not the extermination of the enemy. The narrator continues, "For the fiercest Indian tribes wars had been a never ending part of life. . . . Attacks on wagon trains, settlements and US cavalry-men took thousands of lives. US cavalry forces were spread thinly across the plains committed to protecting the Western migration of the settlers." While native peoples might charac-terize the "settlers" as invaders and the "attacks" as a rational response, the narrator suggests that the conflict resulted in-evitably from the Indians' warlike nature and that the cavalry had no choice but to respond in kind. Of the five documen-taries, *Crossed Sabers* accords most closely with the residual alternative perspective of the Custer buffs and with previously dominant commodified public memory.

By contrast, the other documentaries make greater ef-forts to include Native American voices, or more correctly, the Euro-American representation thereof, and accord with what I have hypothesized will become the newly emerging dominant that erases history by blurring difference. The texts emphasize the native peoples' harmony with the land, thus replacing the noble red man prominent in sympathetic texts of the past with the newly fashionable "green Indian" of the nineties. In the standard "green Indian" sequence asserting the native peoples' reverence for nature, Indian-accented nar-rators either comment on their ancestors' relation to the land or quote from oral histories to that effect while we see por-traits of nineteenth-century warriors intercut with contem-porary shots of the plains and hear native flute music. The precredit sequence of A & E's *Real West* episode, "Custer and the Seventh Cavalry," typifies this strategy. An Indian narra-tor says:

> In a past that is now lost forever there was a time when the land was sacred and the ancient ones were as one with it. A time when only the children of the great spirit were here and light their fires in this place with no boundaries. When the forests were as thick as the fur on a winter bear. When a warrior could walk from horizon to horizon on the backs of the buffalo. In a time when there were only simple ways I saw with my heart the conflicts to come and whether it was to be for good or bad what was certain was that there would be change.[34]

191

The soundtrack underscores the narration with a "noble" theme in the brass section, accompanied by strings, and "beautiful," wall poster–like images of an undefiled landscape dissolving one into the other: a rainbow over the prairie, verdant pine forests, a gigantic full moon resting on the horizon of Monument Valley, all letterboxed as if they had been shot wide-screen. In the "Indians" episode of the *Wild West* series, a Native American talking head articulates this "green Indian" position when he remarks that his ancestors thought it was time for the white men to leave because "they had scared away all the antelope and the deer, they were polluting the waters."[35]

While at first glance this evocation of the residual perspective of Native Americans might seem oppositional, it seems less so at second glance. Since a ritualized obeisance to concepts of racial equality, if not a commitment to the practice thereof, has replaced overt racism as a mainstay of the hegemonic order, widely distributed texts are most unlikely to portray Native Americans as wild beasts suitable only for extermination but must acknowledge, if only in token fashion, the injustices perpetrated by Euro-Americans.[36] And, as with racism, a certain degree of lip service to environmental protection has become mandatory. Perhaps more important, market forces are at work here. This vision of native peoples living in a primitivist utopia, at one with the "Great Spirit" and the earth, seems part of a "new age" commodification that hawks flattened and dehistoricized signifiers of a vaguely evoked "spiritual" realm. The same "new age" stores that stock incense and crystals also offer compact disks of Native American flute music, Dreamcatcher earrings, and T-shirts adorned with portraits of Geronimo and Sitting Bull. Rather than celebrating difference, this selling of the Native American constitutes one more marker of the amoebalike potential of commodified public memory for an incorporation that appropriates and elides difference.

But these documentaries are not entirely devoid of oppositional impulses, as at some moments they depict the conflict between Native and European Americans as a confrontation between two different cultures with fundamentally differing concepts of ownership, time, battle, and so forth. "Custer and the Seventh Cavalry," explaining the events leading up to the battle of the Little Bighorn, quotes from the famous oral history recorded by the Lakota holy man Black Elk: "The white man had made a treaty with Red Cloud that said the Black Hills would be ours as long as the grass should grow and the water flow. Later I learned that the Long Hair [Custer] had found there much of the yellow metal that makes the white man crazy and that is what caused the bad trouble." Several of the programs point out that the government's offer to resolve the conflict by buying the Black Hills simply made no sense to the Native Americans, who conceived of the region in religious rather than economic terms. The "Indians" episode of the *Wild West* goes even further in its illustration of contrasting value systems. The narrator says, "Indian and white beliefs over the land were fundamentally different and so were their ideas of battle and honor." He goes on to explain that Indians fought primarily for honor, so warriors strove to count coupe (hit the opponent with the coupe stick) rather than to kill the enemy. But, the narrator continues, as a result of the European invasion, "Red Cloud realized that the rules of battle must change and that they must kill the white enemy."

Many of these documentaries, however, acknowledge, even if they do not support, the previously dominant commodified public memory produced by the culture industries, featuring images from Hollywood films as well as other widely circulated texts, such as nineteenth-century lithographs that show a band of ever-dwindling white men futilely but bravely resisting a horde of onrushing savages. The implication seems to be that these images still constitute an important element in the commodified public memory of Custer and the Little Bighorn, and that their centrality demands acknowledgment. In other words, the producers seem to grant that long-standing and widely circulated representations of commodified public memory can to some extent be disarticulated from current ideological configurations: Certain images of the Last Stand remain prevalent and familiar despite shifts in perceptions of Custer and Native Americans.[37]

Hence we must examine the various documentaries' different contextualizations of similar images, particularly that of the Last Stand, which has since 1876 been subject to varied and numerous ideological appropriations.[38] Are the images used to construct the Little Bighorn as a noble defeat, or does the program deconstruct the images and counterpoint them with others to offer a competing representation of the battle as Native American victory and/or white military blunder in

193

which the command structure disintegrated and the soldiery panicked? The former support while the latter negotiates or contests what have been the dominant commodified public memories of the event, centered around the image of beleaguered white men fighting a brave but hopeless battle. The contextualization also entails presenting the images as relatively transparent or as historical documents arising from particular cultural circumstances.

Crossed Sabers employs noncontextualized images from familiar commodified texts, primarily Hollywood films, as if to situate itself within while at the same time reinforcing the previously dominant commodified public memory of Western history. For example, as the narrator discusses white versus Indian conflicts, a colorized clip from the 1941 Custer bio-pic *They Died with Their Boots On* shows a charging cavalry regiment pursuing the fleeing foe. Like the other Custer documentaries, *Crossed Sabers* includes a sequence on the so-called Fetterman massacre, in which a band of Lakota led by Crazy Horse ambushed and killed eighty soldiers, as a precursor of the hostilities leading to the Little Bighorn. The image track includes another colorized clip, this time from the 1948 John Ford film *Fort Apache,* in which Colonel Thursday (Henry Fonda) and a small band of soldiers meet their doom at the hands of an onrushing horde of Indians. The producers do not address the fictional status of this clip, identifying it neither by video-font nor end credits, and seem to have chosen a particularly inappropriate illustration. The historical incident took place in the winter on the plains and involved the Lakota, while the film's events take place in the summer in the Southwest and involve the Apache. This is not to dispute the "accuracy" of the program's facts, for the narrator does provide the requisite historical details. It is rather to suggest that the clip serves primarily not as direct illustration of the narration but rather as invocation of the previously dominant commodified public memory of westward expansion in which good white guys battled the bad red guys. Granted, the program's voice-over narration has acknowledged the injustices suffered by the Native Americans: "Behind it all was the dislocation of a great and proud people. . . . The Indian nations sought to break free of unbearable living conditions." But might not the images, by deliberately activating an extensive intertextual frame for those viewers whose knowledge of Western history comes primarily from Hollywood films, work against and perhaps even overpower the words?

The program's Little Bighorn sequence accords absolutely with previously dominant commodified public memories of the event. The sequence begins with the opening shot of John Ford's 1949 film, *She Wore a Yellow Ribbon,* which shows the tattered guidon of the 7th Cavalry fluttering in the wind. The on-screen host, John Agar, tells us, "All of the great battles fought in the sea of grass pale in the imagination alongside one that took place near Montana's Little Big Horn river on June 26 [*sic*], 1876," pointing to the privileged place this militarily insignificant battle occupies in commodified public memory.[39] Then, as the narrator discusses Custer's tactics and speculates about what might have occurred, the program uses illustrative clips from several Custer films, none of which is identified as fictional, but none of which deviates from the standard heroic imagery.

The sequence ends with the colorized climax of *They Died with Their Boots On.* Surrounded by his dead troopers, Custer (Errol Flynn) stands alone next to the regiment's guidon. Running out of ammunition, he throws away his pistols and picks up a saber, awaiting the Indians' final charge. In medium shot, the oncoming Crazy Horse (Anthony Quinn) fires his rifle and, also in medium shot, Custer staggers at the force of the bullet. In long shot, Custer collapses by the guidon, which Crazy Horse seizes as he rides by. The scene ends with a high-angle, overhead shot of the victorious Indians galloping away from the camera. The documentary provides a voice-over: "The final Indian assault at the Little Bighorn bought a fatal storm of arrows and a hail of deadly rifle fire, much of it from repeating weapons, to overwhelm the gallant Seventh Cavalry with its single-shot Springfields. Custer and members of the five companies under his command died to the last man." The narration, with its use of the phrase "gallant Seventh Cavalry" and implication that inadequate weaponry rather than bad tactics or inadequate training caused the defeat, reinforces the familiar image that is consonant with so many of the depictions of the heroic Last Stand in previously dominant commodified public memory.

Crossed Sabers, situated firmly within previously dominant commodified public memory, excludes competing constructions of the battle derived from, for example, archaeolog-

ical evidence or Native American oral histories or pictographs
that might suggest that Custer died near the beginning of
the fight, or that the Indians remained safely hidden in the
ravines rather than foolishly exposing themselves to rifle fire,
or that several troopers panicked and were cut down trying
to escape. Others of the documentaries, such as the "Custer
and the Seventh Cavalry" episode of the *Real West* series, do
include pictographs and oral histories as well as the more
familiar images. Rather than challenging the construction of
the "gallant Last Stand," however, they accord with what I have
suggested is the emerging commodified public memory by
asserting that there was courage and heroism on both sides.
In fact, the *Real West* hedges its epistemological bets by having
on-camera host Kenny Rogers say, "It will never be known
precisely what happened to Custer and his troops. No man
under his command lived to tell the story," the implication
being that only a white man's testimony could conclusively fill
lacunae in the historical record, despite the fact that there
were Indian eyewitnesses whose testimony was preserved by
Indian oral traditions.

"A Good Day to Die" is based almost entirely on these
oral traditions and other materials that represent the Native
American alternative residual perspective. One of the documentary's Native American "talking heads," Mike Her Many
Horses, says, "I think Custer represents the real evil side of
the American people, vainglorious, victory at any cost, I think
that's what he represents to Indian people. He's basically a
villain."[40] The Battle of the Little Bighorn is presented entirely
from the Native American point of view. A voice-over accompanying shots of Native American pictographs says, "Eyewitness
accounts of what happened at the Little Bighorn have been
handed down from one generation to another. Some of the
Lakotas at the battle recorded their experiences firsthand
in these rare ledger drawings." The battle is presented as
a montage of quickly intercut and camera-animated ledger
drawings, accompanied on the soundtrack by rifle fire, whin-
nying horses, bugles, and quotes from Indian eyewitnesses.
The sequence ends with another talking head, Joe Marshall,
of the Lakota, saying, "The soldiers were outfought because
the warriors were defending their families."

By presenting the battle entirely from the Indian perspective, "A Good Day to Die" refrains from challenging the

previously dominant image of the gallant Last Stand. The the fact that only one of the documentaries, "Last Stand at Little Big Horn," part of the PBS *American Experience* series, consciously deconstructs the gallant image of the Last Stand may attest to the endurance of certain images even in the face of reformulations of commodified public memory to incorporate previously subordinate values, meanings, and practices. A press release claimed that the program "re-examines Custer's Last Stand from White and Native American perspectives." The release continues, "Using point-of-view photography, Indian ledger drawings, and the reminiscences of witnesses and their descendants, Last Stand at Little Big Horn recreates what most likely happened to Custer and his final command on the morning of June 25, 1876. . . . The surprised 7th Cavalry panicked, and Custer and his 210 soldiers were killed to the last man."[41]

Drawing upon archaeological evidence and Indian oral history, the program most flagrantly challenges previously dominant commodified public memory in its description of the troopers' behavior at the Battle of the Little Bighorn. The narrator says that, as their comrades fell around them, the soldiers no longer behaved in military fashion, and "all semblance of order collapsed."[42] Accompanied by war whoops and labored breathing on the soundtrack, a shaky subjective tracking shot moves closer to the present-day tombstones on Custer Hill, as the narrator continues: "Terrified soldiers ran toward Custer's position."

The program also deconstructs the gallant Last Stand of previously dominant commodified public memory by showing how the conventional image of the encounter became frozen and abstracted from historical process. Near the outset, the narrator says, "Generations of Americans remembered them as heroes, part of a legend called Custer's Last Stand." As did *Crossed Sabers,* the image track shows the climactic scene of *They Died with Their Boots On,* but this time to very different effect, since a panning shot of an Indian pictograph of the battle, accompanied by drums and war whoops, follows the clip, the direct cut from one representation to the other challenging the popular image. The narrator reinforces the point, saying, "but for native peoples who remember this battle in stories, songs and ledger art the last stand had a different meaning."

After the program has presented an account of the Plains Indian wars and the Little Bighorn that draws extensively on Native American sources as well as Euro-American accounts, the conclusion returns to the construction of commodified public memory, offering a metaperspective that seems rare in the historical documentary genre by asserting that, although many Native American survivors of the battle passed on their accounts to their descendants, Euro-Americans "wrote history." Following the Little Bighorn battle sequence, the image track shows contemporary newspaper stories and cartoons depicting "savage Indians" as the narrator says, "Overnight newspapers transformed the utter defeat into a vision of heroic martyrdom." Piano chords deliberately evocative of the nineteenth-century melodrama introduce a montage of popular representations of the battle as the narrator discusses their provenance: William de la Montagne Cary's "The Battle of the Little Big Horn River—The Death Struggle of General Custer, 1876"[43]; a program for Buffalo Bill Cody's *The Red Right Hand;* the 1896 Otto Becker lithograph *Custer's Last Fight,* so widely circulated by Anheuser-Busch that it was said to hang above every bar in America; and a poster for Buffalo Bill's Wild West Show. After a discussion of the role Elizabeth Custer played in creating her husband's legend, the program returns to perhaps the most influential of all the texts of commodified public memory, the movies. The film clips show several "Last Stands," all, unlike those in *Crossed Sabers,* identified by supered titles, including those from *Custer's Last Fight* (1912), *The Plainsman* (1937), *They Died with Their Boots On, Fort Apache, Little Big Man* (1970), and *Son of the Morning Star* (1991). The narrator refers both to the persistence of previously dominant commodified public memory and to its challenge by the alternative residual perspective of Native Americans.

> Custer is no longer a hero to a nation troubled by its treatment of native people and yet our image of his last stand persists. Custer in his buckskins with the flags with his cavalry men. But for the Plains Indians the memories were different. The fight with Custer was but one of many battles that led to the theft of their lands. . . . Through the hard years that followed their stories and songs kept the history alive.

198

That history is now acknowledged by and perhaps incorporated into a newly emerging commodified public memory that will mark a temporary cessation of contestation over the dominant representation of the Battle of the Little Bighorn.

Notes

1. George A. Custer, *My Life on the Plains* (Lincoln: University of Nebraska Press, 1966), 26–27.
2. On Custer's reputation in the 1960s, see my "White Network/ Red Power: ABC's *Custer*," in *The Revolution Wasn't Televised: Sixties Television and Social Conflict*, ed. Lynn Spigel and Michael Curtin (New York: Routledge, 1997).
3. James Welch, with Paul Stekler, *Killing Custer: The Battle of the Little Bighorn and the Fate of the Plains Indians* (New York: W. W. Norton and Co., 1994), 109.
4. Karen Lynch, "Custer Loses Again," *Progressive* (September 1991): 11.
5. "Custer Loses Again at Little Bighorn in Montana," *Sunset Magazine* (May 1992): 207.
6. William Plummer, "Bill Shaw at the Custer Battlefield," *People,* February 12, 1990, 93, 96.
7. Michel Foucault, "Film and Popular Memory," in *Foucault Live* (New York: Semiotext[e], 1989), 91–92.
8. Alvin M. Josephy, Jr., "Soldiers and Indians," *New York Times Book Review,* July 3, 1966, 6.
9. Michael Bommes and Patrick Wright, "'Charms of Residence': The Public and the Past," in *Making Histories: Studies in History-Writing and Politics,* ed. Richard Johnson, Gregor McLennan, Bill Schwarz, and David Sutton (London: Hutchinson, 1982), 255.
10. Raymond Williams, "Base and Superstructure in Marxist Cultural Theory," in *Problems in Materialism and Culture* (London: Verso, 1980), 38.
11. Pierre Nora, "Between Memory and History: *Les Lieux de mémoire*," *Representations* 26 (Spring 1989): 8.
12. Bommes and Wright, "'Charms of Residence,'" 265.
13. Michel-Rolph Trouillot, "Good Day Columbus: Silences, Power and Public History (1492–1892)," *Public Culture* 3.1 (Fall 1990), 3.
14. Michael Kammen, *Mystic Chords of Memory: The Transformation of Tradition in American Culture* (New York: Alfred A. Knopf, 1991), 669.

15. A copy of the CBS report was obtained from the Vanderbilt Television News Archives; the author made her own transcript. All quotations are taken from this transcript.

16. *Congressional Record*, v. 136, no. 49 (April 27, 1990).

17. See "As the Crow Fights," *Newsweek*, July 13, 1964, 56, and Anne Chamberlain, "Bad Day Ahead for the Army's Greatest Loser," *Saturday Evening Post*, August 27, 1966, 70–73.

18. Avis Little Eagle, "Custer Revisited: Group Calls for Last Stand of Reenactment," *Indian Country Today*, June 6, 1993, A-1.

19. Tzvetan Todorov, *The Conquest of America: The Question of the Other* (New York: Harper Torch Books, 1987), 146.

20. Todorov, *Conquest of America*, 42.

21. "House Approves Monument for Indians Who Killed Custer," *Detroit Free Press*, September 18, 1990, 5A.

22. *Congressional Record*, v. 136, no. 92 (July 18, 1990).

23. *Congressional Record*, v. 137, no. 98 (June 24, 1991).

24. *Congressional Record*, v. 136, no. 92 (July 18, 1990).

25. Williams, "Base and Superstructure," 39.

26. Williams, "Base and Superstructure," 40–41.

27. "Honor Indians as Well as Custer's Troops in Battle Monuments at Little Bighorn," (Minneapolis) *Star Tribune*, November 11, 1990, 33A.

28. *Congressional Record*, v. 137, no. 98 (June 24, 1991).

29. Quotations are taken from the author's transcript of this report.

30. My thanks to Stephanie Dyer for this term.

31. Tony Bennett and Janet Woollacott, *Bond and Beyond: The Political Career of a Popular Hero* (London: Macmillan, 1987), 281–82.

32. Quotations are taken from the author's transcript of this documentary.

33. Richard White, "Trashing the Trails," in *Trails: Toward a New Western History*, ed. Patricia Nelson Limerick, Clyde A. Millner II, and Charles E. Rankin (Lawrence, Kansas: University Press of Kansas, 1991), 30.

34. Quotations are taken from the author's transcript of this documentary.

35. Quotations are taken from the author's transcript of this documentary.

36. The "wild beast" trope has, in fact, never totally dominated, since, from the moment of first encounter in the fifteenth century, Europeans and Euro-Americans have oscillated between portraying native peoples as "ignoble" or "savage savages" and "noble savages," the choice of trope dependent on the referents' degree of proximity and potential for resistance. Since the clear victory of Euro-Americans over native peoples in the

1890s, after the failure of the Ghost Dance movement and the massacre at Wounded Knee, a romantic regret for the passing of the "noble savage" has become prevalent, even while the impoverished descendants of those "vanished Americans" are still very much with us. Only a very few of the Custer films that I have seen paint an entirely negative picture of the Lakota and Cheyenne, and these tend to be from the early silent period (*Custer's Last Fight* [1912], for example). Even those films that portray Custer as a shining martyr (*They Died with Their Boots On* [1941], for example) do admit that Native Americans had some justice to their cause.

37. This assumption of disarticulation accords with my earlier work on the cinematic representation of history. In interrogating the connection between historical films and the hegemonic order in *Reframing Culture: The Case of the Vitagraph Quality Films* (Princeton, N.J.: Princeton University Press, 1993), my coauthor, William Uricchio, and I argued that historical representation often takes the form of widely circulated images of key events, such as, for example, the Emmanuel Leutze painting of *Washington Crossing the Delaware*. While such images connote vague notions of history or country or patriotism, they bear no essentialist relationship to the hegemonic order but are rather subject to a number of potential ideological appropriations within any particular historical moment.

38. At the turn of the century, some have argued, Last Stand imagery recorded easterners' fears of immigration. Richard Slotkin, *The Fatal Environment: The Myth of the Frontier in the Age of Industrialization* (Middletown, Conn.: Wesleyan University Press, 1985), and Alex Nemerov, "Doing the Old America," in *The West as America: Reinterpreting Images of the Frontier, 1820–1920,* ed. William H. Truettner (Washington, D.C.: Smithsonian Institution Press, 1991).

39. Curiously, Agar gets the date wrong: The battle took place on June 25, not June 26.

40. Quotations are taken from the author's transcript of this documentary.

41. "'Last Stand at Little Big Horn,' on *The American Experience,* RE-examines Custer's Last Stand from White and Native American Perspectives," press release, Michael Shepley Public Relations, October 1992.

42. Quotations are taken from the author's transcript of this documentary.

43. The program does not identify the illustration, the first representation of the Last Stand, which appeared in the *New York Graphic Illustrated Newspaper,* July 19, 1876.

7

"You Must Remember This . . ."; or, Libraries as a Locus of Cultural Memories

Daniel Traister

In memory of Thomas Lask

Introduction

In this essay,[1] I consider some tensions between our society's perceived need to preserve its cultural memories and the workings of one of the increasingly large and complex bureaucratic institutions, libraries, that contain and preserve them. For my purposes in this essay, *memories—cultural memories—are anything you can find in books, in libraries*.

They are not only that, of course.[2] Alvin B. Kernan, recalling his youth as a sailor during World War II, clearly distinguishes between two different forms of memory:

> My great-grandfather William Lott Peters served through the Civil War in Company D of the Fiftieth Georgia Infantry—the fact is proudly registered in brass on his gravestone—which fought, among other great battles, at Gettysburg. I have often longed for his version of the kind of personal memories I have tried to write [in the book which this paragraph concludes], but he left no such record. But using the official history of the Civil War, I once traced the movements of his regiment in that battle. It was on the right wing in Longstreet's Corps, and on the second day of the battle, July 2, 1863, it went down in the afternoon from the woods on Seminary Ridge, across the Emmitsburg Road, down through the Wheatfield, pushed to the north of Devil's Den,

and stopped finally at the narrow stream that runs along the base of Little Round Top (known thereafter as Bloody Run), as the battle petered out in the darkness. I have walked along that route and wondered what William Peters, nineteen years old at the time, ever found again in the seventy-three years of his long and prosperous life on an isolated Georgia farm to match the experience of that day. Still, it must have remained locked up inside him, having nothing to do with the quiet productive life he lived, but making everything else feel slightly unreal.[3]

Whatever William Peters's memories of Gettysburg may have been, they were and remain private and inaccessible. Only through his great-grandson's conjectures can they be imagined. His great-grandson's great-grandchildren, however, able to read *Crossing the Line* whenever they wish, will have immediate access to their ancestor's memories of naval combat in the Pacific during World War II. Written down and published, they have entered the arena of public and accessible cultural memories in a way that Peters's memories have not.

Passages like this one from Kernan may suggest that the role of the library as an institution dedicated to the collection and preservation of cultural memories is, if cultural memories are defined as I have just defined them, very simple indeed: acquire, catalog, make accessible, and preserve the books that constitute this kind of cultural memory. I do not think things are quite this simple, however.

In this essay, I begin by looking at a kind of memory that libraries may not be able to contain. I next look at a kind of memory that libraries can—but which many choose not to—contain. I conclude by observing that librarians, and hence libraries, collect and preserve cultural memories far more haphazardly than most library users appear to realize. My two examples function primarily to buttress my argument that librarians' decisions about what shall be contained by the institutions in which they work are frequently accidental and contingent, dependent on a host of factors, most of which are unaffected by any considerations of the significance of cultural memory. The repositories that librarians build are, in consequence, constructions that only partially represent— not "reconstructions" that faithfully re-present—the vast universe of potentially salvageable memories that print and its surrogates have produced.

For whatever reasons, library users almost never examine either librarians' collection-building processes or their results (which is not to say that they never complain about these results). Librarians themselves agitate about such issues, of course, and rightly: these issues are significant.[4] But their examination ought not to be in the hands only of those whose work it is to build library collections. If, as it seems to me, a culture's recollections depend on its collections, then users as well as librarians need to consider such issues.[5]

I suspect, however, that few people are certain about what they expect libraries to provide. I also suspect that very few people—specifically, very few academics—ever ask such a question. Thinking about libraries is not part of an academic's job. Using them is.

But academics in the historical humanities depend on libraries. The degree of this dependency is normally unstated or admitted only as a pious expression of general indebtedness. It is dispiriting for academics to notice that their ability to pursue easily a line of inquiry depends in a most literal sense on what nonacademics—librarians—decide to acquire and catalog; how they organize, shelve, and reveal the presence of the materials they have acquired; and how successfully they prevent the materials they have acquired from ceasing to exist. Yet, as they do these things well or ill, librarians make teaching, studying, and research and scholarship possible— or *im*possible. No library collects all, or even a large fraction, of the possible materials that document our many cultures' many memories. How do their staffs choose from among the vast possibilities they confront? Academics rarely ask.

A library, an archive, a museum, or any other analogous repository exists in an institutional context at once social, bureaucratic, and responsive to its own imperatives. In most institutions of higher education, libraries are inadequately housed, understaffed, and poorly financed; by and large, national and public libraries are in no better shape. At the time this essay is being written, improvements that would depend on improved financing for such institutions seem an increasingly distant and unlikely prospect. Growing numbers of books and journals, to say nothing of manuscript and archival collections, seek admittance to library collections, but too few employees are able to select new or retrospective acquisitions with an expertise that academics recognize as academically respectable, and few have time for genuinely considered selection decisions. "Selection" is itself an aspect of librarians' work frequently left unanalyzed, unproblematized, even by the academics who are most at its mercy—and even though, as I have argued elsewhere, the selection process is deeply problematical, deeply suspect.[6]

One last word about my procedure. I address academic library users most particularly, but I do not write about an academic *subject*. I am concerned instead with an academic *place*, a university library where people work. I take an anecdotal and personal approach to discuss how the work performed in this place affects the availability, even the survival, of the cultural memories that the varied labors of students, teachers, and scholars may examine.[7] I hope my generally colloquial style will discourage either a romanticized or a mystified view of my topic.

Uncontained Cultural Memories

I begin with an example of the sort of information— "cultural memory"?—that will *not* be found in libraries or in the books they contain.

In 1967, Dutton published a novel "by Helen Hudson" called *Meyer Meyer*. I first read the book that year, in a copy loaned to my parents by the person to whose memory this essay is dedicated, Thomas Lask. Lask had reviewed *Meyer Meyer* for the *New York Times*,[8] where he worked for many years as, among other things, a daily book reviewer, a member of the reportorial staff, and poetry editor during the years when the *Times* printed a daily poem on its editorial page. Tom Lask had been my father's student in high school during the 1930s. They and their families remained friends through their own and into their children's (my) generation. When I was growing up, our families lived in apartment buildings across the street from one another and were very close.

Meyer Meyer offers a critical, feminist view of a male history professor. The author depicts his behavior, amorous and otherwise, with his students, colleagues, and mistress, an artist, as selfish and unpleasant. Largely forgotten, the book nonetheless has much to recommend it. Its acerbic view of its central character, somewhat severe for the time, would now strike most readers (I think) as relatively mild. Both ordinary readers and historians interested in how the revived American women's movement of the 1960s found new literary expression (the novel postdates Betty Friedan's *Feminine Mystique* by three years) would find it readable. Readable or not, however, the book has some documentary significance for the history of feminist American literature in its period as well as for its depiction of academic life and mores.

The author's name on the book's title page—"Helen Hudson"— is a nom de plume. As recently as 1988 (the latest reference I have found for her), the author lived in New Haven, where she continued to write. She was also married to a professor of political science at Yale University, Robert Lane.[9] Thomas Lask may not have known who "Helen Hudson" "really" was when he reviewed the novel. He did know, but could not say in print, that it tells (imagines?) a tale about other "real people."

The book's title character, Meyer, was modeled closely on another friend of my father's, a Brooklyn College history professor named Solomon F. Bloom. In 1962—five years before *Meyer Meyer* was published—Sol Bloom had been hit and killed by a bus while visiting Columbia University to give a lecture.[10] Sol was one of my father's childhood friends. They had known one another since Sol's emigration from Romania shortly after World War I. Like Tom Lask, Sol Bloom was part of the adult orbit in which I was raised; and Sol and Tom knew one another through their mutual friendship with my parents.

Another of Hudson's characters was modeled on Bloom's long-term mistress, Olga, a sculptor from Orange, Connecticut, who also taught at Yale. I never knew—and, despite inquiries to the Yale Archives, have not yet learned—Olga's last name. At Yale, one supposes, she got to know one or both of the Lanes.[11] A third character was modeled on a colleague of Bloom's, the late Samuel J. Hurwitz, with elements, perhaps, of Moses Rischin (now a professor of history at San Francisco State University), as well.[12] As a teenager—I believe in the summer of 1958 or 1959—I visited Olga's home in Orange with my parents and Sol Bloom, an occasion I remember in part because that was also my first visit to New Haven and Yale.

My mother read Tom Lask's review of *Meyer Meyer*. As she later told me, she suspected immediately from what his review managed to say about the novel's characters that the book concerned Sol Bloom (about whom, as it happens, her feelings would have been closer to Helen Hudson's—if *Meyer Meyer* represents those views accurately—than to my father's). Curious, she called Tom with her suspicions. He confirmed them and loaned her his review copy. She read it, gave it to my father to read, and then gave it to my wife and me to read, too. By then, we lived in New Haven where my wife was a graduate student at Robert Lane and Olga's university; the book's setting, my mother thought, would interest us. Moreover, although I had known Sol Bloom, my wife had not, and my mother (I can at this date only assume) hoped, through providing her with books such as this one, to acculturate to "our" world. We did read it; and we now have our own copy of the book.

What does one do with such "knowledge"? What status does it have *as* knowledge? How do I even know, why should a reader believe, that any of this is "true"? In truth, even for me it is all hearsay—and I have actually *met,* as almost none of my readers will have done, most of the people just mentioned (with the exceptions of Samuel J. Hurwitz, Robert Lane, and Helen Hudson). If anyone thinks this stuff *is* knowledge, it is still worth asking how any library might contain it. My reader may happily grant (is it not merely obvious?) that *Meyer Meyer* is a book that an academic library with a responsibility for documenting the history of American women's fictions, or academic novels, or just plain old American literature, might want to have. But would my reader also agree that a library that owns the book ought also to possess somewhere a text about it that includes such highly speculative, unpleasant, personally damaging, and unfounded gossip as this?

Why not? Modern editions of eighteenth-century novels or poems, as is also "merely obvious," are always provided with such contextualizing annotation. *The Dunciad* is unthinkable, in any of its myriad forms, in a modern text that omits any effort to identify the "real" human beings whom Pope pillories. We can not imagine such a beast. Neither, indeed, could Pope, although he might not have foreseen annotations of his own annotations. Yet such annotations do no more than I have just done, pulling together and presenting a mixture of truths that include both documentable "facts" (Bloom as a history professor at Brooklyn College) and the

207

kind of "gossip" (Olga as Bloom's long-term mistress) I have just purveyed about people referred to in Hudson's novel. They recall "cultural memories" (even though most people do not share or keep these specific memories within their own individual memories) that mingle, indiscriminately, memories with completely different referential statuses: "Bentley" as famous textual scholar versus "Bentley" as pretentious horse's ass. Editors and scholars go to libraries for the information they can dredge up to bring such memories back to some semblance of life for those people—our students, our colleagues, even, occasionally, ourselves—who find it necessary or pleasurable to read works such as these once in a while. Editors and scholars do not doubt that such notes are necessary. For textbook purposes, if not for critical purposes, almost no one doubts their utility. Teachers will, of course, wonder if their students really pay as much attention to these notes as they hope they do. They should also wonder (but, in my experience, rarely do) if those students who do pay attention will then uncritically misunderstand annotations that gather together and present Pope's mixed cultural memories by reading them as if they were "the truth"—a distillation of "our memories"—about such people as, say, Bentley or Cibber.

For such notes, generations of scholars have ransacked published works and unpublished letters, diaries, and journals, seeking just the sort of gossip I have here provided—without cost in time or labor to anyone—for *Meyer Meyer.* Uncorroborated, however, my information must remain suspect. What would constitute corroboration? Sol Bloom, Olga, and Sam Hurwitz, primary witnesses, and Tom Lask and my parents, secondary ones, are all dead. Should I write Helen Hudson and ask? I *have* written to Professor Rischin, a slight acquaintance. His reply, as I have already remarked (note 12, above), was perfectly polite . . . and completely uninformative. Yale's archives has found neither Olga's last name nor any other biographical information about her. Unless the novel excites interest from later generations of readers, documents that might provide corroboration—Hudson's correspondence or diaries; Sol Bloom's; Olga's; Hurwitz's; Rischin's (*if* any of these survive!)—will never be searched. And, of course, if those sources have not been or do not get saved in libraries, searching them is likely to be impossible. Whatever confirmatory or contradictory information they might have contained will never rise to the level of anyone's (let alone "the culture's") memories.

And yet, will our understanding of a fiction not be enriched or altered if we are allowed a peek at some of the materials from which its writer constructed that fiction? I have phrased this question in a way that suggests that "yes" is the only answer it can receive; but such a "yes" cannot, in fact, remain uncontested. My question elides some extremely basic questions about how we read fictions. To what degree, for instance, does "insider" knowledge of a book's genesis affect the ways in which we read it, especially by comparison to readers who lack the inside perspective? Argued in other terms, this question was a staple during the days when the then New Criticism was attempting to supplant a more traditionally historical approach to reading. In the tradition in which I was trained, the opposing views on such matters were presented with crystalline clarity by Douglas Bush, Historian, and Cleanth Brooks, New Critic, arguing with one another about how best to understand the depiction of Oliver Cromwell in Marvell's "Horatian Ode."[13] They are not simple views nor are they simple to decide between. Of course, memories can inform reading; and perhaps they should. Yet memories get lost, the urgency of what they were supposed to recall gets transmuted—or just muted—with the passing of time, and, at some point or other, a future generation is no longer able to pick up on the conditions out of which a work was born and to which it tries to speak. No longer knowing what it has lost, that future generation and its successors may read the book anyway (finding other things of value in it?); or, no longer knowing what it has lost, it may instead simply discard the book from those it keeps in its consciousness as works that matter and remain worth collecting and reading. Thus, for these as well as for other reasons, do works drift in and out of canonical status over long periods of time.

My implicit "yes" to the question whether information concerning its genesis will affect our understanding of a work assumes something else, the significance of which is by no means obvious. It derives from the (only partially illusory) tangibility of the sheer *stuff* with which a librarian deals: both the physical copies of the book in which *Meyer Meyer* is embodied and preserved and the documents, whether they exist somewhere or not, which I have *imagined* might exist

209

and which, if they did, might contain material to "confirm" or "contradict" my remembered (constructed?) excursus on one aspect of the book's (possible) genesis. Had we the book alone, discussion of its genesis would be neither possible nor relevant. The book would be read or forgotten for other reasons. But had we as well the additional documentation I have imagined might exist—and which I have reconstructed, without documentation, from memory—then the sheer presence of such stuff, in some collection somewhere, would eventually make a scholar happy as it emerged from its Hollinger boxes into the light of day. Thus would these documents affect understanding of the work—whether or not they should do so; for of course the tangibility of documents is only an inert fact about them, not a reason to think that they help readers decide between ways of reading fictions elaborated by either Douglas Bush or Cleanth Brooks. Granting this objection, tangibility is nonetheless something to be reckoned with. As Richard Terdiman appositely notes, "Normally objects have an intimate relation to remembrance" (13). Of the objects we call books and papers—that very tangible "stuff" with which librarians work—this relation is especially characteristic. Everything in the world, as Mallarmé said, exists in order to end up as a book.[14]

Unclaimed Cultural Memories

I want to begin this section by quoting a poem that deals with memory while leaving its author unidentified, at least for a bit—although if the reader *must* look at my endnotes, the author is there identified, a source provided. This chapter, after all, uses much of the apparatus that print technologies long ago generated to relieve readers of the anxieties caused by some of the fallibility of human memories. Surrounded by print, we call this apparatus "documentation" and rely on it as a prophylactic against drowning in that sea.

The poem, called "Meditation on a Bone," bears an initial note. Somewhat obliquely, the note explains that the poem was occasioned by its author's encounter with a reference to "A piece of bone, found at Trondhjem in 1901, with the following runic inscription (about A.D. 1050) cut on it: *I loved her as a maiden; I will not trouble Erlend's detestable wife; better she should be a widow."*

> Words scored upon a bone,
> Scored in despair or rage—
> Nine hundred years have gone;
> Now, in another age,
> They burn with passion on
> A scholar's tranquil page.
>
> The scholar takes his pen
> And turns the bone about,
> And writes those words again.
> Once more they seethe and shout,
> And through a human brain
> Undying hate rings out.
>
> "I loved her when a maid;
> I loathe and love the wife
> That warms another's bed:
> *Let him beware his life!"*
> The scholar's hand is stayed;
> His pen becomes a knife
>
> To grave in living bone
> The fierce archaic cry.
> He sits and reads his own
> Dull sum of misery.
> A thousand years have flown
> Before that ink is dry.
>
> And, in a foreign tongue,
> A man, who is not he,
> Reads and his heart is wrung
> This ancient grief to see,
> And thinks: When I am dung,
> What bone shall speak for me?[15]

The poet, born in 1907, produced work that lies well out of the stylistic mainstream of modernist poetry.[16] Nonetheless, I have enjoyed and read it ever since, early in the 1960s, I first encountered it. I did so thanks to another review by Tom Lask in the daily *New York Times* of the poet's *Selected Poems* (1962).[17] Indeed, as with *Meyer Meyer*, I first read the very copy of the *Selected Poems* that Tom had used for review and then passed to my parents. His review was a wild rave ("Not since Wallace Stevens' 'Harmonium' have diffidence and excellence combined to produce a first book of such high quality")—one of very few wild raves, or even notices, for a book of poetry that had appeared in the daily book review columns of the *Times* in my memory to that date.

People who worked for the book's publisher, Viking, were astonished. In those days (as, one presumes, now), a good review in the *Times* sold books. This, not merely a good but a positively glowing review, extolled a book for which its publisher had not expected to receive any notice at all. Speaking by telephone a few days after the review's appearance with a person at Viking—as Tom later told me the story—he was warmly thanked for his notice. In fact, the person told him, Viking had, the very day the review appeared, put its printer on alert to await the rush reprinting that would be required by the interest the *Times* review was naturally expected to generate. Some time after that first conversation, as Tom continued this story, talking once again with his acquaintance at Viking about an altogether different matter, he learned that the publisher had been forced to conclude that these hopes had been somewhat overoptimistic. Whatever difference a rave in the *Times* might make to sales of a novel or a work of nonfiction, its impact on sales of poetry proved nonexistent. The publisher was unable to detect any sign that the *Times* review had affected what it had originally projected as the prospective sales of the book.

None of my readers is likely to have a memory so bad that this story will prove even moderately surprising. Even though some of us may once have specialized or still specialize in the study of poetry, we all know its marginal role in modern literary culture, even if we are so courageous or benighted as to attempt to "teach" poetry to students in some academic setting or another.

Has any reader yet recognized the contemporary poet whose work I have quoted? I am making a (rhetorical) bet that a large majority will not have done so; and this bet provokes me to a small *bizarrie*. In an autobiographical memoir published in 1992, the same poet wrote about a literary hoax which, its readers are told, they will recall so well that only a few details will instantly bring it back to mind: It is, as the poet remarks in passing, part of "common history." *Really*? I ask.

212

The poet is writing—alas, in language that displays neither the dispassion nor the charity that readers might have expected of a writer by now both long in years and heavy with honors— about "the famous Ern Malley Hoax."[18]

> . . . it was by mere chance that I became involved in the hoax. An arrogant and stupid literary magazine was jointly produced by Max Harris and John Reid under the title of *Angry Penguins*. It aimed to be more avant-garde than most progressive theories of the day[,] . . . among these Surrealism. . . . [The poet recalls setting about concocting *faux*-"surrealistic" poetry for this magazine and being quickly warned off this project by some "ingenious friends" who already] had invented poor Ern, using Stewart's sister's address from which to send to Max Harris a semi-literate letter posting supposed poems and some covering matter. Max fell for it at once. The poems, composed in one idle afternoon at the office, [were] supplied with a mish-mash of all the then popular *avant-garde* theories of poetry, surrealist vomit, Marxist propaganda, "obscure" so-styled intellectual verse, free verse techniques, multiple meaningless references to irrelevant objects, pictures, ideas and what have you. They then roughed up the papers to make them appear to have been written over some time and sat and waited until *Angry Penguins* exploded with two numbers hailing Ern Malley as the greatest poet of our day. . . . Finally the news [of the hoax] was released and the rest belongs to common history. Both here and abroad there were a number of eminent critics whose faces must have been very red. Max Harris and his friends tried to put a good face on it by claiming that McAuley and Stewart were simply mistaken.[19]

Et cetera, et cetera. We catch the drift of the poet's tale without difficulty. We are all knowledgeable about hoaxes; the joke is not one of surpassing originality, difficulty, or even wit.

Yet, if you are like me, even as you grasp its drift, you are nonetheless wondering: *Who are these people? Max Harris? John Reid?* The one who died in Russia spelled his name differently and surely lived too early in the century anyway; could this be the same person who wrote the biography of John Quinn?[20] And who are Stewart and McAuley? If you are like me, you love the target magazine's title, *Angry Penguins*— would anyone dare to make up that title for an avant-garde periodical in a novel? But, like me, you've never heard of it. In fact, if you are like me, you have, till now, heard of none of this stuff, none of these people, at all. This is, it would appear, a case not of failed memory: it is a case of sheer ignorance. And not, I think, just my own ignorance.

But I am concerned not by the vagaries of individual people's knowledge but rather by "libraries and cultural memories." Even readers who have adhered to my request and avoided looking at my endnotes till now have at least seen that they are there and guessed that I am not making this stuff up out of whole cloth. Quite so; but this is not material the majority of us was ever taught. No one will ever test us on it, few of our colleagues think it matters in any way, we don't have to know it. It may be *someone's* "cultural memory." But it isn't ours.[21]

It is now time for identifications: The "we" in the preceding paragraph is by no means universal. The poet and memoirist is A. D. (Alec Derwent) Hope. He grew up in Hobart, Tasmania, was educated at Sydney, earned a second (bad) university degree at Oxford, and spent the rest of his professional life in Sydney and Melbourne. He has published numerous books. They have won a number of awards, but very few people read them—they are, after all, mostly books of poetry or literary criticism. Most of those who do read them are Australians.

The hoax about which Hope writes in his memoir concerned a literary periodical published during the 1940s in Adelaide. I can locate a copy of this periodical at my near neighbor, Pennsylvania State University, where there happens to be a Center for Australian and New Zealand Studies. But my own institution was far from unique among American libraries in failing to own it (until I bought a copy for it while this essay was in progress). Only after 1994, when our library cataloged Michael Heyward's study of *The Ern Malley Affair*, published and acquired in 1993, could we teach this episode in the history of English-language surrealism or literary hoaxes even had we wanted to.[22] By and large, however, we don't want to. People in Sydney, Melbourne, or Adelaide may have the inestimable advantage of speaking and, it would appear, of writing in a language of whose fundamental seriousness for literary purposes we can be in no doubt. Nonetheless, they rarely do so in a way we notice.[23]

The majority of those who, for one reason or another, in one way or another, care for "English literature"—who get paid to teach this subject to young people or to write, or to buy, books and periodicals that are in some way of or about it for the libraries young people and their teachers use; or who, perhaps, merely read as much as possible of the stuff with an airy or ignorant disdain for its place of intellectual origin—do not bother much about *Australian* English literature, unless we are Australians or, perhaps, New Zealanders. Were we for any reason otherwise inclined, the state of our library resources does not permit us the option, by and large, in any case. Can one imagine why this state of affairs—so normal that, really, even to point it out must seem slightly deranged—might matter to anyone at all? Thomas Kenneally, who has recently succeeded Patrick White in the "Australian-writer-we-notice" category, owes much to the happy accident of having ascended to the attention of metropolitan Mr. Spielberg; he is said now to spend part of every year in Los Angeles. A. D. Hope has ascended, outside Australia, to very nearly no one's attention, except Tom Lask's and mine.

Really, we cannot—and, of course, we do not—expect our libraries to concern themselves with most of what passes for culture throughout the world. And this is only as it should and must be. Otherwise, their shelves, already cluttered, would collapse.

Contingency in the Construction of Library Collections

What these two examples indicate first of all is our uncertainty—*my* uncertainty, since I have no right at all to assert through a linguistic trick any scope whatsoever for my views or my doubts—about what constitutes a "cultural memory" in general or a "cultural memory" specifically fit, first, for a library and, second, for its users.

Some things, known to others, are unknown to most of "us": who wants, who needs, to know them? to learn them? Terry Caesar recalls an Israeli poet's comment about the difference between himself and W. H. Auden: "I have to be aware of him, whereas he doesn't have to be aware of me."[24] "We" are "Auden," of course. Hope and the creators, dupes, aficionados, and historians of the Ern Malley hoax, by contrast, are all in the position of Caesar's Israeli poet. They do—they have to—know about us: we are metropolitan. Their very *hoaxes* respond to us. By and large, we know nothing about them: they are provincial. We don't feel the worse for not knowing anything about them.[25]

Some things are unknown to anybody. Who besides me— now that Sol Bloom, Olga, Samuel J. Hurwitz, Tom Lask, and my parents are all dead, and without "confirmation" from Helen Hudson or Moses Rischin (whatever such confirmation might consist in)—knows about the "historical" background to *Meyer Meyer*? Who—since my readers now know about it, too (*if* you trust my memory!)—cares? Who has read the book? Who will read it? There is relatively little a librarian can do about the kind of lacunae represented by this example. *Meyer Meyer* is probably typical of a great many novels that, presented to their readers as "fictions," are made in significant measure out of their writers' perceptions about the lives of "real" people, including themselves, whom they know. Unless documentation survives to link those real people with the fictional events of the novels in which they appear, however, readers, students, teachers, and scholars will never know about such extrafictional referents. The significance of their ignorance will be slight. Most of these books, as has been true of most other books of all sorts throughout history, will disappear from consciousness without ever attracting either a search for such documentation or even just plain and simple attention. There is some potential here for a self-confirming argument: *Because* scholars are not struck by questions about a book's relation to its author's milieu, it *may* die of neglect more quickly than it should. Who can tell? Our library's shelves are full of books unread for this reason— and for many others: *dead books.* Some deserve rediscovery. Who will find them? Who is even looking, unimpelled by a specific (nowadays usually gender-, class-, or race-based) agenda? (And in any case, what do my *shoulds* and *deserves* in these last sentences actually *mean*?)

Because there is relatively little that librarians can do about such lacunae, there is not, however, *nothing* we can do about them (if we agree that these lacunae ought to concern us in the first place). An essay such as this one represents at least one thing that one librarian can do. Others include

writing inquiries, where they remain alive, to people one suspects of having been a writer's models, or to authors, seeking additional information. (I have tried the former course; I
have thus far lacked the temerity for the latter.) In fact, many
passionate collectors and enthusiasts do just this. On their
efforts to gather *all* possible data relevant to the subjects they
collect, many of our great research collections depend. We
normally distinguish collectors from librarians and, while we
tend merely to ignore the latter, we too often positively malign
the former, stereotyping them, for instance, as mere rich accu-
mulators who remove materials from public accessibility for
no reason other than self-aggrandizement through property-
based and sentimental association with the outer trappings of
"culture." That without their enthusiastic interest and willingness to invest their own funds—indeed, without their sheer
knowledgeability—many materials that seem ephemeral and
of no interest to others would perish is not always something
that scholars *or* librarians bear in mind, although both benefit
clearly and directly from such activities.

Collectors practice their propaedeutic to scholarship,
however, on a model analogous to an extreme free-market
economy. Utterly unregulated and without joint or cooperative
planning, they acquire and gather together materials on the
basis of purely individual decisions. Thus, a few enthusiasts
may be interested in a relatively obscure writer named Franz
Kafka, while almost none is interested in another more or less
contemporaneous obscure writer named Robert Walser. Vol-
umes of Kafka's "ephemeral" writings survive to be published;
these fill out and illuminate Kafka's more narrowly defined
"literary" works and represent a major enhancement of what
readers can bring to bear in thinking about the writer and his
work. What, by comparison, happened to Walser's ephemeral
writings? Is Kafka "better" or "more important" than Walser?
We all know not to ask such a question: who could ever imagine, or provide, an absolute answer to it? And what does it
mean, anyway? Writers are not playing some kind of sport;
literature is not a zero-sum game; to value Tolstoy does not
require one to denigrate Dickens. True enough; and yet there
very definitely is an objective, materially based answer to this
question: What has survived of the works of both writers, as
well as the tortuous routes both took to publication, makes
Kafka the "more important" writer without any doubt at all.

We are now no longer likely to retrieve any materials that might enable or encourage general readers and specialized scholars to reconsider Walser's claims on our attentions.[26] The sheer *accident* of an author's attraction of early sympathetic attention has, in this example, as in surprisingly many others to which we no longer pay any attention,[27] a major impact on what scholars and readers read and value.

This accident has its analogue among those people charged formally (as collectors are not) with the creation of research library collections: librarians. As a library collection officer, I pay attention to Helen Hudson and A. D. Hope as the result of a personal history that few other people who do what I do in other libraries can possibly share. They are, of course, doing the same with other writers, other writing cultures, that my colleagues and I routinely overlook in acquiring materials for the library that employs us. An army of people doing the acquisitions work we all do, and whose idiosyncrasies balanced one another, might—in a world also characterized by unlimited budgets—create truly comprehensive libraries that enabled scholarship to proceed unhindered by selectors' blindnesses or prejudices. No library is able to afford the payroll such an army would require (or the space to house the materials they would bring in). Each is thus at the mercy of selectors with blindnesses, prejudices, and idiosyncratic backgrounds and enthusiasms just as peculiar as, though differently peculiar from, mine. This situation might not matter were library users aware of and able to correct for such inherent biases; or were they interested in interrogating library institutional practices (as they interrogate the practices of many other societal institutions) that justify, by seeing them as if they really are "inherent" biases, what may not need to be inherent at all. But most readers, most scholarly and academic readers, never think about such questions.

My second example seems to me less understandable— less excusable—than my first. It stresses in an even more obvious (because more wholesale) way the role of accident in the construction of research libraries. As my reader will by now have noticed, this is the second point my two examples exist to suggest, following upon uncertainty about what constitutes anything we might call a cultural memory in the first place.

The general lack of interest in the provincial is not new. American literature itself long suffered under this general excuse for its dismissal (see note 25). Even today, no one needs to look as far afield as Australia, New Zealand, India, Africa, or the Caribbean for examples of English-language writers whose works and history—this at many English-language universities with serious pretensions as research-supporting institutions and active and productive Departments of English—students cannot study or teachers teach. Works defined as "regional" or "generic" simply do not get *selected* for inclusion in library collections. At the university from which Zane Grey graduated, how many Westerns are part of its library's collection? or books of any sort published in Salt Lake City or Reno by publishers other than the universities located in those two cities? How many books are stigmatized (and hence uncollected) by library selectors because they can be subsumed under rubrics that consign them to automatic oblivion: "science fiction," "mysteries," "romances," "bestsellers"? In terms of their collecting interests, how many American research libraries find the literature of anglophone Canada (to say nothing of francophone Canada) to be just as distantly compelling as that of Australia?[28] There are exceptions in all of these categories, of course, but the exceptions are just that: they are unusual. They result from geography (Canadian institutions collect Canadian writers; Nevada institutions Nevada writers); from odd institutional contexts (the existence of a center for study of Australian and New Zealand issues at Penn State); or from odd institutional selectors (one who, for instance, has read A. D. Hope, suspects that there may be more at home like him, and thus bumps into Judith Wright and Lily Brett—"like" him because they are Australian?!—or another who, having read Joanna Russ, has never been able to dismiss science fiction from his selection concerns). The exceptions, in short, result from accidents. The collections those accidents produce are contingent upon the presence, and continued existence, of noninstitutionalized selection practices and practitioners able, in their acquisitions, to follow up on their own partialities as well as to acquire the obvious, the mainstream, and the central without which selectors are invited to seek alternative employment.

If, as Mary Warnock writes, personal identity is a function of an individual's memory, then a society's identity may similarly be considered as at least partly a function of its retrievable cultural memories. (Finkielkraut discusses the

219

intersection of individual and societal memories and identity [see note 1].) "Cultural memory" is a concept that needs far more definition than I have bothered to give it here. The plural "-ies" ending in my title indicates that I think there are many such memories. I hope I have also indicated that I imagine no single "culture," out of the many in which we are embedded or by which we are surrounded, that is an uncontested monolith. I have concentrated on literature, with the assistance of two minute examples that happen to be peculiar snippets from my own knowledge, simply because it is "my field" and because both examples (dependent as they are on a specific family relationship to a book reviewer for the *New York Times*) happen so perfectly to suit my argument. Countless other examples illustrative of the multiple operations of contingency in library collection-building might have been used, from this, from related, or from altogether different subjects.[29]

All memories—personal, societal, cultural—are a construct. Neither a single individual nor a single institution can remember everything or provide for total recall. Individuals, institutions, academics: all choose what is worth remembering and on the basis of their choices construct their personal or cultural memories and identities. But they can do so only from among the materials made available to them by circumstances and opportunities for choice that are only partially under their own control. Those materials are the result, that is, of a construction—of many constructions—made prior to the individual's, the institution's, or the academic's.

How individuals construct their own memories is not my topic. I am concerned rather with the almost completely unexamined nature of the constructs which, by their acquisition decisions, librarians who staff libraries (and, what is even more obscure to most academics, the employees of specialized library book vendors) build, as they go about the quotidian task of selecting and acquiring the materials that constitute the library collections with which present and future scholars work and on which they will continue to rely. Daily, these selectors accumulate the materials from which contemporary cultures' memories will be gleaned. Quite literally, they *construct* those memories with each item-by-item decision about what is and what is not worth acquiring and preserving. How they relate materials to one another by their classification systems and subject analyses will also affect how and what memories can be recalled. A vast bureaucracy exists to build the research libraries on which scholars depend. That bureaucracy is almost completely unstudied, not by its own constituents—whose noses are constantly to be found stuck in their own navels—but rather by those whom it ostensibly serves. This despite the fact that, increasingly, those scholars whom it serves have come to recognize how other bureaucracies and social organizations, especially those with functions that can be broadly grouped together as intellectual or ideological, demand scrutiny and interrogation. Academics pay so little attention to the libraries in which they pursue their work, however, that even to speak of libraries and (worse) librarians as outside the control of academics, *and thus uncontrolledly choosing what it is academics are able to attend to,* must raise a prospect that is, at first blush, disgustingly improbable.

Meanwhile, those books most in danger of getting lost while the process remains unexamined—can this possibly come as a surprise to anyone?—are those books that might have preserved as "cultural memories" texts and discourses that are overtly resistant, transgressive, disapproved, or just plain marginalized. Even at a time when far more attention is paid such works than up until very recent times indeed, relatively few scholars work with the books that preserve such discourses. Thus relatively few library vendors or selection officers seek them out. Those who may do so often do so only within the few areas where they have found some reason or prod in the oddity of their own backgrounds or interests. Thus I may pay attention to chronologically somewhat removed women novelists, poets, and dramatists and to Australians. Other selection officers with special interests in lesbian pornography, travel writers, or Anglo-Indian literature will strengthen collections with which they work in these specific fields. Few people complain. Fewer still consider that decisions made in this way, day in and day out, have a long-lasting, perhaps permanent, impact on what survives to become a "cultural memory."

Every decision to buy a book is, consciously or unconsciously, a decision *not* to buy many other books: financial and space constraints make every acquisition decision contestatory in nature. Academic indifference (or the appearance of such indifference) to the institutional practices that determine acquisitions decisions results in the "normalization" of the

221

collections that libraries accumulate. The gap between what is published and what is collected does not lessen, it widens, from year to year—as does the gap between the collected conventional and the uncollected unconventional. This gap has consequences for what "we" can remember and teach. Every student, teacher, and scholar in the historical humanities today knows that this is a time when the scattered, disregarded, unedited, or unrepublished materials that still live in this gap provide the substance for some of the most exciting (and literally reinvigorating) historical and literary scholarship of our time.[30] Almost none has noticed, however, that almost all "research" libraries are perpetuating this gap for future scholars to struggle against. Accidents are not method; they do not "cancel each other out" in some mystical way. The institutional structures through which libraries collect the materials that will ultimately be part of the memories that document our own age need analysis. They need it not only from those who work within and accept as givens the constraints of these structures but also from those who retain the capacity to be surprised by these structures, perhaps even to find them annoying.

Notes

1. My title, of course, recalls memory as one of the thematic constituents of a now-classic American movie, Michael Curtiz's 1942 *Casablanca*. The theme is, in the words I quote, expressed in song ("You must remember this, / a kiss is just a kiss").

2. I proceed from the direction of "memory," not "culture," but I know that writing is not the only repository for cultural memories and agree that culture may be defined (far more broadly than what I say here about writing and books) as "the *nonhereditary memory of the community*" (Yuri M. Lotman and B. A. Uspensky, "On the Semiotic Mechanism of Culture," *NLH* 9 [1978]: 211–32, at 213; quoted in Richard Terdiman, *Present Past: Modernity and the Memory Crisis* [Ithaca, N.Y.: Cornell University Press, 1993], 3). Much of what is nonhereditary is preserved and transmitted in ways that have nothing to do with libraries. Books, repositories of *written* memories, clearly contain and preserve a special subset of memories of all sorts. Edward Shils, *Tradition* (Chicago: University of Chicago Press,

1983 [1981]), is one of many studies to consider forms of cultural memory broader than those I am concerned with here; more recently (in English), see also Alain Finkielkraut's marvelous essay on the politics of cultural memory, *The Imaginary Jew*, trans. Kevin O'Neill and David Suchoff (Lincoln: University of Nebraska Press, 1994 [originally *Le Juif imaginaire*, 1980]).

James Fentress and Chris Wickham, writing in Social Memory: New Perspectives on the Past (Oxford: Blackwell, 1992), are quite explicit about this point: "people use books as only one out of many sources for their representations of the past. Writing on one level transforms memory, by fixing it; but . . . no society is an entirely literate culture, including our own (and even including the heavily text-oriented microsocieties of academics); and shared memory, whatever its sources, tends to be communicated above all in the arena of the oral, through anecdote and gossip, with narrative patterns that can owe as much to oral as to literate tradition" (97). Recent support for such views is found in, e.g., Karal Ann Marling and John Wetenhall, *Iwo Jima: Monuments, Memories, and the American Hero* (Cambridge, Mass.: Harvard University Press, 1991); and Ian Buruma, *The Wages of Guilt: Memories of War in Germany and Japan* (New York: Farrar Straus Giroux, 1994). Nonetheless, in our society, a very great deal of "culture" is also stuff that you have to *look up*—and to look up in books that most people rely on finding in institutions that exist for this purpose: libraries. Consideration of books in their institutional setting is thus highly relevant to issues of cultural memory; and these issues are, themselves, of concern not only to scholarly but also to general public discourse.

Marling and Wetenhall and Buruma indicate this currency and the interplay between written and nonwritten forms of memory. But a striking additional example of the currency of these matters appeared early in the writing of this essay, a single section of a single issue of the *New York Times* (January 26, 1995) containing: (1) a front-page article by Henry Kamm, "Poland Reawakens to Its History as Communism's Mirror Shatters: Reclaiming the Past" (A1, A10), about efforts to reconstruct a sense of Poland's recent national past now that "history . . . [need no longer be] falsified to justify Soviet dominance"; (2) Jane Perlez's "Separate Auschwitz Services Highlight Jewish-Polish Disputes: A Question That Will Not Go Away—Impressions vs. History" (A10); (3) Eric Schmitt's "80 Lawmakers Demand Ouster of Director of Air Museum" (A12), on controversy aroused by the text intended to accompany the proposed exhibition at the Smithsonian's National Air and Space Museum of Enola Gay, the B-29 that dropped a nuclear bomb on Hiroshima; (4) "British Royals' Antics Are Hardly New" (A20), a letter to the editor by theater critic Eric Bentley on the ways in which memories of the often indecorous behavior of members of Britain's royal family have been distorted over time; (5) an editorial, "Remembering Auschwitz" (A20); and (6) "Eating Her Offspring" (A21), Frank Rich's column about the controversy aroused by the "National History Standards" produced by the National Endowment for the Humanities.

Underlying all this interest in memory—Henry Ford's notion that history is bunk notwithstanding—is, of course, our sense that memory is implicated not only in the past but also in the future. See Michael Perlman, *Imaginal Memory and the Place of Hiroshima* (Albany: State University of New York Press, 1988), 3 et passim, who makes this point with impassioned force. So does Finkielkraut (above).

3. Alvin B. Kernan, *Crossing the Line: A Bluejacket's World War II Odyssey* (Annapolis: Naval Institute Press, 1994), 166–67.

4. A particularly interesting example of such worry from within a particular subfield of librarianship came to hand as I last revised this essay before publication. See Jan Paris, "A Conservator Reflects," in Jan Paris, Liz Holdzkom et al., *The Invisible Process: Ingenuity and Cooperation in Finding Women's Lives* (Chapel Hill, N.C.: Academic Affairs Library, University of North Carolina at Chapel Hill, 1997), 3–8. The larger work is a library exhibition catalog (itself an ephemeral, often uncataloged, and hence inaccessible form of publication), the topic of which relates directly to mine.

5. Mary Warnock, *Memory* (London: Faber and Faber, 1987), deals with memory as an individual phenomenon, ascribing the value we place on memory to its contribution to people's sense of "personal identity" (vii et passim). She does not consider memory's social or cultural aspects. Only a librarian, I fear—a person who must consider what his or her society and culture will manage to remember—would notice that her publisher has printed her book on paper so acidic that, a bare decade after the book's publication, both cased and paperback copies show severe discoloration and embrittlement. Concerned that people have continued access to her book as a representative intellectual product of its times, that librarian wonders how to preserve it.

A short essay by Peter Burke discusses social and cultural memory, its converse (which he calls "social amnesia" [106]), and the dependence of both on "conscious and unconscious selection" and "[socially conditioned] interpretation and distortion" (98; on 108, he mentions "the *social organization* of forgetting" [my emphasis]). However, Burke never discusses the major "social organization" in his world (and ours) that is the primary repository for the memories (and forgettings) he studies: libraries and archives. See his "History as Social Memory," in *Memory: History, Culture and the Mind,* ed. Thomas H. Butler, Wolfson College Lectures, 1988 (Oxford: Basil Blackwell, 1989), 97–113. Rather more alert in this respect is Arthur C. Danto who, in "The Shape of Artistic Pasts: East and West" (in *Philosophical Imagination and Cultural Memory: Appropriating Historical Traditions,* ed. Patricia Cook [Durham, N.C.: Duke University Press, 1993], 125–38), notes how important was the lack of art museums—"that crucial institution," Danto calls the museum, which is clearly analogous in function to the library—for an eighteenth-century Chinese artist, Wan Shang-Ling, trying to work in the tradition of fourteenth-century artist Ni Tsan.

6. See "What Good Is an Old Book?" *Rare Books and Manuscripts Librarianship,* 7.1 (1992): 26–42.

7. To one of the charges used to discredit such an approach—"anecdotal individualism"—I plead guilty. In collegiate and university academic institutions, however, where most displays of hierarchically based dismissive superiority are (at least for the nonce) generally disapproved, it remains easy for faculty to regard librarians as a particularly disreputable form of "the other." Shelvers, re-shelvers, checkers-out, and book stampers, librarians, in this view, are people who *do* think you can tell a book by its cover. As a result, they frequently know no more about books than the color of their covers; or are, at best, people who, every so often, prove willing to order the odd *good* book an academic person wants (if the academic person remembers to tell the librarian to do so). Thus, although my resemblances to (let us say) women of color would, in most contexts, leave a certain amount to the imagination, I nonetheless find myself able to empathize quite well—at least, in the context within which I spend my working hours—with something of what I take Patricia J. Williams to mean when she writes, explaining her own devotion to "anecdotal individualism" (6): "Since the self's power resides in another, little faith is placed in the true self, in one's own experiential knowledge. It is thus that children's, women's, and blacks' [and librarians'?] power is actually reduced to the 'intuitive' rather than to the real: social life is based primarily on the imaginary" (*The Alchemy of Race and Rights* [Cambridge, Mass.: Harvard University Press,

225

1991], 63). More entertainingly, for the congenitally mordant—although because of its length not quotable here—see Williams, *Alchemy of Race,* 44–51. See also Michel Foucault: "Whenever I have tried to carry out a piece of theoretical work, . . . it has been on the basis of my own experience, always in relation to processes I saw taking place around me. It is because I thought I could recognize in the things I saw, in the institutions with which I dealt, in my relations with others, cracks, silent shocks, malfunctionings . . . that I undertook a particular piece of work, a few fragments of autobiography" ("Practicing Criticism," in *Politics, Philosophy, Culture: Interviews and Other Writings, 1977–1984,* ed. Lawrence D. Kritzman [New York: Routledge, 1988], 156).

8. Thomas Lask, "He Knew What He Wanted" [review of Helen Hudson, *Meyer Meyer* (New York: Dutton, 1967)], *New York Times,* March 6, 1967, 31.

9. See the article on Helen Hudson (s.v. "Hudson, Helen") in *Contemporary Authors,* 123 (1988), 219–20.

10. See his obituary ("History Professor Is Killed by Bus") in the *New York Times,* January 7, 1962, 76; his funeral is reported two days later ("Rites Held for Prof. Bloom," 47). A brief article about Solomon F. Bloom appears as the "Introduction" (5–12) to a posthumous collection of Bloom's papers, *A Liberal in Two Worlds: The Essays of Solomon F. Bloom,* ed. Samuel J. Hurwitz and Moses Rischin (Washington, D.C.: Public Affairs Press, 1968).

11. A later novel by Helen Hudson is dedicated "To the memory of Mary and Olga" (*Farnsbee South* [New York: Holt, Rinehart and Winston, 1971], dedication leaf [vii]). I can only guess that this "Olga" is the same person who figures as a model for Meyer's mistress in *Meyer Meyer.*

12. Hurwitz and Rischin are the editors of the posthumous collection of Bloom's papers cited above (note 10). Professor Rischin's response to a letter of inquiry I sent him about the people in Hudson's book avoided replying to any of my questions.

13. See Cleanth Brooks, "Marvell's 'Horatian Ode,'" originally in *English Institute Essays, 1946* (New York: Columbia University Press, 1947), 127–58; Douglas Bush, "Marvell's 'Horatian Ode,'" *Sewanee Review* 60 (1952): 363–76; and Brooks's reply, "A Note on the Limits of 'History' and the Limits of 'Criticism,'" *Sewanee Review* 61 (1953): 129–35. William R. Keast reprinted these essays (with the titles I have followed here) in *Seventeenth Century English Poetry: Modern Essays in Criticism* (New York: Oxford University Press, 1962), 321–58. His 1971 second edition omits them entirely.

14. " . . . tout, au monde, existe pour aboutir à un livre." Stéphane Mallarmé, *Écrits sur le livre (choix de textes)*, préface Henri Meschonnic, Collection philosophie imaginaire, no. 3 (Paris: Éditions de l'éclat, 1985), 5.5 (131).

15. A. D. Hope, *Collected Poems 1930–1970*, A&R Modern Poets (North Ryde, N.S.W.: Angus and Robertson, 1977 [1966]), 96–97.

16. Hope's self-conscious "insistence on metrical formality, stanza forms and rhyme" becomes the starting point for the useful brief discussion of his work by Andrew Taylor, "A. D. Hope: The Double Tongue of Harmony," chapter 6 in his *Reading Australian Poetry* (St. Lucia: University of Queensland Press, 1987), 70–84.

17. Thomas Lask, "Books of the Times" [review of A. D. Hope, *Selected Poems* (New York: Viking, 1962)], *New York Times*, April 2, 1962, 29.

18. A. D. Hope, *Chance Encounters, with a Memoir of A. D. Hope by Peter Ryan* (Carlton, Victoria: Melbourne University Press, 1992), 91. Hope describes the Ern Malley Hoax at 91–94. See, generally, the recent study by Michael Heyward, *The Ern Malley Affair* (London: Faber and Faber, 1993).

19. Hope, *Chance Encounters*, 91, 93.

20. Heyward spells this name "John Reed"; Hope may merely have got it wrong. No matter for me: I would still not recognize the name.

21. The Ern Malley Hoax was not completely unknown outside Australia; it proved a brief diversion for the American and British press in late 1944 (see Heyward, *Ern Malley Affair*, 162–63) and, at the beginning of the 1960s, Harry Mathews, an American writer then editing *Locus Solus* in Paris, and, in New York, John Ashbery, Kenneth Koch, and James Schuyler, were all interested in "Ern Malley's" poetry (Heyward, *Ern Malley Affair*, 232–34). Scholarly references outside Australian works that show their author's knowledge of the hoax are difficult to find; I have also failed to find examples of "Malley's" poems in standard anthologies. In view of my argument here about who pays attention to whom, it is notable that Heyward attributes "Malley's" revived influence on *Australian* poetry to the promptings of *American* interest in the poems (233). Danto (n. 5, above) speaks usefully about the question of "who is the agent and who is the patient" in the matter of artistic "influence" ("Shape of Artistic Pasts," 130–31; he quotes—as I do, from him—Michael Baxandall on this point).

22. The year 1993 also saw republication of Ern Malley's *Col-*

lected Poems, with commentary by Albert Tucker et al. (Pymble, N.S.W.: Angus and Robertson, 1993).

23. So hopelessly upside down are some antipodean critics that they seem to feel Australia to be sufficient unto itself. Thus, for example, John Docker has actually suggested that Hope's "dilemma" is that "he cannot relate himself to the Australian society and nature around him," "only half-jokingly" calls it a "barbarous" land, and finds "Europe . . . the only and abiding reality for the spirit" ("The Image of Woman in A. D. Hope's Poetry," chap. 3 in his *Australian Cultural Elites: Intellectual Traditions in Sydney and Melbourne* [Sydney: Angus and Robertson, 1974], 43–44).

24. Terry Caesar, *Conspiring with Forms: Life in Academic Texts* (Athens: University of Georgia Press, 1992), 149. See, similarly, Williams, *Alchemy of Race,* 28: "There is great power in being able to see the world as one will and then have that vision enacted. But if being is seeing for the subject, then being seen is the precise measure of existence for the object."

25. I owe thanks to Patrick Buckridge, who teaches Australian literature at Griffith University (Brisbane), and who tells me that, when he teaches Australian literature of the 1950s, he includes literature and history that refer to McCarthy, Dies, the Hollywood Ten, and other American events of the era. Can anyone even begin to imagine an *American* teaching a class on American literature of that decade supposing, for even the merest flicker of a moment, that an *Australian* reference or text might be relevant?

The things "we" do not need to know are legion. "Pushkin, a historian as well as a poet, . . . told the tsar that he wanted to write about the eighteenth-century peasant leader Pugachev. The tsar's reply was brutally simple: 'such a man has no history'" (Burke, "History as Social Memory," 107). Thus class. Here geography: "[Stranded by the Second World War in Australia, the English scholar J. I. M.] Stewart . . . created a minor controversy in 1940 when, after being asked to lecture on Australian literature, he declared the category did not exist" (Heyward, *Ern Malley Affair,* 66).

Stewart was speaking in the direct line of pom descent from Sydney Smith who, writing in the *Edinburgh Review* of December 1818, remarked: "Literature the Americans have none—no native literature, we mean. It is all imported." In January 1820, in the same journal, Smith continued in this vein: "In the four quarters of the globe, Who reads an American book? Or goes to an American play?" I quote Smith from Jay B. Hubbell's relentlessly—and, I hope, consciously—hilarious book, *Who*

Are the Major American Writers? A Study of the Changing Literary Canon (Durham, N.C.: Duke University Press, 1972), 4.

26. I owe these examples to Siegfried Unseld's *The Author and His Publisher: Lectures Delivered in Mainz and Austin*, trans. Hunter Hannum and Hildegarde Hannum (Chicago: University of Chicago Press, 1980). See especially, on Kafka, 24–27, and, on Walser, Unseld's final chapter, 191–273. Although Unseld compares Kafka and Walser from what seems to be a strikingly different point of view from mine, looking mainly at how their relationships with their publishers affected their writing careers and their lives, I think his point not very different from mine at all. The implications of his comparison are directly relevant to a consideration of the ordinarily unexamined role of contingency, of accident, in determining what we come to value and think worth preserving.

27. The locus classicus for English literature is almost never remarked upon in quite this way, for the very nearly (literally) sacred as well as merely literary canonical status of the author in question simply removes such concerns far beyond our capacity for either question or doubt. Nonetheless, even if only as a mere thought experiment, try to imagine what we would know about—and thus read as and value in—the "works" of William Shakespeare if we did *not* have the results of the pious early intervention into the preservation of his texts of Heminges and Condell, who edited the 1623 folio. Enough of the printing history of this book is known so that we can say that the presence in it of *Troilus and Cressida* and the absence from it of *Pericles*—to give only two obvious examples—are both accidental. That arguments continue to swirl about the attribution or nonattribution to Shakespeare of a good number of other plays and poems testifies not only to the power of his authorial name but also to the tinge of deep uncertainty that still touches many of the attributions of plays now commonly accepted as his.

28. I am grateful to Professor Germaine Warkentin of the University of Toronto for sending me a diatribe on the subject of American views of Canada and its history. We have, on several occasions, spoken about American attention to Canada's literature, which occasionally attains to the tepid—and which the sorry state of Canadian literature, as represented in American research library collections, is unlikely to prompt Americans to reconsider in the near future.

29. I had thought at one point, for example, of looking up all the books by someone named Traister which most research libraries do not have. A large number of them are by a Traister

named Robert, whom I do not know, and purport to instruct their readers in how to use various personal computers and computer programs. "Cultural memories" indeed! I would argue, of course, that they *are* indeed "cultural memories"—and of a very valuable sort, in fact, for they document some of the ways in which our society has accommodated to a new mechanism with which many people have in a very short time learned to live and work. Awareness of the quotidian effects of the automobile, now generally known, if as yet incompletely understood, means that handbooks for the owner of a Pierce-Arrow or a 1913 Minnesota roadmap do "count" as the stuff of "cultural memories." Robert Traister's various guides to early versions of the personal computer have the same potential.

30. Does such a statement require documentary justification? Just consider, as one example, the reinvigoration of our sense of what "counts" as "American literature" that has resulted from our changed sensitivity to what African-Americans, women, and the political left have all contributed to that construct. Cary Nelson's *Repression and Recovery: Modern American Poetry and the Politics of Cultural Memory, 1910–1945* (Madison: University of Wisconsin Press, 1989) undergirds this essay in many more ways than one. Alan Wald indicates what may be the single most crucial aspect of Nelson's importance for my point here when, in his 1991 review of Nelson (originally in the *Minnesota Review* and now in Wald's collection of essays, *The Responsibility of Intellectuals: Selected Essays on Marxist Traditions in Cultural Commitment* [Atlantic Highlands, N.J.: Humanities Press, 1992], 126–30), he comments: "a key lesson of Nelson's book is that partisans of cultural, economic, and political equalitarianism cannot count on the internal dynamics and networks of extant institutions to preserve even the most rudimentary material artifacts of oppositional cultures" (130).

8

Placing Race at Jefferson's Monticello

Robert Blair St. George

Going to the Mountaintop

Early in 1994 I visited Monticello, Thomas Jefferson's celebrated estate outside of Charlottesville, Virginia. Although I had known about Monticello since childhood, I had never before made the trip. But courses in American architectural history in both undergraduate and graduate school had long ago whetted my appetite to see Jefferson's remarkable house. High on a mountaintop, a place apart: no doubt Jefferson worked hard to achieve its Palladian rationalism, pastoral landscape, and sense of studied calm amid the treacherous political terrain of post-Revolutionary America. I imagined all this while driving there. Little did I expect that the tourist's path to this pilgrimage site would so radically reframe reality.

Pulling off the interstate highway, the first place I stopped was the Thomas Jefferson Visitor's Center, a Frank Lloyd Wright-ian transition zone perhaps intended to ease the motorist's modern sense of speed back at least into the early twentieth century. As I began my ascent of Jefferson's mountain, the next landmark was the "Meadow Run Mill and General Store," a restaurant and retail shop that trades on a fake overshot waterwheel, the sort used by small textile operations in the early nineteenth century. A strange image, I thought, given Jefferson's plea to "let our workshops remain in Europe" while harnessing instead the uncorrupted virtue of dirt farming at home. The next sign I spied halfway up to

231

Jefferson's home was at the entrance of "Jefferson's Lake," a protected residential estate—a warning, I thought, of the protected residential enclave to come. Finally, I made it to the entrance to Monticello. The late eighteenth century must be just around the corner. But no: the gate house was a Gothic cottage that could have come from a page of Andrew Jackson Downing's *Cottage Residences; or, A Series of Designs for Rural Cottages and Cottage Villas* (New York, 1842). I turned in. More signs ensued: a list of tourist options, a map of the entire Monticello site, and, finally, on top of the hill, a sign telling me which ways I could turn. To the right, I could find "Jefferson's Grave (1/4 mile)," and the "Trail to Shuttle Station Parking (3/5 mile to Station)." On my left, an arrow pointed to the "Garden (Straight Ahead)," "Shuttle Bus," "Gift Shop," and "Rest Rooms."

At this point I in fact needed to rest, since two questions were gradually raising my anxiety level. The first question, recalling my vision of Monticello as a place that had always been valued as a "place apart," borrows a line from Kenneth Lynch: What time *is* this place? The welter of passing architectural styles, the shifts in speed from highway to mountainside, the simultaneity of Jefferson's late-eighteenth-century architectural statement and the strange, fragmenting pace of cultural tourism made me wonder: How were past and present related here? My second question, the focus of the present essay, is more specific: How was an American construction of "race" placed already in the Monticello I was seeing, walking through, trying to capture in a camera? Placement, I suggest, is a historically continent process in which the production of spaces and social positions are coterminous with the articulation and exercise of personal interest and political power. The difficulty of placing race at Monticello hit me in eccentric ways that warrant more exploration.[1]

For example, I quickly discovered that the interpretive museum about the African-American archaeology project that has been underway at Monticello since 1980 and about specific slaves is now located in the "bowels" of the big house, implicitly preserving a hierarchy of significance in interpretation, despite the difficulties of allocating space within the great man's home. Instantly I recalled Palladio's apt summary of architectural anthropomorphism, a statement especially appropriate to Monticello given both Jefferson's keen appreciation

232

8.1. Gift shop complex, with ca. 1770 surviving stone house at right, Monticello, May 1994. Courtesy of Robert Blair St. George.

of the Italian architectural theorist and his probable naming of his "little mountain" after the *fiumicello* or "little stream" that ran below the hilltop site of Palladio's Villa Rotunda near Vicenza. "An edifice may be esteemed commodious," Palladio argued, "when every part or member stands in its due place and fit situation, neither above nor below its dignity and use. . . . Beauty will result from the form and correspondence of the whole, with respect to the several parts, of the parts with regard to each other, and again to the whole: that *the structure may appear an entire and compleat body*, wherein each member agrees with the other."[2] African-American culture is here in the grotesque lower body, the realm of the "low other" in Jefferson's symmetrical, enclosing frame. In the house above, Jefferson entertained in his dining room, read in his private library, and hosted visiting dignitaries in the salon overlooking his specialized collection of plants and trees in the gardens beyond. Yet while down below, household slaves moved meat, vegetables, fruits, wine, and ice from the quarters and outkitchens into the lower entrails of the house's body. From there such supplies were processed, cooked, set on fine china, and hoisted in Jefferson's dumbwaiters to the

dining room, with its overlapping echoes of enlightened political discourse, Augustan wit, and Rabelaisian laughter. Yet
while an impressive archaeological project aimed at exca-
vating and interpreting African-American culture along "Mulberry Row" (Monticello's quarter) had been underway since
1980, the only building actually still standing from the original
row—one of a group of stone dwelling houses Jefferson built to
house his "servants" (a term he used for both free and enslaved
members of his extended "family")—is now part of the gift
shop complex (fig. 8.1).[3] Gifts and chattels, commodities and
souvenirs: the ironies of imagining missing social relations, of
memorializing loss in such a context, hit me hard.

At one level, the strange refraction of the tourist's gaze
at Monticello surely relates to broader problems facing museums concerning the representation of race in America's increasingly present past. Monticello is not the only place where
strange erasures and grotesque placements occur. At the Colonial Williamsburg Foundation, research over two decades has
resulted in the painstaking reconstruction of slave quarters
at the Carter's Grove plantation site (fig. 8.2). The quarters
themselves are interpreted by a costumed African-American
staff with a high level of historical precision and detail; the
scene is nuanced, the spoken dialect evocative and varied.
Yet the entire system of cultural domination and class pre-
rogative these quarters implicitly reference never appears:
the mid-eighteenth-century "big house" of the Carter family,
while close enough at hand to be visible from the quarters,
is instead deflected away from the 1770s, to talk about the
way its last residents used it in the 1930s. (The term "last
residents" is used on the tour of the property to reference
the owners of the property who willed it to the foundation;
it is charged with the romantic and nostalgic overtones of
claims to the value of many "last" phenomena.) Without the
big house or, in its interpretive absence, at least an overseer's
house, the discipline of the slave economy that gave social
meaning to the reconstructed quarters is effectively erased.
Instead, there remains a strange bifurcation of time that keeps
Colonial Williamsburg weirdly colonial in actual experience;
the African-American "museum" interpretation has emerged
as a critical intervention in consensus history, but alongside it
remains the lived, ongoing representation of racial inequality.
In "colonial" Williamsburg, tourists are driven everywhere by

8.2. Slave dwelling, Carter's Grove plantation site quarter, Colonial Williamsburg, March 1994. Courtesy of Robert Blair St. George.

black bus drivers, the kitchen help in all the restaurants is black, the porters and maids at the hotels are black, the staff at the Colonial Williamsburg laundry is black. This "splitting" of time, with the present and past locked in a dance of ambivalent meanings, is what placing race at Monticello must examine. We need to locate race in Jefferson's Monticello if we are to correctly place it in "our" Monticello.

Making Plans

A compressed history of Monticello: The house we encounter now represents construction activity up to around

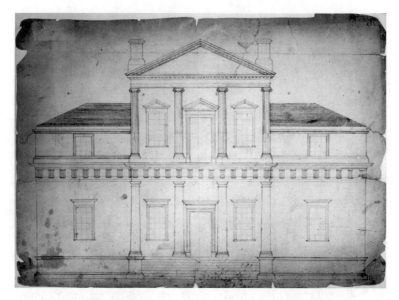

8.3. Thomas Jefferson, elevation of the first Monticello, probably prior to March 1771. Courtesy of Massachusetts Historical Society.

1803 and consists of a central block, two side dependency wings, and two service wings. As stated above, a subterranean passage through the "bowels" of the house allows for circulation in service spaces without disturbing activity in the house above. Yet this Monticello is actually the end result of a sustained building campaign. As Isaac, one of Jefferson's slaves recalled in 1847, "Monticello-house was pulled down in part & built up again some six or seven times. . . . They was forty years at work upon that house before Mr Jefferson stopped building."[4]

Jefferson inherited the land for Monticello from his father, and by 1767—at age twenty-four—he began working on the drawings. During the next year he leveled the mountaintop and by late 1769 began building. What ideas swirled through his imagination? As Rhys Isaac has suggested, they were drawn from a learned but eclectic blend of traditions. His fondness for MacPherson's Ossianic verse perhaps drew him to the misty and craggy heights of his mountain home. He also envisioned grottoes and temples. He even pondered

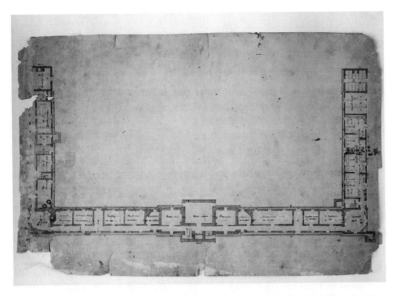

8.4. Thomas Jefferson, final drawing of the dependencies, prior to August 4, 1772. Courtesy of Massachusetts Historical Society.

other names for the estate: the "Hermitage" perhaps implied his preference for a romantic, isolated retreat. He had also briefly considered giving it the name "Rowanty," after the Nottowa Indian word for the place.[5] But his fondness for Roman republican architecture triumphed. Surviving drawings show the initial facade of 1771, an essay in classical discipline and virtue materialized (fig. 8.3). A plan of the entire complex from 1772 shows Jefferson's original scheme to incorporate domestic functions under the house and in side wings (fig. 8.4); this scheme was not fully realized in fact until the final phase of construction at the turn of the nineteenth century, perhaps because Jefferson himself had difficulty deciding what functions these wings might best contain. Another sketch of 1772, for example, shows him playing with such "enlightened" spaces for the dependency corridors as "school room," "nursery," "museum," "laboratory," "writing office," and "hospital." The first version of the house was finished by 1782. Alongside its construction, work on the gardens and grounds also advanced. Jefferson terraced the south side of the mountain for garden plots, an orchard, and a vineyard; a drawing of

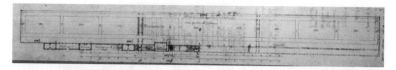

8.5. Thomas Jefferson, study for outbuildings along Mulberry Row and kitchen gardens, ca. 1776–78. Courtesy of Massachusetts Historical Society.

1776–78 shows his plan for Mulberry Row, flanked by kitchen gardens (fig. 8.5). Thus, by the time he left for Paris in 1784, Monticello was fully imagined, but partially built. The service wings proposed earlier had not yet been built. Some service buildings and slave houses were standing. He returned from France in 1789, began work on a totally new house to replace the first, and by 1803 his vision—parts of which had remained on the drawing board since the early 1770s—was largely realized.

During the 1790s, in particular, Jefferson was busy with construction that both replaced and added to earlier work. Fortunately, the progress of building along Mulberry Row is clearly shown in a drawing Jefferson made to accompany a policy he purchased from the Mutual Assurance Society of Virginia in 1796 (fig. 8.6). According to Fiske Kimball, this drawing shows the buildings on the estate just prior to "the drastic remodelling begun in 1796," many of which were also present on the 1776–78 sketch of outbuildings. The structure designated as "E" on the 1796 plat is identical to the stone structure still standing in the gift shop complex, and was the only one of eight classical "servant" or slave houses designed by Jefferson in September 1770 that was actually built, using in this case plan "No. 1" (fig. 8.7). According to Jefferson's declaration on the policy, this was "a stone. outhouse 34. by 17. f. the floor of brick, the walls & chimney of stone, the roof of wood, one story high." To this remaining structure, indicative of Jefferson's early intention to build substantial housing for his "servants," he had during the ensuing twenty-five years added a stable, a nailery, a joiner's shop, and several smaller slave houses. The four slave houses designated by the letters "o," "r," "s," and "t" in the upper left-hand corner of the 1796 plat are those on which archaeological research has focused.

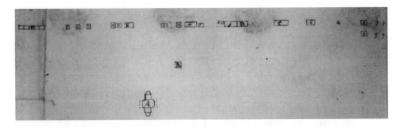

8.6. Thomas Jefferson, plat of the buildings at Monticello, attached to insurance declaration dated 1796. Courtesy of Massachusetts Historical Society.

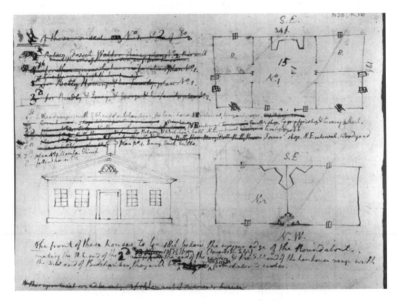

8.7. Thomas Jefferson, drawing of "servant" or slave house at Monticello, September 1770. Courtesy of Massachusetts Historical Society.

Interesting ceramics and faunal remains, in particular, have emerged; the ceramics in particular are often of surprising range and quality, suggesting perhaps that Jefferson either treated his slaves well by giving them discarded wares from the house or that his household slaves managed covertly to steal desired items and put them to their own uses.[6] But a more

239

basic issue warrants our attention. What were these small houses like?

The terse descriptions of these small cabins on the 1796 plat itself reveal important details. According to Jefferson's declaration on the policy, structure "o" was a "servant's house 20 1/2 f. by 12 f. of wood, with a wooden chimney, & earth floor. from o. it is 102 feet to E." Archaeologists have confirmed the presence of the "wooden chimney," a stack made of woven sticks or "cats" coated with mud, clay, or plaster along the eastern end of the structure. At the same end, just inside the foundation line, a small brick-lined storage pit or root cellar appeared. According to archaeologist William Kelso, this small house was similar to one still standing at the Bremo Recess Plantation not far from Monticello, a single-pen structure with a rectangular plan, a brick-lined root cellar, a chimney standing at one gable end, and walls of horizontal log; his suggestion that the Monticello cabin was similarly constructed is supported by a letter written in 1809 from Jefferson to overseer Edmund Bacon instructing him to move his former cook, Peter Hemings, into "any one of the log-houses vacant on Mulberry Row." One-room rectangular slave houses do not survive in great numbers in contemporary Virginia; one example from the William Gaines plantation in Hanover County, while it has had additions made at either side of the chimney bay, offers a useful point of comparison (fig. 8.8).[7]

What of the remaining three slave houses labeled "r," "s," and "t" on the 1796 insurance plat? According to the description, they "are servants houses of wood, with wooden chimnies, & earth floors, 12. by 14 feet, each and 27. feet apart from one another." Given the dimensions of these small houses, they must each have been intended to house a separate slave family. These three houses were probably constructed in 1792. In that year Jefferson instructed his overseer, Clarkson, to build "log houses . . . at the places I have marked out of chestnut logs, hewed on two sides and split with the saw and dovetailed . . . to be covered and lofted with slabes."[8] In other words, these houses were made of logs that were then covered over with sawn boards or "slabes." Each also had a clay-covered chimney centered on their south wall.

Despite having been constructed for Jefferson's slaves, these structures were very similar in form and construction to houses owned by poor whites. They, too, were often small,

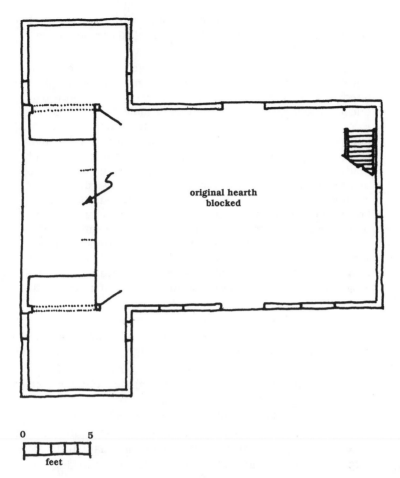

original hearth
blocked

0   5

feet

8.8. Plan of slave quarter at William Gaines's plantation, Hanover County, Virginia. Drawing by Robert Blair St. George after Historical American Building Survey drawing by A. A. Davis, 1941.

one-room structures with a loft overhead and a stick chimney parged with clay running up one gable end. From a strictly theoretical point of view, Jefferson must have looked up from his copy of Palladio's *Four Books of Architecture* and disapproved of ordinary houses that made no effort to uplift the morality and aesthetics of their residents through stylistic reference

241

to classical forms. The houses of poor whites at the foot of Monticello's slopes felt the harsh glare of his critical gaze:

> The private buildings are rarely constructed of stone or brick; much the greatest portion being of scantling and boards, plaistered with lime. It is impossible to devise things more ugly, uncomfortable, and happily more perishable. There are two or three plans, on one of which, according to its size, most of the houses in the state are built. The poorest people build huts of log, laid horizontally in pens, stopping the interstices with mud. . . . The genius of architect seems to have shed its malediction over this land. Buildings are often erected, by individuals, of considerable expence. To give these symmetry and taste would not increase their cost. It would only change the arrangement of materials, the form and combination of the members. This would often cost less than the burthen of barbarous ornaments with which these buildings are sometimes charged. But the first principles of the art are unknown, and there exists scarcely a model among us sufficiently chaste to give them an idea of them.[9]

With their clayed chimneys situated along their southern walls, the three slave houses ("r," "s," and "t") at Monticello would have stood with their blank gable end facing Mulberry Row; the door to each house would have been positioned along the side perpendicular to the lane. The image of the quarters would have looked very much like those at Roseberry plantation in Dinwiddie County, Virginia (fig. 8.9); these poorly constructed buildings, set in a row with their gable ends to the quarter road, convey a sense of fiscal austerity and spatial discipline typical of tidewater society. Already running out of money, Jefferson in the early 1790s turned from his early vision of a classical row and built slave housing exactly like that seen on many Virginia plantations during the period; his careful notation in the 1796 insurance policy to the linear distance between each house also suggests he was aware of the ways in which spatial segregation can enhance discipline and control.

The one-room log houses Jefferson built for slaves in around 1792 were only one such measure of the degree to which he followed customary practices. On other Virginia plantations, landowners also built double houses, in which two families shared a central chimney, as in the surviving eighteenth-century Virginia quarters near Broadnax, and at

8.9. Row of slave quarters at Roseberry plantation, Dinwiddie County, Virginia. Beckstrom for Historic American Building Survey, Library of Congress, 1936.

Tuckahoe and Howard's Neck plantations (fig. 8.10), both in Goochland County near Monticello. It is precisely this double-house plan with central chimney that Jefferson sketched as the "servants" houses when he began to remodel the south dependency wing in the mid-1790s. Archaeological investigations also indicate that a slave dwelling of "double-house" proportions had occupied the site of structures "r," "s," and "t" prior to the early 1790s, but had been cleared to provide space for the new housing. One-room houses offered Jefferson an opportunity to combine an apparent improvement in his slaves' domestic life—allowing them a greater sense of "privacy," perhaps, from the master's perspective, and an improved standard of living consistent with Jefferson's desire to treat his slaves well—with a new form of spatial surveillance that was then coming into vogue with planned housing schemes for workers in early industrial communities. And with the other types of buildings along Mulberry Row, Monticello in the 1790s looked more like a small industrial community, complete with a nailery and forge, than a Virginia plantation. Jefferson himself seems to have not only ignored

243

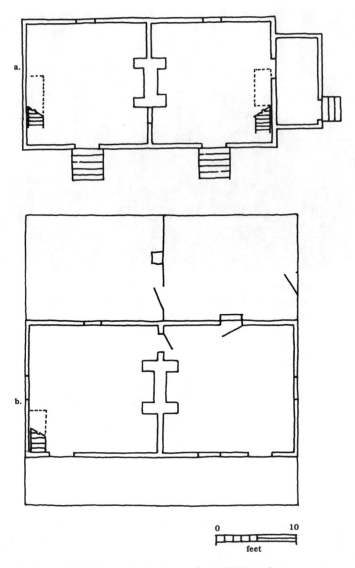

8.10. Central-chimney, two-room slave houses in eighteenth-century Goochland County, Virginia: *a.* plan of slave house at Tuckahoe plantation; *b.* plan of slave house at Howard's Neck plantation. From *Material Life in America, 1600–1860,* ed. Robert Blair St. George (Boston: Northeastern University Press, 1988), 358–61. Drawing by Robert Blair St. George.

his own advice about industrial production ("for the general operations of manufactures, let our workshops remain in Europe"[10]), but in fact integrated industry into his own domestic economy. Indeed, as Joyce Appleby has recently argued, Jefferson embraced the market economy and manufacturing as a key frame in which human potential for moral action could be exercised; his republican rhetoric was rationally consistent with Lockean logic.[11]

At this point, where does our tour of Monticello place "race"? For one thing, we see that, despite his lofty visions and designs of the early 1770s, Jefferson actually housed his slaves in hovels that occupied the cellar of the architectural spectrum. He treated them as did many other Virginia landowners. For another, we learn that his extensive record-keeping and monitoring of domestic productivity reveals a very calculating economic instinct, a person keenly aware of profit, investment, and loss; here Jefferson seems the ancestor of Thoreau, whose close tallying of building costs and domestic economy in *Walden* betrays any literal belief in his critique of materialism's moral wickedness. But how do these structures at Monticello—and the strange erasure of interpretation at the one surviving stone house—contribute to our understanding of race for the towering Enlightenment myth of "Mr. Jefferson"?

"Beyond the Reach of Mixing"

Jefferson's concept of race during the period when the slave houses were built was complicated, and at many points his own writings seem contradictory. Most scholars describe Jefferson as a heroic moral philosopher struggling to reconcile his enthusiasm and commitment to natural rights and the republican writings of Locke, Sidney, and Rousseau with his being "trapped" or "caught" in an economy that demanded he retain his slaves. They also point to the fact that Jefferson emancipated seven of his house slaves as a sign that he tried to live up to his best philosophical inclination. This is also the version of Jefferson one typically hears from the interpretive staff at Monticello should one ask about the "race problem." Yet only two of Jefferson's slaves were actually manumitted prior to his death, and these were from a total of some 220 slaves, on average, that he owned on his several properties.

To paint Jefferson as an emancipator seems premature, to say the least. The critical passage on slavery in his *Notes on the State of Virginia*—drafted in the early 1780s and published in 1787—offers a point of reference. Jefferson began by filling in a few numbers. The estimated number of blacks in Virginia society, he asserted, was almost equal to that of whites. After careful tabulation and correction for biased reports, Jefferson offered the following numbers: 270,762 slaves to 296,852 free whites. He also noted with caution that the number of slaves "increases as fast, or faster, than the whites." But Jefferson soon moves on to other, more difficult matters: the "physical and moral" qualities of blacks as compared with whites, and his plans for a "solution" to the issue. On the relative attributes of whites and blacks based on complexion, Jefferson wondered, "Are not the fine mixtures of red and white, the expressions of every passion by greater or less suffusions of colour in the one, preferable to that eternal monotony, which reigns in the countenances, that immovable veil of black which covers all the emotions of the other race?" On their hair and bodily form, he noted: "Add to these, flowing hair, a more elegant symmetry of form, their own [i.e., the slaves'] judgment in favour of the whites, declared by their preference of them, as uniformly as is the preference of the Oranootan for the black woman over those of his own species. The circumstance of superior beauty, is thought worthy of attention in the propagation of our horses, dogs, and other domestic animals; why not in that of men?" Jefferson goes on to compare such "objective" scientific factors as perspiration and the amounts of sleep required by blacks and whites. He then turns to the slaves' sexuality: "They are more ardent after their female: but love seems with them to be more an eager desire, than a tender delicate mixture of sentiment and sensation." Finally, after suggesting of blacks that "their existence appears to participate more of sensation than of reflection," he weighs the "physical and moral" attributes of blacks against those of whites as follows:

> In general . . . Comparing them by their faculties of memory, reason, and imagination, it appears to me, that in memory they are equal to the whites; in reason much inferior, as I think one

could scarcely be found capable of tracing and comprehending the investigations of Euclid; and that in imagination they are dull, tasteless, and anomalous.[12]

Thus, from the comparative perspective of an "enlightened" science, Jefferson suggests an inequality of body and mind between whites and their slaves. Still, he made allowances for the restricted opportunities slaves had for learning, but even these were cast in ethnocentric terms. "Most of them have been confined to tillage, to their own homes, and their own society," he observed, "yet many have been so situated, that they might have availed themselves of the conversations of their masters." He noticed their ability in music, but expressed doubt that mastery of a simple "catch" or tune would ever lead "to the composition of a more extensive run of melody, or of complicated harmony." He derided Phyllis Wheatley, maintaining that "the compositions published under her name are below the dignity of criticism." Yet he excused slaves that stole from their masters, which he ascribed "to their situation, and not to any depravity of the moral sense."[13]

Jefferson did not stop with an inventory of racial "characteristics." Beginning in 1779, Jefferson was on a committee charged with transforming the laws in effect under the monarchy to ones consistent with the new republican form of government. Among the issues the so-called Report of the Committee of the Revisors addressed was the emancipation of the slaves. This was a particularly vexing issue, for while the laws and form of government had changed, the economy of Virginia had not. After reviewing his description of slaves' physical qualities and moral status (both as property and thieves of property), Jefferson backed off from some of his more prejudicial statements about the slaves' lack of reason and "dull, tasteless" imaginations, and suggested their parity on the basis of equal but "different" natures. "To our reproach it must be said," he maintained,

> that though for a century and a half we have had under our eyes the races of black and red men, they have never yet been viewed by us as subjects of a natural history. I advance therefore as suspicion only that the blacks, whether originally a distinct race, or made distinct by time and circumstances, are inferior to the whites in the endowments both of body and mind. It is not against experience to suppose, that different species of the same

247

genus, or varieties of the same species, may possess different qualifications.[14]

This appreciation of equality amid "different qualifications" lay behind Jefferson's committee report, a report that argued the emancipation of slaves could occur in a republic if they were properly trained in a productive trade or craft and then sent elsewhere. As the committee report advised, all slaves born after the passage of the act (1779) "should continue with their parents to a certain age, then be brought up, at the public expence, to tillage, arts or sciences, according to their geniusses, till the females should be eighteen, and the males twenty-one years of age, when they should be colonized to such a place as the circumstances of the time should render most proper." The plan was to guarantee the slaves emancipation by exporting them to a "colonized" locale; there Jefferson felt sure the United States would "declare them a free and independent people." As part of the plan, the committee report also called for sending vessels "at the same time to other parts of the world for an equal number of whites" to fill the vacated places in the labor market. The end result would be a white America, where conflicts over the reality of slavery and the imagined world of classical virtue would not exist. The solution was unprecedented in Jefferson's experience: "When freed, he is to be removed beyond the reach of mixture."[15]

Thus the so-called paradox of race that Jefferson sought to reconcile was in fact a profound ambivalence about race and racial mixture. While he in principle recognized the natural equality of blacks and whites, he felt that equality could only be realized through deportation and by admitting the color line was an insurmountable barrier. As he put it, "This unfortunate difference of color, and perhaps of faculty, is a powerful obstacle to the emancipation of these people."[16] From this perspective, Jefferson's legacy to the practice of racism in America is mixed. He penned clear indictments of the institution of slavery, though less of the economy supporting it. But his reasoned solution as a landowning member of the educated gentry antedates the segregationism of the New South by almost a century.

Jefferson clearly anticipated criticism. "It will probably be asked," he admitted, "why not retain and incorporate the blacks into the state, and thus save the expence of supplying, by importation of white settlers, the vacancies they leave?" His answer swelled with the anger and pain of a slave economy.

> Deep rooted prejudices entertained by the whites; ten thousand recollections, by the blacks, of the injuries they have sustained; new provocations; the real distinctions which nature has made; and many other circumstances, will divide us into parties, and produce convulsions which will probably never end but in the extermination of one or the other race.[17]

It is important to note that Jefferson's plan addressed the concern of large landowners who, like himself, needed to find a way to replace the labor lost on their plantations when emancipated slaves left for their new nation. Because it addressed the anxieties of the Virginia gentry, Jefferson's scheme perhaps was popular with old Anglican families and identified with high church politics in the post-Revolutionary period. At least such an argument helps make sense of the major critical rejoinder that followed shortly after *Notes on the State of Virginia* was published in 1787.

A prominent Presbyterian and future president of the College at New Jersey (Princeton), Samuel Stanhope Smith wrote *An Essay on the Causes of the Variety of Complexion and Figure in the Human Species* (1787), in which he argued that racial mixing—rather than racial segregation through resettlement—was the only solution to Virginia's racial and, by extension, political problems. Smith had been born in Lancaster County, Pennsylvania, had graduated from Princeton, and between 1773 and 1779 had preached among the Scotch-Irish in the new western counties of Virginia. In his 1787 tract Smith took a liberal position on the question of race, and contradicted with force the prevailing belief held by Jefferson, among many others, that the different races had been independently created. Instead, he asserted a genetic unity of all people. "The doctrine of one race," he stated, "renders human nature susceptible of system, illustrates the powers of physical causes, and opens a rich and extensive field for moral science. The unity of the human race I confirmed by explaining the causes of its variety." In his text, he attributed variation among physical appearance and custom to the imprint of either "climatic influence" or "the state of society" among a certain group. To be sure, Smith's argument was predicated

249

on his implicit trust in the superiority of European society and the positive effects that sustained contact with its cultural centers might have on marginal groups whose "state of society" was less developed. Racial mixture, far from weakening white peoples, would for Smith have had the obvious effect; it would gradually strengthen individuals whose own society was conceived as less stable. As the following quote suggests, this was a baldly ethnocentric perspective: "Carry the nation of Africa or America to Europe, and mix the breed, as you do that of horses, and they will acquire in time, the high perfection of the human form seen in that polished country. Men will acquire it in the same number of descents as these animals." Still, in its own time, Smith's belief in the genetic unity of human people established a means to find strength in miscegenation rather than weakness. As Rhys Isaac has argued, if Presbyterians and Baptists emerged from the Revolution as popular political groups that embraced both poorer white landowners and blacks, it is no wonder that Smith's pamphlet—grounded in part on his experiences among the Scotch-Irish Presbyterians in the Virginia piedmont—sought social stability through the mixture of the races rather than through continued segregation. For Smith, racial mixture would enhance the young republic's society, not undercut it.[18]

This last point recalls Jefferson's approach to the black slave more pointedly: "he is to be removed *beyond the reach of mixing*"—mixing not in the social sense alone, but more important, through the mixing of blood and the generation of boundary-blurring mulattoes. Here lies the core of Jefferson's ambivalence over race, the aspect of race that is never discussed at Monticello. It is not mentioned by guides in the house. It is not referenced in either the recent pamphlet for "The Worlds of Thomas Jefferson at Monticello" exhibition or the special handout interpreting "Mulberry Row: The Story of Monticello's plantation industries and workers, both slave and free, with a self-guided tour," the latter of which seeks to interpret both black slaves and white workers, but not the mulatto culture where they collided.[19] It is also rendered strangely invisible through the conversion of the sole remaining structure associated with both mulatto people and those charged with overseeing them—the precise point of disciplining the "partial-self, partial-other" into compliance—into the gift-house complex.

Jefferson was insistent on the danger of "mixing" precisely because he had lived in the midst of mixture since at least the 1760s. In September 1769 he had placed an advertisement in the Virginia Gazette that read: "Run away from the subscriber in *Albermarle,* a Mulatto slave called *Sandy,* about 35 years of age, his stature is rather low, inclining to corpulence, and his complexion light." The next spring he stood before the General Court of Virginia in Williamsburg, defending pro bono a mulatto slave named Samuel Howell, whose great-grandmother was a white woman. On the basis of his mixed heritage, Howell had filed suit against his master for his freedom. As Jefferson presented his argument to the court, he revealed a familiarity with practices of miscegenation that could only have come from experience. An "act of 1705 makes servants of the first mulatto, and that of 1722 extends it to her children," with the gendered pronoun "her" suggesting here that mulattoes were normally the issue of white men and women of color. Yet Jefferson, eager to criticize any further extension of enslavement across later generations, added that "it remains for some future legislation, if any should be found wicked enough, to extend it to the grandchildren and other issue more remote."[20] Although the court rejected Jefferson's plea and returned Howell to slavery, the case demonstrates that Jefferson by 1770 had considered carefully the definition of a mulatto under Virginia law.

Jefferson's most sustained contact with mulattoes came soon after his marriage to Martha Wayles in 1772. At that point, as part of her dowry, Martha brought 135 slaves and 11,000 acres of land to their marriage; they actually became Jefferson's property when the estate of his father-in-law, John Wayles, was divided in early 1774. When added to the fifty-two slaves Jefferson had already inherited from his own father's estate in 1752, his holdings made him the second-largest slave holder in Albemarle County on the eve of both the Declaration and the Revolution. Not all of these slaves worked at Monticello. In 1776, when Jefferson completed a census of the "Number of souls in my family," the actual number residing at the estate was 177, a total that included his own wife and daughter, sixteen free men (his overseers and their families), and eighty-three slaves. Among these slaves were several members of the Hemings family, including the mother, Elizabeth (Betty), and four mulatto children fathered

251

by John Wayles, Jefferson's father-in-law. Martha Wayles Jefferson had, in other words, brought her late father's mistress, Betty, and four of her half-sisters and half-brothers into their estate. Betty Hemings was herself also a mulatto, having been born around 1735 to an English mariner named Hemings and a black (probably African) woman owned by John Wayles. Hemings attempted to buy his daughter from Wayles but was denied because, as his great-grandson described, "Just about that time amalgamation [interracial mixing] began, and the child was so great a curiosity that its owner desired to raise it himself that he might see its outcome."[21]

The early kinship ties of all the Hemingses remain elusive. Betty Hemings's children at Monticello included Robert (Jefferson's valet), Martin (a butler), Nance (a weaver), Bett (a personal servant), Critta (a domestic servant and nurse), Sally (a domestic servant), Peter (a cook), and John (a joiner). But there were other Hemingses in her children's generation, too—perhaps later children—including Bob, Martin, James, and Mary. These individuals were privileged among Jefferson's other slaves because they were taught skilled trades and to read and write. They were also, with one exception, the only slaves who lived on top of Jefferson's mountain, and they and their children were the only people who initially occupied the slave housing on Mulberry Row. They were all, in varying degrees, mulattoes. According to the reminiscences of Isaac Jefferson, a blacksmith living in Petersburg, Virginia, when he was interviewed in 1847, "Sally Hemings's mother Betty was a bright mulatto woman & Sally mighty near white . . . Jim & Bob bright mulattoes, Martin darker."[22]

Strictly on the basis of Betty Hemings's own history, it is clear that some of the slaves at Monticello were already three-quarters white. While at Monticello Betty had another mulatto child with John Nelson, an English carpenter employed by Jefferson. And it was this John Nelson who lived in the existing stone house, most likely with Betty while they were raising their mulatto child; Jefferson's own later notes on the 1770 drawing of the "classical" servants houses even specifies that he planned on her living in one of the "no. 1" plans—exactly like that of the surviving house. The benevolence with which Jefferson favored his household "servants" also makes clear that within the slave population as a whole, having more "bright" or "fair" skin was also indicative of one's higher class position.

Certainly racial "mixture" in eighteenth-century Virginia was not restricted to Jefferson. Indeed, many references could be marshaled to demonstrate it was a fairly widespread practice, and one that in large part involved white men and slave women. But Jefferson's Monticello was singled out for comment by the French traveler Rochefoucauld-Liancourt, who suggests that not only slaves were ardent lovers. After visiting Monticello in 1796, the Frenchman recorded that

> in Virginia mongrel negroes are found in greater number than in Carolina and Georgia; and I have even seen, especially at Mr. Jefferson's, slaves, who, neither in point of colour nor features, shewed the least trace of their original descent; but their mothers being slaves, they retain, of consequence, the same condition. . . . But the public opinion is so much against this intercourse between the white people and the black, that it is always by stealth, and transiently, the former satisfy their desires, as no white man is known to live regularly with a black woman.[23]

Jefferson's ambivalence toward slavery—and his abiding concern that whites and black not "mix"—was wrapped up in the very closeness of his relationship with the mulatto slaves at Monticello, and perhaps from the shame that might have attached to it for a person of his exalted status. On one hand he could confidently state that "the improvement of blacks in body and mind, in the first instance of their mixture with whites, has been observed by every one, and proves their inferiority is not the effect merely of their condition of life." Mulattoes may be close to white, but they still lived in slave houses of logs and sticks. Yet on the other hand, he depended on their skills, their willingness to incorporate into his family, and, if debates over the paternity of Sally Hemings's children are taken into account, was himself directly implicated in the continued "whitening" of mulatto culture and thereby its changing legal status. The case of "mighty near white" Sally Hemings makes this point clearly. Having formed a relationship with a white man, her children were of seven-eighths white heritage and were thus considered white under Virginia law, which held that a mulatto must be one-quarter or more "of negro blood." As Lucia Stanton observes,

Jefferson consulted this statute in 1815 and, after thinking through its implications, wrote that "our Canon considers 2. crosses with the pure white, and 3d. with any degree of mixture, however small, as clearing the issue of negro blood." Yet, he warned, "this does not establish freedom, which depends on the condition of the mother." If the concern over the third cross were eliminated, or if the third cross was also with "pure white," however, Jefferson concluded "he becomes a free white man, and a citizen of the US. to all intents and purposes." For Jefferson to emancipate the children of Sally Hemings, as he did before his death, therefore did not involve "freeing slaves" in any simple sense; in legal terms, it instead meant freeing white people whose enslavement or continuing status as Jefferson's "children" (as he termed them) was itself unconstitutional.[24]

Departures

There are of course other points to remember about placing race in Jefferson's Monticello: the endless talk during tours of the house about Jefferson's books and reading, his extensive knowledge of gardening and plants, his exquisite furnishings, his insights as a collector of "natural history" specimens, the exquisite period room settings that make it seem as if spectacles of lavish consumption are always about to happen, material proofs of Joyce Appleby's assertion that Jefferson's republicanism was fully consistent with an enthusiastic embrace of the world's markets. Each in their own way plays a part in the construction of the Enlightenment patriarch in such a way that renders invisible the issue of racial mixture at the center of Jefferson's complex racial politics. A case in point comes from Jefferson himself, writing to Henry Remsen in October 1794, amid a spate of building, economic expansion, and landscaping: "I am so much immersed in farming and nail-making (for I have set up a nailery) that *politicks are entirely banished from my mind.*"[25] As with Jefferson himself, so too does the museum "distract" visitors from problematic issues by naturalizing them

8.11. Gift shop in image of a double slave house, Monticello, May 1994. Courtesy of Robert Blair St. George.

in details of planting schedules, production costs, and furniture styles.

Finally, as I leave Monticello, I walk along the path charted for Mulberry Row and stop for one last look in the gift shop, which I suddenly realize is labeled "slave house" on the site plan posted nearby. The new structure itself is meant to look on one side like a double slave house, with a chimney placed centrally on the roofline (fig. 8.11); in Jefferson's 1796 insurance description, a building on the identical spot is marked "q" and was indeed a small "servant's house 14. f, by 17. f. of wood, with a wooden chimney, the floor of earth" that was seventy-two feet away from house "r." But like "r," "s," and "t," this was a single-room structure, and not the double-house type modeled by the "slave house/gift shop." (Since this building had been built prior to 1980 and disturbed the underlying site, the archaeological team could not make any attempt to excavate house "q"). From the other side, when viewed from the garden or Jefferson's vineyard, the slave house/gift shop looks strikingly like a California winery (fig. 8.12).

Inside the slave house/gift shop, we discover another enlightened marketplace. A replica of Houdon's bust of Jefferson is suitably surrounded by books (fig. 8.13). Souvenirs

8.12. Rear elevation of gift house complex in image of a winery, Monticello, May 1994. Courtesy of Robert Blair St. George.

of Jefferson's other domesticated passions—viniculture and gardening—surface in the bottles of "Monticello Riesling" (fig. 8.14) and souvenir canvas bags (fig. 8.15) that promise, if purchased, vicarious attachment to his Enlightenment aura. There are even intertextual references to the other legacies indexed through the world of commodity purchase and collections, as reproductions from other museums surface amid those from Monticello itself; an amber glass bowl bearing the tag "Created by Pairpoint from the Winterthur Museum Collection" was on exhibit in the aisle directly across from the wine and bags. Such commodities, however, can be as much about loss as about gain, and objects presented as "gifts" can constitute power relations as well as sunder them.

Placing race at Jefferson's Monticello entails reading the deflections and "dis-placements" as well as illuminations of the present in the past. The ambivalence toward racial "mixture" that pulsed through Jefferson's own life and shapes Monticello's invisibility strategies today suggests that the meanings of miscegenation are still uncertain as America struggles to reconcile multicultural realities with an essentially Eurocentric conception of political economy.

8.13. Gift shop interior, showing reproduction of Houdon's bust of Thomas Jefferson, Monticello, May 1994. Courtesy of Robert Blair St. George.

8.14. Detail of label, "Monticello Riesling," in gift shop, Monticello, May 1994. Courtesy of Robert Blair St. George.

8.15. Canvas bags celebrating Monticello as a gardening mecca, in gift shop, Monticello, May 1994. Courtesy of Robert Blair St. George.

Notes

An earlier version of this chapter was presented at "The Question of Race in the Americas" symposium held at the University of Pennsylvania, September 29–October 2, 1994. The author is indebted to Carroll Smith-Rosenberg for inviting him to participate in this conference, and to Anne Norton, Eric Lott, Dana D. Nelson, Simon Newman, and J. Crockett-Smith for their comments and reactions to the argument.

1. Kevin Lynch, *What Time Is This Place?* (Cambridge, Mass.: MIT Press, 1972). On place and power, see Allan Pred, *Place, Practice, and Structure: Social and Spatial Transformation in Southern Sweden, 1750–1850* (Totowa, N.J.: Barnes & Noble, 1986), and Pred, *Lost Words and Lost Worlds: Modernity and the Language of Everyday Life in Late Nineteenth-Century Sweden* (New York: Cambridge University Press, 1990). See also Robert Harbison, *Eccentric Spaces* (New York: Knopf, 1977).

2. Andrea Palladio, *The Four Books of Andrea Palladio's Architecture*, trans. Isaac Ware (New York: Dover, 1965 [London, 1738]), bk. I, 1 (italics added). On the cultural resonance of Palladio's *fiumicello* for Jefferson, see Rhys Isaac, "The First Monticello," in *Jeffersonian Legacies*, ed. Peter S. Onuf (Charlottesville: University Press of Virginia, 1993), 84.

3. On the movement of materials and people through Monticello's lower bodily courses, I am indebted to Alice Gray Read, "Monticello's Dumbwaiters," *Journal of Architectural Education* 48.3 (February 1995): 170–72. On the excavations of the slave dwellings, see William M. Kelso, "Mulberry Row: Slave Life at Thomas Jefferson's Monticello," *Archaeology* 39.4 (September–October 1986): 28–35; and Kelso, "The Archaeology of Slave Life at Thomas Jefferson's Monticello: 'A Wolf by the Ear,'" *Journal of New World Archaeology* 6.4 (June 1986): 5–20; and most recently, Anna Gruber, "The Archaeology of Mr. Jefferson's Slaves" (M.A. thesis, University of Delaware, 1990).

4. *Memoirs of a Monticello Slave, as Dictated to Charles Campbell in the 1840's by Isaac, One of Thomas Jefferson's Slaves*, ed. Rayford W. Logan (Charlottesville: University Press of Virginia for the Tracy W. McGregor Library, 1951), 12. For a history of the shifting ownership of the estate between Jefferson's death in 1826 and the sale of the property for $500,000 to the newly formed Thomas Jefferson Memorial Foundation in 1923, see Merrill D. Peterson, ed., *Visitors to Monticello* (Charlottesville: University Press of Virginia, 1989), 4–10. A general survey of the estate is available in William Howard Adams, *Jefferson's Monticello* (New York: Abbeville Press, 1983).

5. Isaac, "The First Monticello," 84.

6. Fiske Kimball, *Thomas Jefferson Architect: Original Designs in the Coolidge Collection of the Massachusetts Historical Society* (New York: Da Capo Press, 1968 [New York, 1916]), 159. Kelso, "Mulberry Row: Slave Life at Thomas Jefferson's Monticello," 32; see also Eric Klingelhofer, "Aspects of Early Afro-American Material Culture: Artifacts from the Slave Quarters at Garrison's Plantation, Maryland," *Historical Archaeology* 21.2 (1987): 112–19; and the essays in Theresa A. Singleton, ed., *The Archaeology of Slavery and Plantation Life* (Orlando, Fla.: Academic Press, 1985).

7. Quoted in Kelso, "Mulberry Row: Slave Life at Thomas Jefferson's Monticello," 33. The Gaines farm was measured by the Historic American Building Survey (HABS) in 1941, and is illustrated in John Michael Vlach, *Back of the Big House: The Architecture of Plantation Slavery* (Chapel Hill: University of North Carolina Press, 1993), 172.

8. Quoted in Kelso, "Mulberry Row: Slave Life at Thomas Jefferson's Monticello," 34.

9. Thomas Jefferson, *Notes on the State of Virginia* (written ca. 1781, first pub. 1787), in *The Portable Thomas Jefferson*, ed. Merrill D. Peterson (Harmondsworth: Penguin, 1977), 202–3. Hereafter: Jefferson, NSV.

10. Jefferson, NSV, 217.

11. For information on the houses at Tuckahoe and Howard's Neck, see Dell Upton, "White and Black Landscapes in Eighteenth-Century Virginia," in *Material Life in America, 1600–1860*, ed. Robert Blair St. George (Boston: Northeastern University Press, 1988), 358–61; see also Upton, "Slave Housing in Eighteenth-Century Virginia," report submitted to the Department of Social and Cultural History, National Museum of American History, Smithsonian Institution, 1982. On the interchangeability of slave house forms on plantations in the tidewater and worker's housing in early industrial communities, see Bernard L. Herman, "Slave Quarters in Virginia: The Persona behind Historic Artifacts," in *The Scope of Historical Archaeology: Essays in Honor of John Cotter*, ed. David G. Orr and Daniel G. Crozier (Philadelphia: Temple University Press, 1984), 271–72. See Joyce Appleby, *Without Resolution: The Jeffersonian Tensions in American Nationalism* (Oxford: Clarendon Press, 1992), 8–10, 19–24; and Appleby, "Introduction: Jefferson and His Complex Legacy," in *Jeffersonian Legacies*, ed. Onuf, 7 ("The Jeffersonian Republicans cast their longest shadow over American political thought by linking scientific rationalism to free trade"), 9 ("The market for the Jeffersonians, however, was never merely an economic system; it represented a new sphere

of action for the unfolding of human potential"). For a slightly later period, see also Larry McKee, "The Ideals and Realities behind the Design and Use of 19th-Century Virginia Slave Cabins," in *The Art and Mystery of Historical Archaeology: Essays in Honor of James Deetz*, ed. Anne Elizabeth Yentsch and Mary C. Beaudry (Boca Raton, Fla.: CRC Press, 1992), 195–214.

12. Jefferson, NSV, 187, 188.

13. Jefferson, NSV, 189, 191.

14. Jefferson, NSV, 192–93.

15. Jefferson, NSV, 186, 193.

16. Jefferson, NSV, 193.

17. Jefferson, NSV, 186.

18. Samuel Stanhope Smith, *An Essay on the Causes of Complexion and Figure in the Human Species* (Philadelphia, 1787), 110, 129. For biographical information on Smith, see *Dictionary of American Biography*, ed. Dumas Malone, vol. 17 (New York: Charles Scribner's Sons, 1935), 344–45. See also Michel Sobel, *The World They Made Together: Black and White Values in Eighteenth-Century Virginia* (Princeton, N.J.: Princeton University Press, 1987), 285, n. 66. Rhys Isaac, *The Transformation of Virginia, 1740–1790* (Chapel Hill: University of North Carolina Press for the Institute of Early American History and Culture, 1982), 143–80, 243–72, 299–301.

19. "The Worlds of Thomas Jefferson at Monticello," pamphlet accompanying exhibition, April 13–December 31, 1993; "Mulberry Row: The Story of Monticello's plantation industries and workers, both slave and free, with a self-guided tour," pamphlet which offers through word and image "A Self-Guided Tour of Monticello Row and Monticello," undated [1992–94].

20. Quoted in Isaac, "The First Monticello," 88–89.

21. Edwin Betts, ed., *Thomas Jefferson's Farm Book* (Princeton, N.J.: Princeton University Press, 1953), 27; Lucia Stanton, "'Those Who Labor for My Happiness': Thomas Jefferson and His Slaves," in *Jeffersonian Legacies*, ed. Onuf, 148. Quoted in Joel Williamson, *New People: Miscegenation and Mulattoes in the United States* (New York: Free Press, 1980), 43.

22. *Memoirs of a Monticello Slave as Dictated to Charles Campbell in the 1840's by Isaac, One of Thomas Jefferson's Slaves*, 13. On the genealogy of the Hemings family, see the convenient summary in Susan R. Stein, *The Worlds of Thomas Jefferson at Monticello* (New York: Harry N. Abrams with the Thomas Jefferson Memorial Foundation, 1993), 87–91.

23. Duc de la Rochefoucault-Liancourt, "A Frenchman Views Jefferson the Farmer," in *Visitors to Monticello*, ed. Peterson, 30.

24. Jefferson, NSV, 190. Quoted in Stanton, "'Those Who Labor for

My Happiness,'" 152. On the paternity of Sally Hemings's children, it is interesting to note that while many (though not all) white scholars have chosen to remain "cautious" of Jefferson's involvement—citing the lack of hard documentary evidence besides the politicized accusation by James Thomson Callender in the Richmond *Recorder* in 1802—most African-American historians have argued on the basis of oral history that Jefferson indeed was the father of such mulattoes as Joseph Fossett, beginning with Fossett's descendant Lerine Bennett, "Thomas Jefferson's Negro Grandchildren," *Ebony* 10 (November 1954): 78–80. The literature on the debate, itself racialized to protect interests from diverse perspectives, is well summarized in Stanton, "'Those Who Labor for My Happiness,'" 172, n. 5, 173–74, n. 20. I am indebted to Stanton's excellent work in documenting this debate. On Jefferson and the changing interpretations of his relationship with Sally Hemings, see Annette Gordon-Reed, *Thomas Jefferson and Sally Hemings: An American Controversy* (Charlottesville: University Press of Virginia, 1997).

25. Quoted in Frederick D. Nichols and James A. Bear, Jr., *Monticello: A Guidebook* (Monticello, Va.: Thomas Jefferson Memorial Foundation, 1967), 59.

9

Critical Memory and the Black Public Sphere

Houston Baker, Jr.

Temporally, modernity is always situated before or after the revolution. Black modernity in the United States—like modernity in general—is articulated through the twin rhetorics of *nostalgia* and *critical memory*. Nostalgia does not here mean arrested development, a distraught sentimentality ever pining for "ole, unhappy, far-off things, and battles long ago." Rather, it suggests *Heimweh*, or homesickness. Nostalgia is a purposive construction of a past filled with golden virtues, golden men, and sterling events. Nostalgia plays itself out in two acts. First, it writes the revolution as a well-passed aberration. Second, it actively substitutes allegory for history.

Critical memory, by contrast, is the very faculty of revolution. Its operation implies a continuous arrival at turning points. Decisive change, usually attended by considerable risk, peril, or suspense, always seems imminent. To be critical is never to be safely housed or allegorically free of the illness, transgression, and contamination of the past. Critical memory, one might say, is always uncanny; it is also always in crisis. Critical memory judges severely, censures righteously, renders hard ethical evaluations of the past that it never defines as well passed. The essence of critical memory's work is the cumulative, collective maintenance of a record that draws into relationship significant instants of time past and the always uprooted homelessness of now.

Black modernity is figured in the textural interweavings of nostalgia and critical memory. Hence, it is ceaselessly dependent on the peculiar light and responsiveness brought to bear on it. Black modernity's stylistic and political resonances are ever-varying in their appearances. With respect to the politics of style, only a sweet and beautiful reasonableness of future expectations can nostalgically write the past. Reason pats the present on the back for its good intentions. With this optimistic gesture of good cheer occurs the primal scene of black conservative modernity. Absent from this beautifully constructed scene—normally marked by black-and-white social and professional camaraderie of a discreet, controlled temper—is the noise or even a fleeting memory of the black masses.

The masses should not be taken as a code phrase, but should be conceived in terms of the cultural style or lifeworld of the overwhelming majority of black people in the Americas. In relation to the black public sphere, it is this majority and its interests that make the work of critical memory so crucial. Black conservative nostalgia offers an exclusively middle-class beautification of history designed to erase the revolution, lay blessings on the heads of white people, and give a rousing cheer for free-enterprise individualism. The time frames of conservatism are a congratulatory present and a shamelessly revisionist past in which the black masses play, at best, a boisterously misguided role.

But the black majority and its institutions have always provided the only imaginable repository for the formation of a self-interested and politically engaged black public sphere in the United States. Furthermore, the resources of the black majority have enabled both the emergence of effective (self-, or better, community-interested) leadership and radical redefinitions of black publicness itself. Critical memory works to illustrate the continuity, at a black majority level, in the community-interested politics of black publicness in America. It also seeks to reclaim from conservative revisionism and nostalgia the organic interconnections between black leadership, such as that of the Reverend Dr. Martin Luther King, Jr., and the black majority.

Critical memory operates to save Dr. King from arrest in a golden allegory of the past. In so doing, it sets in motion a critique of the very notion of the public sphere, and calls black

265

conservative nostalgia to serious scholarly account. The following discussion is excerpted from a larger work in progress. It commences at a primary site of public sphere scholarship and proceeds to a critical reading of King and the black public sphere.

No matter how critical the topic, a discussion of blacks in the public sphere might start out in a somewhat lighthearted way. The following comes to mind:

> Be eloquent in praise of very dull old days
> which have long since passed always, And
> convince 'em if you can, that the reign of good
> Queen Anne was Culture's palmiest day.
> Of course you will pooh-pooh whatever's fresh
> and new, and declare it's crude and mean,
> For Art stopped short in the cultivated court of
> the Empress Josephine.
> And everyone will say,
> As you walk your mystic way,
> "If that's not good enough for him which is
> good enough for *me*,
> Why, what a very cultivated kind of youth
> this kind of youth must be!"[1]

This is from Bunthorne's song in Gilbert and Sullivan's *Patience*, a wonderful light opera parody of 1890s English aestheticism. Bunthorne is the opera's arch aesthete, appearing on stage dressed in the style of Oscar Wilde. The stanza's time frame—from the ascension of Anne in 1702 to the close of Josephine's reign in 1809—coincides with the valorized moment specified by Jürgen Habermas for the development of the bourgeois public sphere as a historical category.

Bunthorne's privileging of "Art" and cultivation of a bygone era strikingly represent a conscious, simultaneous mystification of the actual "dullness" of the "old days." It also expresses the aesthete's mystification of himself. His "eloquent praise" is meant precisely to distance him from the common sense, the politics of everyday life, and the newly emergent phenomena of his times. He thus ransacks the past for gold. Moreover, he engages in a purposive self-fashioning, including that of sexual orientation, which enables him to be singularly at home amid the militarism and revolutionary incumbencies of his age. In the world of Gilbert and Sullivan, public opinion rewards Bunthorne with the sincerest form of flattery: imitation.

Habermas's work in that monumental moment of critical social theory, *The Structural Transformation of the Public Sphere: An Inquiry into a Category of Bourgeois Society*, sets forth an intriguing valorization of a bygone era along with a peculiarly anachronistic self-fashioning in the vein of the Frankfurt School. Habermas can be as much a detractor of the culture industry as his friend Theodor Adorno. Like Bunthorne, he also sometimes seems far too elaborate in his praise of dull old days when distinctive structures and relationships of the conjugal family, economic markets, and state authority allowed the emergence of a bourgeois public sphere. Habermas writes:

> The bourgeois public sphere may be conceived above all as the sphere of private people come together as a public; they soon claimed the public sphere regulated from above against the public authorities themselves, to engage them in a debate over the general rules governing relations in the basically privatized but publicly relevant sphere of commodity exchange and social labor. The medium of this political confrontation was peculiar and without historical precedent: people's public use of their reason.[2]

Habermas elaborates further: "A public sphere that functioned in the political realm arose first in Great Britain at the turn of the eighteenth century. Forces endeavoring to influence the decisions of state authority appealed to the critical public in order to legitimate demands before this new forum" (56). At a specific historical moment, then, a rational public forms itself out of a congeries of structural arrangements. These arrangements produce public debate in sites such as coffeehouses, reading societies, clubs, and salons. The public formed in these locations takes, as grist for its conversational mills, legitimate, subjective, rational responses to issues of the day as they occur to participants (votaries of coffeehouses) from their scrutiny of the press and literature. Bourgeois subjectivity is created, according to Habermas, in the intimate sphere of the family. But it is projected or mirrored in literary genres such as letters and diaries. It is also reflected in the commodification of both of these genres when Samuel

267

Richardson combines them into his bestseller *Pamela.* The press, in Habermas's view, is represented by public organs like the *Tatler, Spectator,* and *Guardian.*

What ultimately emerges as Habermas's ideal of the early public sphere is an associational life of male property owners gathered to exchange rational arguments and critical opinions shaped and mirrored by novels and the press. This translates into an influential bourgeois public sphere. And what is the outcome? Habermas answers:

> Because it turned the principle of publicity against the estab-
> lished authorities, the objective function of the public sphere in
> the political realm could initially converge with its self-interpre-
> tation derived from the categories of the public sphere in the
> world of letters, the interest of the owners of private property
> could converge with that of the freedom of the individual in
> general. (56)

Hence, the democracy of the bourgeois public sphere became normative because:

> The cliches of "equality" and "liberty," not yet ossified into revolu-
> tionary bourgeois propaganda formulae, were still imbued with
> life. The bourgeois public's critical public debate took place in
> principle without regard to all preexisting social and political
> rank and in accord with universal rules . . . intrinsic to the idea
> of a public opinion born of the power of the better argument
> was the claim to that morally pretentious rationality that strove
> to discover what was at once just and right. (54)

Habermas implies that while the sphere of the market was called private, and the sphere of the conjugal family was called intimate, the scene of private, rational persons gathered in contestatory (vis-à-vis the State) argumentation and exchange was actually a public sphere. The publicness of this sphere was, of course, dependent on both (male) ownership and (male) literacy.

This reading of *The Structural Transformation of the Public Sphere* finds Habermas eager to enter a time machine and return to the good old days of London coffeehouses and literary societies: things long ago and far away. Once the structural outlines and historical contours of the bourgeois public sphere's emergence and effects are fully drawn, Habermas proceeds to detail a lamentable decline and fall that brings the reader up to the "pseudo-public sphere" consumerism of postindustrial modernism. (His characterization is enough to make even Gilbert and Sullivan's Captain of the Dragoons weep!) About today's arrangements of life in a welfare-state economy, Habermas writes:

> The disappearance of publicity inside large organizations, both in state and society, and even more their flight from publicity in their dealings with one another results from the unresolved plurality of competing interests; this plurality in any event makes it doubtful whether there can ever emerge a general interest of the kind to which a public opinion could refer as a criterion. A structurally ineradicable antagonism of interests would set narrow boundaries for a public sphere reorganized by the social-welfare state to fulfill its critical function. (234)

"Structural transformation," thus, manifests itself not so much as objective historiography as an affective epic, a wish-fulfillment narrative of now and then, of decline and fall . . . the golden nostalgia of once upon a time.

Habermas certainly does *not* suffer from either methodological sleight-of-hand or an ideological narrative zeal. *Structural Transformation* deftly anticipated qualifications, corrections, and criticism. It adduces far too many caveats for us to interpret it as simply a valorization of the bourgeois public sphere. Habermas understands fully that his most valued notion of "publicity" (*Öffentlichkeit*) is exclusionary, overdetermined both ideologically and in terms of gender, overconditioned by the market and by history, and utopian in the extreme.

He notes, in great detail therefore, that the bourgeois in the pursuit of his private (market) interests never left behind "the unfreedom of the property owner." Hence, the bourgeois was never able to develop into that actual and authentic human being in whose capacity the bourgeois wanted to assume the function of the *citoyen*. In brief, a patriarchal "family" dominated by a property-owning male who claims exclusive rights, via literacy, to both rationality and argumentation in coffeehouses and reading societies may importantly challenge some authority. It scarcely qualifies, however, as a realization of the most valuable associational life for a universal *homme* in quest of a pluralistic and egalitarian world.

The very idea of the bourgeois public sphere is shot through with contradictions, and Habermas's *Structural Transformation* dutifully records them: "the equation of 'property owners' with 'human beings' was untenable; for their interest in maintaining the sphere of commodity exchange and of social labor as a private sphere was demoted, by virtue of being opposed to the class of wage earners, to the status of a particular interest that could only prevail by the exercise of power over others" (124–25). Theoretically, and with a certain willing suspension of disbelief, the idea of a bourgeois public sphere, one compelled by reason alone, free of class and status distinctions and resolutely challenging state authority, is tremendously attractive. Even in a discussion of Habermas's model, however, it is obvious that the *idea* of such an apparatus is far more compelling than its shadowy, exclusive manifestations in history.

If Marx, in the nineteenth century, was so brilliantly clear about the limitations of the model, how can black Americans of the 1990s take it up as a serious analytical construct? Marx regarded the seductions of the idea of the bourgeois public sphere as false consciousness. For black America, the attraction of the idea may result not so much from false consciousness as from, to invoke Gilbert and Sullivan, aesthetic consciousness. Habermas's bourgeois public sphere, in situ, is a beautiful idea. It is grounded in a historiography that claims universal men were once golden citizens, rationally exchanging arguments in a realm between the family and the market—regardless of race, creed, color, annual income, or national origin. But insofar as the emergence and energy of Habermas's public sphere were generated by property ownership and literacy, how can black Americans, who like many others have traditionally been excluded from these domains of modernity, endorse Habermas's beautiful idea?

Black Americans arrived on New World shores precisely as *property* belonging to the bourgeoisie. They were strategically and rigorously prevented from acquiring literacy. And they were defined by Thomas Jefferson and his compeers among America's Founding Fathers as devoid of even a germ in their minds that might be mistaken for reason. Historically, therefore, nothing might seem less realistic, attractive, or believable to black Americans than the notion of a black public sphere. Unless, of course, such a notion was meant to symbolize a strangely distorting chiasma: a separate and inverted opposite of a historically imagined white rationality in action. Such a black upside-down world could only be portrayed historically as an irrational, illiterate, owned, nonbourgeois community of chattel—legally barred from establishing even conjugal families—sitting bleakly in submissive silence before the state. It would be precisely what white America has so frequently represented in blackface: the "b," or negative, side of a white imaginary of public life in America.

Yet, it is exactly because black Americans have so aptly read this flip side that they are attracted to a historically imagined "better time" of reason. They are drawn to the possibilities of structurally and affectively transforming the founding notion of the bourgeois public sphere into an expressive and empowering self-fashioning.

Fully rational human beings with abundant cultural resources, black Americans have always situated their unique forms of expressive publicity in a complex set of relationships to other forms of American publicity (meaning here, paradoxically enough, the sense of publicity itself as authority). The sorrow songs, as expressed and marketed by the Fisk Jubilee Singers, which W. E. B. Du Bois treats so eloquently, became a global currency of black spirituality. In the nineteenth century they *materially* purchased both a building for a Negro college in Nashville and effected changes of the human heart to set against the racist imaginary in American courts of power. What was publicized in the voice, presence, global migratory movements of the Jubilee Singers was a black counterauthority of interpretation. This black authority and montaged composition removed the songs as decisively from an imagined circle of primitive, incoherent, subhuman noise as did the brilliantly contestatory reading of the spirituals by the great Frederick Douglass in his 1845 *Narrative of the Life of Frederick Douglass.*

The public sphere, then, expressively conceived as *black,* can suggest a nostalgic, purely aestheticized fascination with the narrative of a beautiful "time past." Or, in the more critical vein of Habermas himself, it can make its way through the interruptions and fissures of an idealized notion of universal man without class, racial, and gender distinctions. Habermas's own analyses portend a critique of any claim that the public can legitimately be confined to a singular sphere rather

271

than read as a plurality of spheres. From his own critique evolve such clear-eyed readings as the following observation by Bruce Robbins: "Within the concept of the public sphere, there is an unresolved and perhaps unresolvable tension, between a tight, authoritative singleness (the public as object of a quest for a universal collective subject or a privileged arena of struggle) and a more relaxed, decentered pluralism (public as something spread liberally through many irreducibly different collectivities)."[3]

Robbins's assumption of plurality rather than singularity is in some ways like the simple lemon juice that children learn to spread across the invisible ink on a page. His assumption casts light on a variety of "invisible publics": the secret message of social plurality comes to view. We come to see, for example, not simply The (white male) Abolitionists, but The (Plural) Abolitionist Movement, replete with Women Abolitionist Organizers, Black Abolitionist Orators, and Ethnic Immigrant Abolitionist Sympathizers on the Underground Railroad. The publicness of abolitionism, thus, becomes less a golden narrative of white male New England Brahmins than a site of montage: a space where a variety of forms of "talk," to paraphrase Nancy Fraser, come together to constitute "political participation."[4]

Out of critique and modulation, alteration and adjustment, the analytical instrument of the public sphere suggests revised notions of how human interactive modes—other than reason alone—bear on publicity. The "wishes," "desires," and "fantasies," again invoking the work of Fraser, of a subaltern counterpublic always help to shape their appropriation of even the most subliminally resonant mass media propaganda. We might, therefore, following Fraser's lead, and regard the politics, or publicity, of the wish as a conversion process that characterizes inter- or post-media moments of personal, face-to-face interaction and display.

Such wishful publicity is the postmodern, immediate response of black everyday life to, for example, the dominant media culture's attempt to institute black role models for purposes of consumption. Even when Charles Barkley says, "I'm not a role model," black publicity responds with: "You are intended as a role model of media/consumer culture, Sir Charles. You are meant to convince us that you are not role-modeling, so that we, who have thoroughly discredited the notion of role models, will buy the product that you, Sir Charles, are being paid to hustle." The commercial may be regarded as "dope" on the street, but nobody black is buying the product simply because of Sir Charles's slickness in relationship to role-modeling. This short-lived commercial is simply one result. The actual wish for real forms of power can be thought of as a desire for counterauthority. Reading through the commercial is a form of rational and emotional resistance by marginal productions. Within recent years, Chicago Bulls star Scottie Pippin viciously said of Barkley: "He walks around thinking he's the ambassador of the league, but he's a phony person. Until he gets a [National Basketball Association Championship] ring, he's not the ambassador. Until then, I'm considering myself the ambassador."[5] Taking apart reigning commercial models by using the very signs and emblems of publicity, Pippin clearly knows how to "change the joke, and slip the yoke." Outrageous dress—the implicitly "gay oriented" blue jeans advertisements converted to a public "acting up," or the industry-controlled kinesthetics of MTV's rap music converted to insurgent forms of black walking and talking in the city—constitute "reading through." What then seems passively consumed as culture as a whole, whether popular, high, commercial, mass, or otherwise, may be psychologically and affectively appropriated as merely a base/bass line for wildly fanciful counterpublic performances. (Even if they are only "talking the talk," like Pippin.)

Seizing the critical possibilities of Habermas's analyses in their evolving forms of 1990s cultural studies, black Americans are surely in tandem with Arjun Appadurai's suggestion:

The image, the imagined, the imaginary—these are all terms which direct us to something critical and new in global cultural processes: *the imagination as a social practice.* No longer mere fantasy (opium for the masses whose real work is elsewhere), no longer simple escape (from a world defined principally by more concrete purposes and structures), no longer elite pastime (thus not relevant to the lives of ordinary people) and no longer mere contemplation (irrelevant for new forms of desire and subjectivity), the imagination has become an organized field of social practices, a form of work . . . and a form of negotiation between sites of agency ("individuals") and globally defined fields of possibility.[6]

273

Certainly, the white American imaginary's view of public with respect to blackness has made abundantly necessary an agential, black imaginative work of the kind suggested by Appadurai. A different, sometimes invisible, black cultural work can be conceived as ceaselessly inventing its own modernity. In the concrete instance of Southern Jim Crow legality, for example, it had to fashion a voice, songs, articulations, conversions of wish into politics. This creative agency enabled hundreds of thousands of black men, women, and children to gain access to basic public accommodations. The black Civil Rights struggle, particularly during the decade 1955–65, exemplifies the active working of the imagination of a subaltern, black American counterpublic.

In so many ways, the language, the voice, the articulation of Martin Luther King, Jr. captures the peculiar agency of Civil Rights and the movement's effort to recapture and recode all existing American arrangements of publicness. King's voice and language made fully visible and audible the black public sphere in America. He is, in fact, the King of the public sphere.

His was also a double work: simultaneously making visible this sphere and expanding the black public's expression, experience, and influence in globally significant ways. King reached back and took hold of the Reconstruction moment of American defaulted debt concerning forty acres . . . and a mule. His was a *critical* act, and it brought all the implications of Du Bois's modern and informed "laborer" to full black and, ultimately, American consciousness. What black folks most needed, Du Bois had long ago insisted, were opportunities and resources for dignified labor.

King put a black imagination and the resources of its public sphere to work in order to structurally transform the virtually feudal South of the 1950s. His Southern efforts eventually led to an ambitious attempt to rewrite completely the inequitable rearrangements of a late-capitalist global order. His goal, like Du Bois's, was a dignified labor; it is not yet a black reality in America, or elsewhere, as the twentieth century rushes to an end. By 1968, the public status of Memphis sanitation workers in their sphere of labor became for King an icon of American injustice. The struggle of these workers alone signaled for him the desperate requirements, in a postindustrial world, for new and effective forms of counterhegemonic publicity.

274

The historian Taylor Branch, in his magnificent historical account *Parting the Waters: America in the King Years
1954–63* (1988), captures the creation of a new black *publicness*. Branch's work demonstrated how any consideration of
the American public sphere in recent years must account for
this new form of black social and imaginative work. Branch
suggests that, beginning with the famous bus boycott in Montgomery, Alabama, in 1955, Martin Luther King, Jr. increasingly realized and enhanced the most important of his gifts for
leadership: oratory. Of the huge church rally that followed the
first successful day of the Montgomery boycott, Branch writes:

> King would work on his timing, but his oratory had just made
> him forever a public person. In the few short minutes of his first
> political address, a power of communion emerged from him that
> would speak inexorably to strangers who would both love and
> revile him, like all prophets. He was twenty-six, and had not
> quite twelve years and four months to live.[7]

In fascinating detail, *Parting the Waters* chronicles the national print media's captivation with King, a media that only
began to report seriously on a black American general public
with the emergence of the Montgomery Improvement Association.

By 1957, when *Time* magazine published a cover story
devoted to the popular leader of the Montgomery boycott,
Martin Luther King had displaced in the American press's
imagination all of the traditional faces and roles of "Negro
Leadership" in America. The familiar space of Negro Leadership associated with the Executive Director's office of the
National Association for the Advancement of Colored People
(NAACP) was all but cast into the shadows. Comfortably situated in his Northern importance, NAACP Director Roy Wilkins
was seriously annoyed about the success of the powerful up-
start down in Montgomery.

Young, charismatic, and intensely sincere in his commitment to nonviolent direct action in the service of a black collective, King became a national sensation. He also became an
international figure, a model for emerging Third World leaders
and nations of color. In the same year that the *Time* story appeared, one American magazine estimated that King's annual
travel covered 780,000 miles. This would have amounted to

his speaking in public at the rate of four events per week: two hundred talks a year (225)! One of King's close advisors suggested, even at his early moment, that the Montgomery leader had achieved the global recognition and praise for which a younger generation would come stridently to berate him. He had, in fact, become a media star.

Oratory and nonviolent direct action; commitment to, and reliance on, the power of the Southern black American masses; charismatic appeals to racial and religious coalition; the organizational merging of the Southern Christian Leadership Conference (SCLC) with the struggles of the youth-led sit-ins and Freedom Rides—all of these King-endorsed strategies produced a new black American publicity. Branch describes the movement:

> From the Montgomery bus boycott to the confrontations of the sit-ins, then on to the Rock Hill jail-in and now to the mass assault on the Mississippi prisons, there was a "movement" in both senses of the word—a moving spiritual experience, and a steady expansion of scope. The theater was spreading through the entire South. One isolated battle had given way to many scattered ones, and now in the Mississippi jails they were moving from similar experiences to a common experience. Students began to think of the movement as a vocation in itself. (485)

Early in the Montgomery struggle, black preachers realized the only way to unify their efforts was to follow King wherever the struggle led him, including jail. This was the beginning of the ironic creation of a new space of black freedom: the entire criminal justice system of the American South. With the sit-ins, the most thunderous cry of black public resistance was "jail, no bail." This cry indisputably defined a new Southern black public consciousness that instituted a body-on-the-line revolution.

Suddenly, the entire apparatus of white policing and surveillance, which had eloped from the "patter-rollers" in the armed camp of slavery, was converted, mostly by young black students, into a vocational site for liberation. The white-controlled space of criminality and incarceration was transformed into a public arena for black justice and freedom. When, in Rock Hill, South Carolina, black youths were given the option of a one-hundred-dollar fine or a sentence of hard labor for their protest activities, they chose hard labor. Jail, thus, became a primary associational and communicative site for the freedom struggle. The Rock Hill Nine were, in fact, joined by four members of the Student Non-violent Coordinating Committee (SNCC) who made their way to Rock Hill with the goal of being jailed. A new moment of the black public sphere had been instituted. About Rock Hill, Branch writes:

> It was an unforgettable vicarious triumph for thousands of sit-in veterans . . . because the thirteen Rock Hill prisoners set a new standard of psychological commitment to be debated and matched. More important, they introduced the idea of roving jail-goers and mutual support. As students began to think of any jail in any town as potentially their own, a new kind of fellowship took hold on the notion that the entire South was a common battlefield. (393)

Neither anomalous nor accidental, one of Martin Luther King's most poignant and effective Civil Rights documents was, in fact, inscribed from within the new black public sphere of the jail. It was a letter from Birmingham, Alabama. Furthermore, after witnessing the communicative effect, the "group-identity-formation effect" of the white American site of incarceration, how can one be surprised by the emergence of a post–Civil Rights-era "prison" consciousness in black America? From George Jackson to the hyper-success of Sanyika Shakur's *Monster,* there is a continuity in the development of black publicity rather than a recurrent novelty. The Black Muslims, Black Panthers, and such "independents" as Eldrige Cleaver all contributed, as did an accomplished poet like Etheridge Knight, to the resonances of this black public sphere of incarceration.

If there was a paradox in the Southern jail as a rallying place for freedom, there also was an amazing twist of expressive-cultural irony in the fact that music became its own form of cultural and leadership capital during the struggle. In so many historical writings of black America, music is portrayed as the source of spirited religious reverie and inspiration for the most outrageous forms of secular escapism—in dives, jukes, and speakeasies, from Memphis to Mobile, from Atlanta to Los Angeles. But in the moment of the creation of the new black publicity of Civil Rights, sacred and secular traditions coalesced in the office of struggle. Traditional gospels

277

and hymns were rewritten to fit the mounting struggle and spectacle of the movement. A final word from Branch:

> At first, the SNCC leaders accepted the songleader role because of their appreciation for movement singing, and the elders conceded them the role because music was of marginal importance to the normal church program. But the SNCC leaders soon developed a manipulative guile about the music. Their *a capella* singing took the service away from established control by either the preachers or the organist. The spirit of the songs could sweep up the crowd, and the young leaders realized that through song they could induce humble people to say and feel things that otherwise were beyond them. (532)

This was a reshaping of black American media in the service of liberation; song became the expressive mode in which the struggle attracted the voices of the young across the nation. They helped to create a completely different set of associative and communicative norms within black America. School cafeterias and after-school church rallies alike resounded with the new harmonies and lyrics of traditionally black religious songs. These songs were preludes and spurs to committed action in streets, towns, and cities across the American South.

Civil Rights, then, signifies black cultural work of a mass movement: oratory, songs, new and surprising sites of resistance. The movement, in its mass energies and vernacular harmonies, unequivocally pulled the rug out from under the traditional, high *bourgeois* conservative black leadership in the United States. The majority black church did not support King's leadership; indeed, the multi-million member National Baptist Convention relentlessly *opposed* a Civil Rights agenda. Similarly, the NAACP did all in Director Roy Wilkins's and his regional agents' power to keep the spotlight off King and on the organization's own program of legal-defense gradualism. The courts were, in Wilkins's opinion, the best public place for black American advancement. Politicians such as Adam Clayton Powell were cynically opposed to King, refusing during the mid-1960s to allow SCLC leaders actively to support social reform in Harlem.

King did not find at his beck and call an established leadership or a visible public that was in any way ready to make the leap into black modernity which occurred between

1955 and 1965. The insightful historian Clayborne Carson cautions us about encomia for King:

> Although King biographies and King-centered studies of the black struggle continue to appear, serious writers have moved beyond hagiography and have challenged the notion of King as the modern black struggle's initiator and indispensable leader. This reflects a general historiographical trend away from the notion of Great Men either as decisive elements in historical processes or as sole causes, through their unique leadership qualities, of major historical events.[8]

Carson's reminder is sound and timely. At the grass-roots level the struggle had extraordinary leaders such as E. D. Nixon, Amzie Moore, Ella Baker, Septima Clarke, Robert Moses, Fred Shuttlesworth, and so many others.

Yet, at the same time, any adequate reading of the black public sphere during the decade between 1955 and 1965 is unthinkable without the "indispensable" and unique leadership of Martin Luther King. A struggle, and indeed a successful one, may well have occurred, but without King, it could never have been as significantly informed or profoundly inscribed as a modern form of black publicity. For King's oratory was absolutely emblematic of his genius for identifying with a black public constituted in the poverty and exclusion of the Jim Crow system. King felt this economically impoverished public's history, spirit, local knowledge, and leadership like the very beating of his heart. His voice was always tuned by and attuned to its deepest registers. King's goal, therefore, was to transform the invisible deprivations of black day-to-day life into a national *scene.*

A scene such as Birmingham in 1963, with its black masses, white fire hoses, and vicious dogs, became through King's presence and agency a national media *spectacle.* Internationally, Birmingham was read as an American moral scandal. The famous March on Washington of the same year surely qualifies as spectacle in the office of black publicity and liberation. And only King's voice metaphorically and expansively imagined could have achieved such publicity. To analyze King's oratorical engagement enhances understanding of his role in specific forms of black modernity.

In a sermon delivered shortly before his death, King suggested terms for his eulogy. He asked to be remembered not as a Nobel laureate, nor as the recipient of more than three hundred other distinguished awards. Rather, he wanted to be remembered as a Christian practitioner who had fed the hungry, clothed the naked, and refreshed the thirsty. These terms of remembrance were meant to document a harmony between King's life and the New Testament preachments of Christ, specifically those found in Mark 10:35–45. King chose a striking metaphor for his harmony, asking to be eulogized as a "drum major for justice."

The drum major leads a marching band of followers, sometimes with highly unique style. One might say a unique black cultural style if one recalls the high-stepping, smoothly coordinated Florida State A and M Marching Band of the 1960s. This Florida band, in the tradition of Marcus Garvey's remarkable drill teams, with sparks flying from taps on their heels as they paraded down the summer streets of Harlem, combined the precision of military drill teams, the flair of black fraternity step shows, and the choreography of black, post-funeral gyrations in New Orleans. The result was, at least, a revolution in halftime entertainment. The band's drum major fronted and guided a dazzling display with baton-wielding, deep-bowing, downright magical grace. If the field of reference for King's drum major includes such grace and synthesizing energy, then surely it is more than a common metaphor. It can be read as both a vibrant *conceit* and a type of mounting or performative trope for an aesthetics of *montage.*

Conceit is the trade name given by literary critics to figurative language that combines dissimilar images and, in the words of the eighteenth-century lexicographer Samuel Johnson, "discovers occult resemblances in things [that are] apparently unlike." Johnson and his successors have traditionally culled the poetry of writers like John Donne and George Herbert, the Metaphysical poets, for examples of the conceit. Donne's comparison of sorrowfully parting lovers to "stiff twin compasses" and his writing of love's most enduring memorial as "a bracelet of bright hair about the bone" are frequently cited as conceits par excellence.

Conceits negotiate between mental and material worlds. They are designed to make even the most philosophically and theologically complicated thought as immediately present, in the words of T. S. Eliot, "as the odor of the rose." Indeed, Eliot speaks of the conceit as a poetical sign that produces a "direct sensuous apprehension of thought, or a recreation of thought into feeling."[9] The conceit, like the Florida State A and M drum major, makes cultural style and its philosophical implications as palpable as the smell of black Southern cooking at a church homecoming during a week of successful voter-registration activity.

The verbal resourcefulness that produced Martin Luther King's drum major conceit is often viewed by his biographers as a direct outcome of the Civil Rights leader's family background. He was, after all, the product of three generations of black Baptist ministers; he knew the language of the black church and its traditions in their full emotional and metaphorical brilliance. To explain King's verbal dexterity as a family matter is surely correct. Yet, this explanation is incomplete unless we realize that the drum major conceit and, indeed, King's entire repertoire of sparkling oratory are not products of a Christian familial background alone. The language and effectiveness of his Civil Rights leadership also point to a specific habit of mind. This habit of mind enabled him to convert the tortuous, complex, heterogeneous lines and images of U.S. race relations into a strategically conceived and brilliantly articulated program of American social reform that led directly to a new and modern black publicity in America.

The conceit is the linguistic correlative of a mind that imaginatively combines the most seemingly dissimilar things and orders of existence. King's sensibility was metaphysical. It was one of montage or, after the example of Romare Bearden in the graphic arts, collage. It was capable of both effecting and expressing a peculiar synthesis between seemingly disparate walks of American life. Ultimately, King's mind seems to survey a world where the Lord may be the undisputed owner of the field, but He still needs the shrewd, secular drum major to move forward His designs for black liberation.

The bare linguistic bones of conceit may have come to King from Baptist forebears. But the habit of mind that put flesh on the bones was surely a developmental outgrowth of King's participation in and astute understanding of the wider black public sphere in which the Baptist church itself is located. Having come of age in and graduated from a historically black college in the Deep South of the 1950s, King shared a legacy of black collectivity that is virtually inconceivable amid the fragmentation and rubble of today's American world.

Without romanticizing or minimizing the brutal realities of America's Deep South apartheid, it is still possible to acknowledge that racial segregation in the United States both necessitated and gave birth to a remarkable black Southern public sphere. This definitively separate and putatively equal black public sphere of American life comprised a world of civic responsibility, commercial duty, and professional obligations shared by Southern blacks. These behaviors and values were sheltered and nurtured in institutions like the black family and church and at historically black colleges and universities. In its codes of class, patriotism, respectability, dissent, consensus, tolerance, justice, and ethics, the black public sphere offered a sometimes radical critique of the dominant white society with which it coexisted. For example, the Constitution of the United States and the American national flag were valued sites of patriotism and pride for the black public sphere.

Which of us, for example, who attended those awesomely scrubbed black urban public Southern schools of the 1950s that always smelled of disinfectant, can forget the pride and solemnity with which each school day began in recitation of the Pledge of Allegiance to the flag of the United States of America?

How sharply this *Black Federalism*, as it were, contrasts with and critiques the state sovereignty and Confederate nostalgia of, say, 1950s Mississippi. Woven into the very warp and woof of the Mississippi state flag, waving over the capitol in Jackson, were then, and still are, the stars and bars of the Confederacy. Southern state sovereignty meant, in effect, a resolve by the dominant society of the Deep South to preserve Southern whiteness as a separate public sphere.

In *The Souls of Black Folk*, W. E. B. Du Bois captures the spirit and consequences of coexisting black and white public spheres when he analyzes the black church. The church, says Du Bois in his chapter "Of the Faith of the Fathers," is effectively a government of men, reproducing "in microcosm, all that great world from which the Negro is cut off by color-prejudice and social condition."[10] Du Bois does not intend to characterize black religion as a poor substitute for black participation in the American macrocosm. Rather, he seeks to convey the magnificent originality and signal importance of the black Americans' institutionalization of "his higher life." In the black public sphere, the church sustains and expresses the tensions of black American group life. It is at once a social and a religious center, a site of material ownership, a place of frenzied spiritual regeneration, a mecca for intellectual leadership, and a bright oasis for the musical ministry of those who cannot read and write.

The black church negotiates vigorously between the concrete need for black freedom and opportunity in this world and a black theological and philosophical desire for the glories of the infinite. Hence, its mission might be described as psychosocial. Its "twin-compassed" institutionalization is bound to require and produce a special brand of leadership, as Du Bois asserts: "The [black] Preacher is the most unique personality developed by the Negro on American soil" (338). Similarly, the music of the church and its "frenzy" (animated black congregational responses) are seen by Du Bois as significant aspects of its unique, public being-in-the-world. Sociologist Aldon D. Morris astutely notes that when Martin Luther King began his work in black America, "the black church was the only popularly based institution within the black community that was, for the most part, economically and politically independent of the white community. This independence allowed it to serve as the staging ground for the black protest movement."[11]

Black colleges and universities also offer, in the view of Du Bois, prime examples of a creative convergence between black expressivity such as the "Sorrow Songs" of the Fisk Jubilee singers and unique forms of leadership such as the black Talented Tenth. Like that of the church, the mission of black colleges and universities combines or, better, holds in intricate tension, the curriculum for a liberating black economics and programs geared to the "higher life" of black intellectual speculation. Especially significant for the black intellectual, as discussed earlier, is that activism and speculation are seldom mutually exclusive. In the flourishing days of the black university, intellectual speculation was generally held to be a means to a liberatory social end.

Given Du Bois's passionate analyses of black institutions, it seems fair to say he is less interested in condemning the existence of a segregated black public sphere "behind the veil" than in locating the *sui generis* material and spiritual strengths of the sphere. Insofar as these strengths exist in institutional form, Du Bois hopes to decipher their special codes and unique angles of vision. He wants both to read their institutional conceits, one might say, and to present them in his own powerfully figurative language. Du Bois's narrative conceit in *Souls* is that of a black intellectual speaking from "behind the veil." This image provides just the double edge and second sight of verbal mastery that Du Bois required to make his collection of fugitive essays into a black public intellectual document of record. During the 1930s, James Weldon Johnson astutely proclaimed that Du Bois created what had never existed before—a "Negro intelligentsia."[12]

When Martin Luther King was growing up in the Deep South, the truths of black folk, their collective sense of responsibility, and their pride in their public institutions were matters of history and record. In part this was so because Du Bois had achieved the montaged style to take them public. By the time of King's youth in black Atlanta, where Du Bois accomplished some of his most outstanding intellectual work, self-evident truths of the black public sphere rolled trippingly off the tongues of King's Baptist progenitors every Sunday. Such truths were the mainstay of Sunday morning rituals in polished assembly halls of Southern churches from Richmond to New Orleans. The great Civil Rights leader, thus, learned at home in the black public sphere of church, college, and community in a segregated South the contrasting codes and conceits of black American critique.

King came to know that in order to be a drum major, one has first to be touched by the frenzy of black spiritual existence. Du Bois describes this experience: "Finally, the Frenzy or 'Shouting,' when the Spirit of the Lord passed by, and, seizing the devotee, made him mad with supernatural joy, was the last essential of Negro religion and the one more devoutly believed in than all the rest" (339). The words belong to Du Bois, but King's oratorical performances and leadership during the years between Montgomery and Memphis prove that he fully appreciated their wisdom. He understood that before one can be a successful leader in the black public sphere, one must first be instructed in the spirit. This alone allows one to become an instrument of the Lord. The proof of such instrumentality is in the rhetorical effectiveness of the person who, it is provisionally agreed, has been touched. A frenzied style makes one recognizable and resonant before a spirited mass audience. In black public sphere shorthand, King knew

284

that he had to self-consciously model himself as one of "God's Trombones."

Yet his leadership language and development were not simply black recapitulations of, say, Saul's scriptural journey along the road to Damascus. Christian spirituality was pre-eminent in King's life. But this spirituality did not allow him to be satisfied by a simple call to local ministry or clownishly to bellow homespun truths before a gullible audience. Those sacred, black, university ideals expounded by Du Bois at the turn of the twentieth century motivated King. These ideals were as present in the black public sphere of the 1950s as the calling of the black church, and King was fortunate enough to stand intellectually and generationally at the fragile cusp between a closed, nearly feudal South and its inevitable entry into twentieth-century modernity.

In the black public sphere the idea of advanced graduate degrees beyond bachelor's of arts and science credentials was gaining currency. Furthermore, a new black ecumenical spirit was at least as well grounded in the 1950s black American public sphere as the drive to independence by various African nations and the anticolonial struggles of India. Global work awaited, and it seemed in the 1950s that there were global economic possibilities for the black American. New media and communications technologies provided greater access to the world for the South via television and improved telephones services. Conversely, the South and its everyday realities were destined to be internationally telecast.

Finally, there were generational differences that have always marked the black public sphere. Thrust into leadership at twenty-six years of age, King found himself in the midst of a congeries of competing black age groups, mind-sets, ethical orientations, and reform agendas. He was compelled to speak as convincingly to Rosa Parks and her cohort of adult wage earners and domestic laborers as to an adolescent advanced guard of newly middle-class high-school and college sit-in participants. He had to make as much sense to James Lawson of Vanderbilt University as to the Reverend Ralph Abernathy and the SCLC.

King was equal to the challenge. His legacy from the black public sphere, combined with his graduate theological training in Eastern and Western philosophy, enabled him to articulate a new conceit of black moral leadership. His performances before mass audiences made his strategies of leadership irresistible. The pulpit, the podium, and the premiere place in nonviolent protest marches became sites of King's drum-major leadership. He adjusted and keyed his voice and vision to the music of the church and its new SNCC variations, to the values of a Southern black collectivity and to the social and spiritual rhetoric of the black public sphere at large.

Ultimately, King's leadership was a performative occasion. He used it to declare war on American injustice. His performances always combined, after the fashion of the conceit, enormously varied tropological energies. The combinations or montages, which seemed to flow, to be moving images, as naturally fluid as the pulsing of the blood, were powerfully persuasive. On any single occasion, he might move from an explanation of the history of a local protest action, to citations (in layman's terms) of the constitutional supports for the protest, to a parable drawn perhaps from children's literature, to a rollicking exegesis of a scriptural passage relevant to the protest. He then would conclude with a rousingly applauded quotation, half chanted and half sung, from a repertoire that ranged from Aristotle's *Logic* to "The Battle Hymn of the Republic."

King proclaimed clearly and repeatedly that words were not enough. Action—nonviolent, direct action—was the goal of his performances. He was intent on an active gospel designed to correct centuries of American injustice. He knew that his performances would first have to erase a traditional image of black religion that had ruled the white imaginary for decades.

James Baldwin was surely correct when he suggested in his 1955 essay, "Everybody's Protest Novel," that the most valorized image of black religion in the white imagination is Harriet Beecher Stowe's title character from her 1852 novel, *Uncle Tom's Cabin*. "Uncle Tom," writes Baldwin, "is a jet-black, wooly-haired, illiterate; and he is phenomenally forbearing. He has to be; he is black; only through this forbearance can he survive or triumph . . . [and] his triumph is metaphysical, unearthly."[13] For Baldwin, Uncle Tom is indisputably a "category" that white America has substituted for black humanity. Stowe's character represents, in Baldwin's account, a divestiture of both the black American's humanity and his sex.

Stowe's divestiture attempts to nullify evil. According to Baldwin, this New England author's "theology of terror" is widely shared by Americans. It asserts a clear equivalence between blackness and evil; only clothing blackness in the white robes of salvation will redeem America. However, salvation's bright, smothering mantle chokes to death the black personality—and the possibilities for a new and liberating publicity. This theology of terror and the protest novel that it spawns reduce black humanity to a cipher; a will-less, Christian thing incapable of resisting even its own denigration. Baldwin writes: "This tableau [of Stowe's Uncle Tom], this impossibility, is the heritage of the Negro in America: *Wash me,* cried the slave to his Maker, *and I shall be whiter, whiter than snow!* For black is the color of evil; only the robes of the saved are white" (16). Baldwin's terrifying vision of white American Christianity's effect on black America is precisely the image that King designed his own performances and conceits to eradicate.

The genius of King's campaign was its radical, active, uncompromising transformation of the solacing American space occupied by Uncle Tom. Mrs. Stowe's medieval Christian grotesquerie yields figurative right-of-way to King's black public sphere conceits. King's performance of such conceits—working them into his oratory and living them with a drum-major leadership style—produced a new national scene. It was a scene of sharp and ineluctable moral crisis. It was the scene, without a shadow of a doubt, of critical memory in the office of new black publicity and liberation.

King understood that he was compelled to walk and talk in the ways of a Southern, rurally oriented black community that transmitted wisdom as often through oral/aural means as by "the book." He realized that he must carry the church itself and its manifold congregation out of comfortable conservative structural alignments with Southern Jim Crow, such as his own father's Republican ministry. They had collectively to move onto a new national political stage. "Forbearance" and "death," which in Baldwin's account of Uncle Tom serve merely to make Mrs. Stowe's character a quiet casualty of theology, were converted by King's leadership into mass, public, moral weapons.

Weapons were mandatory. King was convinced, from his first engagement at Montgomery, that he had entered a fight, a battle, a war. And he intended to win. "Don't be afraid," he counseled during one memorable speech. "Don't even be

287

afraid to die. . . . For I submit to you tonight that no man is free, if he fears death. But the moment you conquer this fear, you are free."[14] According to King, the "capacity to die" without fear, in the knowledge that you have confronted—without money, power, or the law's protection—the dread, beauty, and rights of your own black humanity, is a mighty weapon against injustice. Furthermore, he proudly, and with the glad endorsement of his constituency, assured his adversaries: "We will wear you down by our capacity for suffering."

King reclaimed those imaginary racial traits of Uncle Tom that caused Mrs. Stowe's "thing" to virtually commit suicide for Christianity. Indeed, he dramatically and performatively refigured them. They were metaphysically refigured in terms of the will, daring, spirit, and institutional strengths of a new black public sphere in formation. King brought this sphere to an intense consciousness of the immediate necessity to achieve full citizenship rights *now,* in *this* world. Economic impoverishment and social segregation had to be eliminated. Only tension and crisis, as King declared in his "Letter from Birmingham Jail," could produce, first, negotiation, and then, new laws offering new opportunities for the black public sphere.

Thus, the conceit of the drum major is far more than a common metaphor or a simple figure for a humble Good (black) Samaritanism. In its black public sphere resonances from the world of King's more than twelve-year battle to open the American South to the sounds of modern justice, the conceit of the drum major assumes a military signification. It gestures toward the point man for a drumming corps of followers. The uniquely black rhythms of such a corps may well guide the stylish strut of a leader. Ultimately, however, King's constituency and its leader were closely akin to the Lord's chosen thousands, in ancient times, across the Jordan, as described in Joshua 6:20. On the seventh day of their occupation, the priests of Joshua sounded their trumpets of rams' horns seven times:

> So the people shouted when the priests blew with the trumpets: and it came to pass, when the people heard the sound of the trumpet, and the people shouted with a great shout, that the wall fell down flat, so that the people went up into the city, every man straight before him, and they took the city.

288

By transfiguring mortality, forbearance, and white America's theology of terror with the intellectual and imaginative resources of the black public sphere, King led his followers in the brilliant (might one say conceited?) sounds of struggle that tumbled the walls of injustice—like the walls of Jericho—and drove the wicked from their seats of power.

Martin Luther King's leadership was so firmly rooted in a black Southern public sphere that it became virtually impossible for King himself, or for America at large, to separate his work from this "publicity." It is a mistake, however, to see the coming of Black Power into the black liberation struggle of the 1960s as a fateful rupture in the work of King's corps that was drumming evil out of the land.

In the far too allegorical historiography of black conservatism, Stokeley Carmichael and the field secretaries of SNCC are charged with substituting a gospel of (evil) armed self-defense and black separatist empowerment for what are held to be Martin Luther King's (good) preachments of integration. But since Jamestown in 1619, notions of black separatism (e.g., emigration) and community empowerment have always coexisted with other orientations in the black public sphere. However, such notions as Carmichael's and H. "Rap" Brown's have only sporadically gained currency with the masses of black America. Their strength of appeal relates to peculiar convergences of American social and economic opportunities with the necessary black leadership to articulate a Black Power agenda.

By the mid-1960s in the United States, such a convergence had come to fruition in the North with the organization of the Black Muslims and the charismatic leadership of Malcolm X. Moreover, the necessity for a new agenda beyond nonviolent, direct action protest in the South had been made clear by the suddenness and ferocity of the Los Angeles Watts riots of 1965. Suddenly visible to national and international publicity were the black Southerners in quest of a promised industrial land. But the new land has all too often left these immigrants from the South abandoned, victims of the death of the smokestack industries. They turned to the meager doles of the welfare state.

Carmichael, Brown, and a Black Power cohort of the 1960s, with King's unhappy agreement, imported "Northern" notions into the black Southern struggle. But the appeal of

Black Power was surely as much generational as regional. If one watches carefully videos[15] of the Black Sanitation Workers' strike in Memphis, which was King's last point of struggle, one sees *young* Southern black men brandishing sturdy clubs in the camera's eye and shouting "Black Power!" When the youth of the corps begin to drum a different cadence, what choice does the drum major have but to rethink his work?

Though Martin Luther King was enveloped in the imagery of the black South at his death—his funeral cortege was led by a mule-drawn wagon—even by 1965 he had moved to a conception of global economic justice and anti-imperialism that forced him to oppose the war in Vietnam and to call for a Poor People's Campaign to be spectacularly staged in Washington, D.C. He realized during his nonviolent 1966 summer campaign in Chicago just how difficult and dangerous urban modernism made the struggle for black liberation, saying, "I've never seen mobs, even in Alabama and Mississippi, as hostile as mobs in Chicago."[16]

In the South, the scene had changed from medieval morality to legally civil twentieth-century premodernity. Blacks could vote in Lownes County, Mississippi, eat at the Woolworth's lunch counter in Greensboro, North Carolina, and ride a Greyhound bus from Durham to Birmingham without being murdered. The South had opened up from feudalism. But the real stakes of modernism were in the ethnically divided cities of the North and West, where there were jobs, economic security, gleaming cars, and sturdy homes: symbols of a fulfilled American dream. In these cities young, black urban dwellers were confronting the forces of racism with combative strategies that they deemed far more appropriate than moral suffering or a courageous capacity to die.

King himself had said that the mobs of the Northern and Western cities were more hostile than those of Alabama and Mississippi. Furthermore, as James R. Ralph reminds us in his fine study of the Chicago Freedom Movement, "By 1965, as Chicago's black population approached one million and accounted for almost a third of the city's residents, more blacks lived there than in the entire state of Mississippi."[17] The scene of black modernity had to be staged, if it was to be meaningful, where most of black America lived.

The black novelist Richard Wright had indeed been prescient in his bestselling work of 1940, *Native Son*, which is set in Chicago. The scene of modernism for blacks was to be a Chicago of the intellect and imagination, an urban space in which an archetypal "Bigger" black consciousness was to find itself caught in a nightmare of acquisitive real estate owners, callous labor leaders, corrupt political officials, and morally blind social welfare workers. Bigger in the electric chair might well have been emblematically and realistically enacted by the Black Panthers' leader, Fred Hampton, who was murdered by the Illinois attorney office in 1969.

Suddenly, the task before young black activists of the mid-1960s, whether in Chicago or Memphis, was to create a new conceit for modernism. It required a figure that could move an urban black public sphere to consciousness and action. The black writer Amiri Baraka states the theme for such modernity in his poem "Return of the Native":

> Harlem is vicious
> modernism. BangClash.
> Vicious the way its made.
> can you stand such beauty
> So violent and transforming.
>
> Each thing, life
> we have, or love, is meant
> for us in a world like this.
> Where we may see ourselves
> all the time. And suffer
> in joy, that our lives
> are so familiar.[18]

Isolated, spatially confined, abandoned by industry, marked by crumbling schools and indifferent teachers, cruelly defined by wretched public housing, the ghetto is its own unique arrangement of black American life. In the 1960s it brought forth from the black publicity of the prison and the ranks of the Black Muslims not only the leadership of a Malcolm X, but also the minimalistic, modern black poetic cadences of a fiery Amiri Baraka.

King had already realized by the mid-1960s that his familiar conceits would have to take account of a far more expansive and complex geographical and imaginative territory than he had previously envisioned. The tragedy for the 1990s is that he did not live long enough to guide us—in the fine energy of his drum major leadership and black public sphere brilliance—through the straits of the past quarter-century. Can anyone doubt that, had King lived, moral tawdriness and black nostalgia would scarcely be as all-consuming as they are in our era?

King's continuing and always transformative leadership might have stood as a bulwark against the disingenuous, conservative black revisionism of the 1990s that seeks to return Mrs. Stowe's Christian martyr to where a mighty drum major of the public sphere lived and had his being-in-the-world. Martin Luther King was the master of conceit. He understood, even as he drew his last breath on that balcony in Memphis, that the language of the black public sphere en masse is the leader's only source of regeneration.

In 1968, that language was Black Power. Aldon Morris writes of King, the Civil Rights Movement, and the media:

> Throughout much of American history blacks were exploited, beaten, and oppressed while most Americans and people around the world went about their daily affairs barely aware of the situation. Indeed, racial segregation and oppression isolated blacks from the American mainstream, making their wretched conditions invisible. The media, however, played an important role in bringing King's leadership and the civil rights movement to national and international attention. (46)

The liberation struggle under King's leadership moved from "invisibility" to legal Civil Rights victories. It also brought black rights the recognition of the highest legislative body in the land. King managed to recuperate a numerical and ideological black public that had been violently erased by the post–Reconstruction South.

The new visibility achieved by Civil Rights was no more than a "recuperation," a small payment of interest on that vast debt noted by Du Bois in 1903. Blacks in 1965 had, in effect, returned to Reconstruction, hoping once again that civil and voting rights would enable them to get ahead with daily life in America without being summarily lynched. The new black visibility scarcely constituted a gain sufficient to satisfy a black majority. This was made abundantly clear as uprisings became normative publicity at the very heart of the Great Society declared by President Lyndon Johnson. New social welfare initiatives designed to end poverty in America were, thus, made more urgent by the international visibility of American cities on fire. King himself realized that a paradoxical return was scarcely more than a Pyrrhic victory. Late in his leadership he angrily declared: "I am appalled that some people feel that the civil rights struggle is over because we have a 1964 civil rights bill with ten titles and a voting rights bill. Over and over again people ask, What else do you want? They feel that everything is all right. Well, let them look around at our big cities."[19] Radically new forms of visibility, or black publicity, were required. Black residents of big cities had decided the only way to gain the nation's attention was by rebellious community action. The theologian James Cone reports that King was shocked, after surveying the destruction of the Watts riots, to hear community residents claiming a victory. How could they think they had won in the face of such wreckage? They answered: "We won because we made them pay attention to us."

Attention, a publicity quite different from any attained by noble sacrifice, was desperately needed if a genuine black modernity was ever to occur. This modernity called for an urban liberation of black America, and for its movement to cultural and economic independence. In July 1967 King proclaimed: "The movement must address itself to restructuring the whole of American society. The problems that we are dealing with . . . are not going to be solved until there is a *radical* redistribution of economic and political power" (emphasis added).[20]

King, thus, moved into harmony with Du Bois by making national indebtedness to the black and the poor a matter of radical American structural concern. Early in the century, Du Bois had outlined the necessities for such structural work. He speculated that, had a "permanent" network of government social organizations and arrangements been established during Reconstruction, the newly emancipated freedmen would have been assured long-term "equal opportunity" and parity in American citizenship with their white brothers and sisters. Instead, the freedmen were handed nothing more than the ballot: "The Freedmen's Bureau died, and its child was the Fifteenth Amendment."[21] The amendment was completely unenforceable in a South where "there was scarcely a white man . . . who did not honestly regard emancipation as a crime, and its practical nullification as a duty."[22] King knew enough history to know that a Voting Rights Act was scarcely enough for black modernity.

Though a fascinating project, I cannot trace here the complex outcomes of what can tentatively be called a "Black Power Agenda," which accompanied the final years of King's life and work. Nevertheless, it is possible to specify results, such as the establishment of Black Studies in American colleges and universities, the birth of nationwide programs designed to foster black business and economic development, the emergence of a new Black Theology circulating in economically independent and popularly based black churches, the exponential increase in new and well-heeled black middle-class professionals, the national recognition and acknowledgment of a new Black Arts and its creativity and criticism, the emergence of a flourishing and internationally influential Black History movement. To these might be added the growth of groups such as the National Bar Association, the National Medical Association, the African Heritage Studies Association—all imbued with cultural and racial pride summed up in the phrase "Black Is Beautiful."

In brief, Black Power led the way and established guidelines for the upsurge in marginal constituency politics in the United States during the last twenty-five years. Black Power decisively broke, sometimes in problematic ways, the lock on national definitions of "America" and "American" that had been held for centuries by wealthy, academically and socially privileged white males. The possibilities of a new and structurally significant visibility became an empowering model for initiatives by women, gays and lesbians, Chicanos and Chicanas, Puerto Ricans, Native Americans, Asian Americans, and other groups in the United States. All followed Black Power's lead into a radical politics of visibility, as that politics has already been defined.

In focus and goals the later leadership of Martin Luther King was commensurate with this Black Power agenda. Only a colossal act of historical forgetting would allow one to envision the King of 1967 as anything but a *black political radical of the first order.* He had become a man temperamentally inclined to radical restructuring rather than slow and noble reform. In the manner of black modernity, critical memory focuses the historical continuities of black majority efforts, strategies, and resources for leadership and liberation. Furthermore, it demonstrates the ever-renewing promise inherent in the contiguity of majority and "leadership" remembrance. Black intellectual and political self-interest, therefore, demands emphasis on an integrity of critical recall. By integrity, I am suggesting a historically verifiable emphasis on how the black public sphere has always been restructured through contiguity: the closeness of King to the black majority, the inevitable segue of Civil Rights into Black Power, the convergence of SNCC activists' secular versions of black church jubilees, and the minimalistic poetics of Black Arts modernism.

The critically imagined closeness of our black majority selves and the birth of black radical modernism must be continually foregrounded. Re-membering King on the far side of the Reagan-Bush era is necessarily a critical and imaginative act. It requires sharp resistance to nostalgia. To the extent that black conservatism dedicated itself to a nostalgic fissuring of continuity and the erasure of contiguity between black majority and black leadership interests, it must be seriously challenged. Such historical revisionism—one that reads King as aloof from or majestically out of touch with the majority at *any* time during his leadership—offers a false reading of the past. Moreover, at this complex moment of late capitalism, such revisionism woefully limits majority interests in a black public sphere, an arena that requires perhaps more urgently than ever before the good offices of critical memory.

Notes

1. William Schwenck Gilbert, from *Patience,* in *Poetry of the Victorian Period,* ed. George Benjamin Woods and Jerome Hamilton Buckley (Chicago: Scott, Foresman and Company, 1955), 745.
2. Jürgen Habermas, *The Structural Transformation of the Public Sphere: An Inquiry into a Category of Bourgeois Society,* trans. Thomas Burger with Frederick Lawrence (Cambridge, Mass.: MIT Press, 1993), 27. Subsequent page citations appear parenthetically in the text.
3. Bruce Robbins, "Introduction," in *The Phantom Public Sphere,* ed. Bruce Robbins (Minneapolis: University of Minnesota Press, 1993), xxi.
4. Nancy Fraser, "Rethinking the Public Sphere: A Contribution to

the Critique of Actually Existing Democracy," in *The Phantom Public Sphere,* ed. Bruce Robbins, 2.

5. *Philadelphia Inquirer,* March 13, 1994, D5.

6. Arjun Appadurai, "Disjuncture and Difference in the Global Cultural Economy," in *The Phantom Public Sphere,* ed. Bruce Robbins, 269.

7. Taylor Branch, *Parting the Waters: America in the King Years, 1954–63* (New York: Simon & Schuster, 1988), 142. Subsequent page citations appear parenthetically in the text.

8. Clayborne Carson, "Reconstructing the King Legacy: Scholars and National Myths," in *We Shall Overcome: Martin Luther King, Jr. and the Black Freedom Struggle,* ed. Peter Albert and Ronald Hoffman (New York: Da Capo Press, 1993), 239.

9. T. S. Eliot, "The Metaphysical Poets," *Selected Essays, 1917–1932* (New York: Harcourt, Brace and Company, 1932), 247, 246.

10. W. E. B. Du Bois, *The Souls of Black Folk,* in *Three Negro Classics,* ed. John Hope Franklin (New York: Avon Books, 1965), 340. Subsequent page citations appear parenthetically in the text.

11. Aldon D. Morris, "A Man Prepared for the Times: A Sociological Analysis of the Leadership of Martin Luther King, Jr.," in *We Shall Overcome,* ed. Peter Albert and Ronald Hoffman, 39–40. Subsequent page citations appear parenthetically in the text.

12. Quoted in W. E. B. Du Bois, *The Autobiography of W. E. B. Du Bois* (New York: International Publishers, 1968), 299.

13. James Baldwin, "Everybody's Protest Novel," in *Notes of a Native Son* (Boston: Beacon Press, 1955), 17. Subsequent page citations appear parenthetically in the text.

14. *Eyes on the Prize II: America at the Racial Crossroads 1965–mid-1980s,* exec. prod. Henry Hampton, Blackside, 1990.

15. Ibid.

16. Ibid.

17. James R. Ralph, *Northern Protest: Martin Luther King, Jr., Chicago, and the Civil Rights Movement* (Cambridge, Mass.: Harvard University Press, 1993), 45

18. LeRoi Jones, *Black Magic: Collected Poetry, 1961–1967* (Indianapolis: Bobbs-Merrill, 1969), 108.

19. James H. Cone, "Martin Luther King, Jr. and the Third World," in *We Shall Overcome,* ed. Peter Albert and Ronald Hoffman, 206.

20. David J. Garrow, "Martin Luther King, Jr. and the Spirit of Leadership," in *We Shall Overcome,* ed. Peter Albert and Ronald Hoffman, 28–29.

21. Du Bois, *The Souls of Black Folk,* 239.

22. Ibid., 238.

AFTERWORD

Dan Ben-Amos

Twenty years ago Pierre Nora remarked that collective memory was "a recent historical problem."[1] No longer. Today collective memory is a problem that transcends disciplinary boundaries, framing research in many humanistic and social scientific fields. None of the contributors to this volume is a historian. They are scholars of folklore, literature, communication, and culture. A glimpse at the Selected Bibliography reveals that collective memory is a viable concept in sociology, anthropology, political science, as well as history. The broad resurgence of this concept, after some fifty years of hibernation in the archives of ideas and on the library shelves, clearly demonstrates that "collective memory" is a problem of our time.

The sheer quantity of articles and books that address this issue, identified either as collective or cultural memory, is on the rise. If the essays in this volume have any collective voice, it is one that calls for a shift in the perception of collective memory from the monumental to the mundane, from the archives to everyday life. In many ways this is a more challenging task, because it counters the social tendency to create storage places for memories, confining them in space and time and preventing them from intruding into daily activities. After all, archives and monuments not only preserve and commemorate the past but also remove it from the daily give and take of social interaction. They enable a society to put memories aside, or to condense a whole history into a single location or a single day of remembrance.

Most of the essays of the present volume do not examine such a social tendency but rather search for collective memories that are diffused and that surround us, blending into our everyday activities in the form of items of clothing, utensils, and tools, or as flickering images on a television set. Even the most horrifying journalistic pictorial images of the Holocaust were served to hurried newspaper readers on their breakfast tables. While past scholarship resonates in these essays as each author, in his or her own way, builds on the notions of the selective nature of collective memory, the subjective construction of the past, and the invention of tradition, they all also point to new directions that would explore the unstructured and culturally diffused nature of collective memory.

Memory is a secondary agent of transformation. It turns a territory of Earth into a motherland and a homeland, a valley into a setting of a battle, and a mountaintop into a location of revelation. Place names engrave on the land the people's memory of their past. Somewhat paradoxically, burial is an elementary form of transforming the Earth into a vessel that contains collective memory. The tombs of ancestors, saints, martyrs, and prophets that are strewn over a land turn a country into holy grounds and into a book of memories. Halbwachs's classical study of the topography of the Holy Land could have been equally applied to many settled territories in which human memory has roots. In all these cases, actions and life were primary, but without memory they would have been lost and faded away, and nature would have returned to its pristine state.

Memory also transforms objects into symbols, infusing them with meanings they did not have on their own, before memory possessed them. Once placed in a historical museum, the old kibbutz tools and utensils do not acquire an aesthetic value, as they would have, as John Dewey proposed, had they been placed in an art museum. Rather, in the local museum that purports to recreate the mundane past, they become the symbols of life gone by. Peter Stallybrass's friend's coat becomes a piece of clothing that is engulfed by a flood of memories. It has been codified as a symbol of friendship, death, and loneliness. Memory, collective and individual, transforms our social and material surroundings into a language that tells us about the past. It intrudes into our daily activities, at times upsetting and at other times rejuvenating our spirit.

The monuments to the victims of the Holocaust, despite their manifest intention to perpetuate their memory in Israel, the United States, and Germany, have a therapeutic, cleansing effect on these societies. In the secular world of the present, museums and monuments to the dead function as shrines where individuals can offer their sorrows as sacrifice and atonement. Obviously, not all museums are alike. They differ in subject and content and consequently in their function in society. However, by the time a theme reaches the exhibition halls, it loses its vitality in people's lives. A display underscores the otherness of the displayed. The local kibbutz museums in Israel, in spite of their alleged intention to promote and celebrate the spirited dedication of the pioneers, are monuments to a fallen ideal that has lost its viability in current Israeli society.

Memorial days and festivals punctuate the calendar and transform it from a linear progression into a repeated cycle. Annual celebrations have been an integral part of local agrarian European societies, and the model that Noyes and Abrahams construct on the basis of the Patum festival in Berga, Catalonia, has, they suggest, a broader application to other localities in Spain and other countries. Today these customs have acquired an additional meaning that memory imparts: they connote the ideology of tradition, casting their own past celebrations into the realm of memory.

The shift from the monumental to the mundane that these essays suggest does not trivialize collective memory. On the contrary, they explore it as a dynamic, positive force that enters into the texture of social life. No longer the negative side of history, it is the bond that unites societies, creating images that attain the truth value of a symbol, even if deviating from facts. As such, collective memory becomes the creative imagining of the past in service of the present and an imagined future. For too long the exploration of memory, private and public, focused on its failure to document, maintain, and communicate events as they happened. Memory and the oral tradition that embodied it were regarded as suffering from an inherent failure to keep accurate records. The anachronistic forces of the present, manipulative and political as they are, were considered as creating myths out of memories; oral tradition, the staple of folklore studies, has been viewed as inherently untrustworthy; and scholars have proposed principles and methods to uncover the historical truth that memory distorts or hides.

However, the acceptance of tradition as the function of memory allows one to consider the selectors of appropriate subjects that a society retains in its collective memory, their public guardians, promoters, and transmitters, not as self-interested producers of social mythologies but as people who, in their professional capacities, whether journalists or storytellers, artists or architects, politicians or scholars, serve society and register on its social landscape of the present the memory of the past. Collective memory is, therefore, not only a "historical problem" but also a problem of social imagination and collective images, of art, language, and literature. Its analysis in society requires an interdisciplinary synthesis that would prepare the ground for a complex ethnography of memory toward which the present essays point the way.

Note

1. "Mémoire Collective," in *La Nouvelle histoire,* ed. Jacques Le Goff, Roger Chartier, and Jacques Revel (Paris: Retz-C.E.P.L., 1978), 400.

SELECTED BIBLIOGRAPHY

GENERAL LITERATURE: HISTORY, MEMORY, AND COLLECTIVE MEMORY

Allan, George. *The Importance of the Past: A Meditation on the Authority of Tradition.* Albany: State University of New York Press, 1986.

Assmann, Jan. *Das kulturelle Gedächtnis: Schrift, Erinnerung und politische Identität in frühen Hochkulturen.* Munich: C. H. Beck, 1997.

————., and Tonio Hölscher, eds. *Kultur und Gedächtnis.* Suhrkamp Wissenschaftliches Taschenbuch No. 724. Frankfurt am Main: Suhrkamp, 1988.

Bastide, Roger. "Mémoire collective et sociologie du bricolage." *L'Année sociologique* 21 (1970): 65–108.

Bender, John, and David.E. Wellbery, eds. *Chronotypes: The Construction of Time.* Stanford, Calif.: Stanford University Press, 1991.

Benson, Susan P., Steven Breir, and Roy Rosenzweig, eds. *Presenting the Past: Essays on History and the Public.* Philadelphia: Temple University Press, 1986.

Blatti, Jo, ed. *Past Meets Present: Essays about Historic Interpretations and Public Audiences.* Washington, D.C.: Smithsonian Institution Press, 1987.

Bourguet, Marie Noëlle, Lucette Valensi, and Nathan Wachtel, eds. *Between Memory and History.* Special issue of *History and Anthropology* 2. London: Harwood Academic Publisher, 1986.

Brown, Donald E. *Hierarchy, History, and Human Nature: The Social Origins of Historical Consciousness.* Tucson: University of Arizona Press, 1988.

Butler, Thomas, ed. *Memory: History, Culture, and the Mind.* Oxford: Blackwell, 1989.

Carruthers, Mary J. *The Book of Memory: A Study of Memory in Medieval Culture.* Cambridge: Cambridge University Press, 1990.

Chartier, Roger. *Cultural History: Between Practice and Representations.* Trans. Lydia G. Cochrane. Ithaca, N.Y.: Cornell University Press, 1988.

301

————. *The Cultural Uses of Print in Early Modern France.* Trans. Lydia G. Cochrane. Princeton, N.J.: Princeton University Press, 1987.

Clanchy, M. T. *From Memory to Written Record: England, 1066–1307.* Cambridge, Mass.: Harvard University Press, 1979.

Connerton, Paul. *How Societies Remember.* Cambridge: Cambridge University Press, 1989.

Cook, Patricia, ed. *Philosophical Imagination and Cultural Memory: Appropriating Historical Traditions.* Durham: Duke University Press, 1993.

Cosgrave, Denis, and Stephen Daniels, eds. *The Iconography of Landscape.* Cambridge: Cambridge University Press, 1988.

Coutau-Begarie, Harvé. *La Phénomène "Nouvelle Histoire": Stratégie et idéologie des Nouveaux Historiens.* Paris: Economica, 1983.

Crane, Susan A. "(Not) Writing History: Rethinking the Intersections of Personal History and Collective Memory with Hans von Aufsess." *History and Memory* 8 (1996): 5–29.

Dorson, Richard M. *American Folklore and the Historian.* Chicago: University of Chicago Press, 1971.

Dunaway, David K., and Willa K. Baum, eds. *Oral History: An Interdisciplinary Anthology.* Nashville, Tenn.: American Association for State and Local History, 1984.

Duncan, James, and David Leys, eds. *Place/Culture/Representation.* London: Routledge, 1993.

Eckardt, Alice L., ed. *Burning Memory: Times of Testing and Reckoning.* New York: Pergamon Press, 1993.

Fentress, James, and Chris Wickham. *Social Memory.* Oxford: Blackwell, 1992.

Ferro, Marc. "Les Oublis de l'Histoire." *Communications* 49 (1989): 57–66.

Finley, M. I. "Myth, Memory, and History." *History and Theory* 4 (1965): 281–302.

Formenti, Carlo. "La Gnose évolutionniste: Matiére, mémoire, oubli chez Bergson et dans les sciences de la complexité." *Communications* 49 (1989): 11–41.

Friedman, Jonathan. "Myth, History, and Political Identity." *Cultural Anthropology* 7 (1992): 194–210.

Funkenstein, Amos. "Collective Memory and Historical Consciousness." *History and Memory* 1.1 (1989): 5–26.

Gauthier, Alain, and Henri-Pierre Jeudy. "Trou de mémoire, image virale." *Communications* 49 (1989): 137–47.

Gedi, Noa, and Yigal Elam. "Collective Memory—What Is It?" *History and Memory* 8.1 (1996): 30–50.

Griswold, Wendy. "A Methodological Framework for the Sociology of Culture." *Sociological Methodology* 14 (1987): 1–35.

Halbwachs, Maurice. *Les Cadres sociaux de la mémoire.* Paris: F. Alcan, 1925. Reprint, New York: Arno Press, 1975.

———. *La Mémoire collective.* Ed. Jeanne Alexander. Paris: Presses universitaires de France, 1950. 2d ed., ed. Jean Duvignaud, 1968. English trans., *The Collective Memory.* Trans. Francis J. Ditter, Jr. and Vida Yazdy Ditter. New York: Harper and Row, 1980.

———. *On Collective Memory.* Trans. and ed. Lewis A. Coser. Heritage of Sociology. Chicago: University of Chicago Press, 1992. Translation of selected sections from the first four chapters and the full text of preface, chapters 5, 6, and 7, and the conclusion of *Les Cadres sociaux de la mémoire,* and the conclusion of *La Topographie des Evangiles en Terre Sainte.*

———. *La Topographie des Evangiles en Terre Sainte. Etude de mémoire collective.* Paris: Presses universitaires de France, 1941. 2d (expanded) ed., 1971.

Handler, Richard, and Jocelyn Linnekin. "Tradition, Genuine or Spurious." *Journal of American Folklore* 97 (1984): 273–90.

Hardtwig, Wolfgang. *Geschichtskultur und Wissenschaft.* Munich: dtv, 1990.

Henige, David P. *The Chronology of Oral Tradition: Quest for a Chimera.* Oxford: Clarendon Press, 1974.

Hobsbawm, Eric, and Terence Ranger, eds. *The Invention of Tradition.* Cambridge: Cambridge University Press, 1983.

Hutton, Patrick H. *History as the Art of Memory.* Hanover: University Press of New England, 1993.

Irwin-Zarecka, Iwona. *Frames of Remembrance: The Dynamics of Collective Memory.* New Brunswick, N.J.: Transactions, 1994.

Kaes, Anton."History and Film: Public Memory in the Age of Electronic Dissemination." *History and Memory* 2.1 (1990): 111–29.

Kaye, Harvey J. *Powers of the Past: Reflections on the Crisis and the Promise of History.* Minneapolis: University of Minnesota Press, 1991.

Kelly, John D., and Martha Kaplan. "History, Structure, and Ritual." *Annual Review of Anthropology* 19 (1990): 119–50.

Kemp, Anthony. *The Estrangement of the Past: A Study in the Origins of Modern Historical Consciousness.* New York: Oxford University Press, 1991.

Kern, Stephen. *The Culture of Time and Space, 1880–1918.* Cambridge, Mass.: Harvard University Press, 1983.

Le Goff, Jacques. *Historia e memoria.* Milan: Einaudi, 1986. English trans. *History and Memory,* Steven Rendall and Elizabeth Claman. New York: Columbia University Press, 1992.

Le Goff, Jacques, and Béla Köpeczi, eds. *Objet et méthodes de l'histoire de la culture.* Paris: Éditions du CNRS, and Budapest: Akadémiai Kiadó, 1982.

Lowenthal, David. *The Past Is a Foreign Country.* Cambridge: Cambridge University Press, 1985.

Melman, Billie. "Gender, History and Memory: The Invention of Women's Past in the Nineteenth and Early Twentieth Centuries." *History and Memory* 5.1 (1993): 5–41.

Nerone, John. "Professional History and Social Memory." *Communication* 11 (1989): 89–104.

Nora, Pierre. "Between Memory and History: *Les Lieux de mémoire.*" *Representations* 26 (1989): 7–25. Reprinted in *History and Memory in African-American Culture,* ed. Geneviève Fabre and Robert O'Meally. New York: Oxford University Press, 284–300.

————. "Mémoire collective." In *La Nouvelle histoire,* ed. Jacques Le Goff, Roger Chartier, and Jacques Revel. Paris: Retz-C.E.P.L., 1978, 398–401.

Nora, Pierre, ed. *Les Lieux de mémoire.* 3 vols. Paris: Gallimard, 1984. English trans., *Realms of History: Rethinking the French Past,* ed. Lawrence D. Kritzman, trans. Arthur Goldhammer. New York: Columbia University Press, 1996.

Norkunas, Martha. *The Politics of Public Memory: Tourist Culture, History, and Ethnicity in Monterey, California.* Albany: State University of New York Press, 1993.

Ohnuki-Tierney, Emiko, ed. *Culture through Time: Anthropological Approaches.* Stanford, Calif.: Stanford University Press. 1990.

Representations 26 (1989). Special issue: "Memory and Counter Memory," ed. Natalie Zemon and Randolph Starn.

Samuel, Raphael. *Theatres of Memory.* Vol I: *Past and Present in Contemporary Culture.* London: Verso, 1994.

Schama, Simon. *Landscape and Memory.* New York: Knopf, 1995.

Shils, Edward. *Tradition.* Chicago: University of Chicago Press, 1981.

Terdiman, Richard. *Present Modernity and the Past Memory Crisis.* Ithaca, N.Y.: Cornell University Press, 1993.

Tonkin, Elizabeth. *Narrating Our Pasts: The Social Construction of Oral History.* Cambridge Studies in Oral and Literate Culture. Cambridge: Cambridge University Press, 1992.

Wood, Nancy. "Memory's Remains: *Les Lieux de mémoire.*" *History and Memory* 6.1 (1994): 123–50.

Yates, Frances A. *The Art of Memory.* Chicago: Chicago University Press, 1966.

Yost, Charles W. *History and Memory.* New York: Norton, 1980.

Zelizer, Barbie. "Reading the Past Against the Grain: The Shape of Memory Studies." *Critical Studies in Mass Communication* 12 (1995): 214–39.

Museum Culture

Bennett, Tony. *The Birth of the Museum: History, Theory, Politics.* London: Routledge, 1995.

Brandt, Susanne. "The Memory Makers: Museums and Exhibitions of the First World War." *History and Memory* 6.1 (1994): 95–122.

Cooke, Lynne, and Peter Wollen, eds. *Visual Display: Culture Beyond Appearance.* Seattle, Wash.: Bay Press, 1995.

Elsner, John, and Roger Cardinal, eds. *The Cultures of Collecting.* London: Reaktion, 1994.

Hooper-Greenhill, Eileen. *Museums and the Shaping of Knowledge.* London: Routledge, 1992.

Karp, Ivan, and Steven D. Lavine, eds. *Exhibiting Cultures: The Poetics and Politics of Museum Display.* Washington, D.C.: Smithsonian Institution Press, 1991.

Karp, Ivan, Christine Mullen Kreamer, and Steven D. Lavine, eds. *Museums and Communities: The Politics of Public Culture.* Washington, D.C.: Smithsonian Institution Press, 1992.

Katriel, Tamar."Remaking Place: Cultural Production in an Israeli Pioneer Settlement Museum." *History and Memory* 5.2 (1993): 104–35.

Luke, Timothy W. *Shows of Force: Power, Politics, and Ideology in Art Exhibitions.* Durham: Duke University Press, 1992.

Lumley, Robert, ed. *The Museum Time Machine: Putting Culture on Display.* London: Routledge, 1988.

Orosz, Joel J. *Curators and Culture: The Museum Movement in America, 1740–1870.* Tuscaloosa: University of Alabama Press, 1990.

Pearce, Susan M. *Museums, Objects, and Collections: A Cultural Study.* Washington, D.C.: Smithsonian Institution Press, 1992.

Senie, Harriet F., and Sally Webster, eds. *Critical Issues in Public Art: Content, Context, and Controversy.* New York: HarperCollins, 1992.

Sherman, Daniel J. *Worthy Monuments: Art Museums and the Politics of Culture in Nineteenth-Century France.* Cambridge, Mass.: Harvard University Press, 1989.

Sherman, Daniel J., and Irit Rogoff, eds. *Museum Culture: Histories, Discourses, Spectacles.* Minneapolis: University of Minnesota Press, 1994.

Vergo, Peter, ed. *The New Museology.* London: Reaktion Books, 1991.

Wright, Gwendolyn, ed. *The Formation of National Collections of Art and Archaeology.* Washington, D.C.: National Gallery of Art, 1996.

Monuments and Commemorations

Ben-Amos, Avner. "Monuments and Memory in French Nationalism." *History and Memory* 5.1 (1993): 50–81.

———. "The Other World of Memory: State Funerals of the French Third Republic as Rites of Commemoration." *History and Memory* 1 (1989): 85–108.

———. "The Sacred Center of Power: Paris and the State Funerals of the French Third Republic." *Journal of Interdisciplinary History* 22 (1991): 27–48.

Boyer, Christine M. *The City of Collective Memory: Its Historical Imagery and Architectural Entertainments.* Cambridge, Mass.: MIT Press, 1994.

Bunzl, Matti. "On the Politics and Semantics of Austrian Memory: Vienna's Monument against War and Fascism." *History and Memory* 7.2 (1995): 7–40.

Don-Yehiya, Eliezer. "Festivals and Political Culture: Independence-Day Celebrations." *Jerusalem Quarterly* 44 (1988): 61–84.

———. "Hanukka and the Myth of the Maccabees in Zionist Ideology and in Israeli Society." *Jewish Journal of Sociology* 34 (1992): 5–23.

Handelman, Don. "The Presence of the Dead: Memorials of National Death in Israel." *Suomen Antropologi* 16 (1991): 3–17.

Schwarz, Barry. "The Social Context of Commemoration: A Study in Collective Memory." *Social Forces* 61 (1982): 374–402.

Yaroshevski, Dov B. "Political Participation and Public Memory: The Memorial Movement in the USSR, 1987–1989." *History and Memory* 2.2 (1990): 5–31.

Remembering the Holocaust

Bartov, Omer. "Intellectuals on Auschwitz: Memory, History and Truth." *History and Memory* 5.1 (1993): 87–129.

Baumel, Judith Tydor. " 'Rachel Laments Her Children'—Representation of Women in Israeli Holocaust Memorials." *Israel Studies* 1 (1996): 100–126.

Don-Yehiya, Eliezer. "Memory and Political Culture: Israeli Society and the Holocaust." *Studies in Contemporary Jewry* 9 (1993): 139–61.

Douglas, Lawrence. "The Memory of Judgement: The Law, the Holocaust, and Denial." *History and Memory* 7.2 (1995): 100–120.

Ezrahi, Sidra DeKoven. "Representing Auschwitz." *History and Memory* 7.2 (1995): 121–54.

Friedlander, Saul. *Probing the Limits of Representation: Nazism and the "Final Solution."* Cambridge, Mass.: Harvard University Press, 1992.

Hartman, Geoffrey, ed. *Holocaust Remembrance: The Shapes of Memory.* Cambridge, Mass.: Blackwell, 1994.

Ludtke, Alf. " 'Coming to Terms with the Past': Illusions of Remembering, Ways of Forgetting Nazism in West Germany." *Journal of Modern History* 65 (1993): 542–72.

Maier, Charles S. "A Surfeit of Memory? Reflection on History, Melancholy and Denial." *History and Memory* 5.2 (1993): 136–52.

———. *The Unmasterable Past: History, Holocaust, and German National Identity.* Cambridge, Mass.: Harvard University Press, 1988.

Reichel, Peter. *Politik mit der Erinnerung: Gedächtnisorte im Streit um die nationalsozialistische Vergangenheit.* Munich: Hanser, 1995.

Roskies, David G. *A Bridge of Longing: The Lost Art of Yiddish Storytelling.* Cambridge, Mass.: Harvard University Press, 1996. Chapter 9, "Estate of Memory: After the Holocaust," 307–44.

Rousso, Henry. *The Vichy Syndrome: History and Memory in France Since 1944.* Cambridge, Mass.: Harvard University Press, 1991.

Skloot, Robert. "Stage Nazis: The Politics and Aesthetics of Memory." *History and Memory* 6.2 (1994): 57–87.

Vidal-Naquet, Pierre. *Les Assassins de la mémoire: un Eichmann de papier et autres essais sur le révisionnisme.* Paris: Découverte, 1987. English trans., *Assassins of Memory: Essays on the Denial of the Holocaust.* Trans. Jeffrey Mehlman. New York: Columbia University Press, 1992.

———. *The Jews: History, Memory, and the Present.* Trans. and ed. David Ames Curtis. New York: Columbia University Press, 1996.

Young, James E. *The Texture of Memory: Holocaust Memorials and Meaning.* New Haven, Conn.: Yale University Press, 1993.

———. "When a Day Remembers: A Performative History of Yom ha-Shoah." *History and Memory* 2.2 (1990): 54–75.

Memory, Individual Cultures, Ethnography

Abercrombie, Thomas A. *Pathways of Memory and Power: Ethnography and History Among an Andean People.* Madison: University of Wisconsin Press, 1997.

Appadurai, Arjun. "The Past as a Scarce Resource." *Man* 16 (1981): 201–19.

Assmann, Jan. "Guilt and Remembrance: On the Theologization of History in the Ancient Near East." *History and Memory* 2.1 (1990): 5–33.

Barber, Karin. *I Could Speak Until Tomorrow: Oriki, Women, and the Past in a Yoruba Town.* International African Library 7. Washington, D.C.: Smithsonian Institution Press, 1991.

Bastide, Roger. *Les Religions afro-brésiliennes.* Paris: Presses universitaires de France, 1960. English trans., *The African Religions of Brazil: Toward a Sociology of the Interpenetration of Civilizations.* Trans. Helen Sebba. Baltimore: Johns Hopkins University Press, 1978.

Boyarin, Jonathan. "Un Lieu de l'oubli: Le Lower East Side des Juifs." *Communications* 49 (1989): 185–93.

———. *A Storm in Paradise: The Politics of Jewish Memory.* Minneapolis: University of Minnesota Press, 1992.

Fabian, Johannes. *Remembering the Present: Painting and Popular History in Zaïre.* Berkeley: University of California Press, 1996.

Fabre, Geneviève, and Robert O'Meally, eds. *History and Memory in African-American Culture.* New York: Oxford University Press, 1994.

Frisch, Michael. "American History and the Structures of Collective Memory: A Modest Exercise in Empirical Iconography." *Journal of American History* 75 (1989): 1130–55.

Gershoni, Israel. "Imagining and Reimagining the Past: The Use of History by Egyptian Nationalist Writers." *History and Memory* 4.2 (1992): 5–37.

Herzfeld, Michael. *Ours Once More: Folklore, Ideology and the Making of Modern Greece.* Austin: University of Texas Press, 1982.

———. *A Place in History: Social and Monumental Time in a Cretan Town.* Princeton, N.J.: Princeton University Press, 1991.

Irwin-Zarecka, Iwona. *Neutralizing Memory: The Jew in Contemporary Poland.* New Brunswick, N.J.: Transactions, 1989.

Kammen, Michael. *Mystic Chords of Memory: The Transformation of Tradition in American Culture.* New York: Alfred A. Knopf, 1991.

Katriel, Tamar, and Aliza Shenhar. "Tower and Stockade: Dialogic Narration in Israeli Settlement Ethos." *Quarterly Journal of Speech* 76 (1990): 359–80.

Keesing, Roger. "Creating the Past: Custom and Identity in the Contemporary Pacific." *Contemporary Pacific* 1 (1989): 19–42.

Küchler, Susanne. "Landscape as Memory: The Mapping of Process and Its Representation in a Melanesian Society." In *Landscape: Politics and Perspectives,* ed. Barbara Bender. Oxford: Berg, 1993, 85–106.

Kugelmass, Jacob, and Jonathan Boyarin, eds. and trans. *From a Ruined Garden*. New York: Schocken Books, 1983.

Linnekin, Jocelyn. "Defining Tradition: Variations on the Hawaiian Identity." *American Ethnologist* 10 (1983): 241–52.

MacCormack, Sabine. "History, Memory and Time in Golden Age Spain." *History and Memory* 4.2 (1992): 38–68.

Malkki, Lisa H. *Purity and Exile: Violence, Memory, and National Cosmology among the Hutu Refugees in Tanzania*. Chicago: University of Chicago Press, 1995.

Miller, Joseph, ed. *The African Past Speaks: Essays on Oral Tradition*. Hamden, Conn.: Archon, 1980.

Moniot, Henri. "The Uses of Memory in African Studies." *History and Anthropology* 2 (1986): 379–88.

Price, Richard. *First-Time: The Historical Vision of an Afro-American People*. Baltimore: Johns Hopkins University Press, 1983.

Rappaport, Joanne. *The Politics of Memory: Native Historical Interpretation in the Colombian Andes*. Cambridge: Cambridge University Press, 1990.

Reddy, William M. "Postmodernism and the Public Sphere: Implications for an Historical Ethnography." *Cultural Anthropology* 7 (1992): 135–68.

Roberts, Mary Nooter, and Allen F. Roberts, eds. *Memory: Luba Art and the Making of History*. New York: The Museum for African Art, 1996.

Sered, Susan S. "Rachel's Tomb: Societal Liminality and the Revitalization of a Shrine." *Religion* 19 (1989): 27–40.

Shapira, Anita. "Politics and Collective Memory: The Debate over the 'New Historians' in Israel." *History and Memory* 7 (1995): 9–40.

Shavit, Yaacov. "Cyrus King of Persia and the Return to Zion: A Case of Neglected Memory." *History and Memory* 2.1 (1990): 51–83.

Shrimpton, Gordon S. *History and Memory in Ancient Greece*. Montreal and Buffalo, N.Y.: McGill–Queen's University Press, 1997.

Thelen, David P. "Memory and American History." *Journal of American History* 75 (1989): 1117–29.

Tonkin, Elizabeth, Maryon McDonald, and Malcolm Chapman, eds. *History and Ethnicity*. ASA Monographs 27. London: Routledge, 1987.

Valensi, Lucette. "From Sacred History to Historical Memory and Back: The Jewish Past." *History and Anthropology* 2 (1986): 283–307.

Vansina, Jan. *De la Tradition orale: Essai de methode historique*. Annales du Musée Royale de l'Afrique Centrale, Sciences humaines, No. 36. Tervuren, Belgium: Musée Royal de l'Afrique Centrale, 1961. English trans., *Oral Tradition: A Study in*

Historical Methodology, trans. H. M. Wright. Chicago: Aldine, 1965.

———. "Memory and Oral Tradition." In *The African Past Speaks: Essays on Oral Tradition,* ed. Joseph Miller. Hamden, Conn.: Archon, 1980.

———. *Oral Tradition as History.* Madison: University of Wisconsin Press, 1985.

Yerushalmi, Y. H. *Zakhor: Jewish History and Jewish Memory.* Seattle: Washington University Press, 1982.

Constructing the Nation-State

Alonso, A. M. "The Politics of Space, Time and Substance: State Formation, Nationalism and Ethnicity." *Annual Review of Anthropology* 23 (1994): 379–405.

Anderson, Benedict. *Imagined Communities: Reflections on the Spread of Nationalism.* 2d ed. London: Verso, 1992.

Ankum, Katharina von. "Victims, Memory, History: Antifascism and the Question of National Identity in East German Narratives after 1990." *History and Memory* 7.2 (1995): 41–69.

Becker, Annette. "From Death to Memory: The National Ossuaries in France after the Great War." *History and Memory* 5.2 (1993): 32–49.

Ben-Amos, Avner. "The Uses of the Past: Patriotism Between History and Memory." In *Patriotism in the Lives of Individuals and Nations,* ed. Daniel Bar-Tal and Ervin Staub. Chicago: Nelson-Hall, 1997, 129–47.

Ben-Yehuda, Nachman. *The Masada Myth: Collective Memory and Mythmaking in Israel.* Madison: University of Wisconsin Press, 1995.

Berdahl, Daphne. "Voices at the Wall: Discourses of Self, History and National Identity at the Vietnam Veterans Memorial." *History and Memory* 6.2 (1994): 88–124.

Bruner, Edward M., and Phyllis Gorfain. "Dialogic Narration and the Paradoxes of Masada." In *Text, Play, and Story: The Construction and Reconstruction of Self and Society,* ed. Edward M. Bruner and Stuart Plattner. Proceedings of the American Ethnological Society. Washington, D.C.: American Ethnological Society, 1983, 56–59.

Confino, Alon. "The Nation as a Local Metaphor: Heimat, National Memory and the German Empire, 1871–1918." *History and Memory* 5 (1993): 42–86.

310

Gillis, John R., ed. *Commemorations: The Politics of National Identity.* Princeton, N.J.: Princeton University Press, 1994.

History and Memory 7.1 (1995). Special issue: "Israeli Historiography Revisited," ed. Gulie Ne'eman Arad.

Litvak, Meir. "A Palestinian Past: National Construction and Reconstruction." *History and Memory* 6.2 (1994): 24–56.

Silberman, Neil Asher. *Between Past and Present: Archaeology, Ideology and Nationalism in the Modern Middle East.* New York: Anchor Books, 1989.

Zerubavel, Yael. "The Forest as a National Icon: Literature, Politics, and the Archaeology of Memory." *Israel Studies* 1 (1996): 60–99.

———. "The Politics of Interpretation: Tel Hai in Israel's Collective Memory." *American Jewish Society Review* 16 (1991): 133–59.

———. *Recovered Roots: Collective Memory and the Making of Israeli National Tradition.* Chicago: University of Chicago Press, 1995.

Memorializing (Historical) Events

Broué, Pierre. "Stalinisme et oubli." *Communications* 49 (1989): 67–79.

Dienstag, Joshua Foa. "'The Pozsgay Affair': Historical Memory and Political Legitimacy." *History and Memory* 8 (1996): 67–87.

Handelman, Don. *Models and Mirrors: Towards an Anthropology of Public Events.* Cambridge: Cambridge University Press. 1990.

Montell, William L. *The Saga of Coe Ridge: A Study of Oral History.* New York: Harper and Row, 1972.

Schwarz, Barry. "Iconography and Collective Memory: Lincoln's Image in the American Mind." *Sociological Quarterly* 32 (1991): 301–19.

———. "Social Change and Collective Memory: The Democratization of George Washington." *American Sociological Review* 56 (1991): 221–36.

Schwarz, Barry, Yael Zerubavel, and Bernice M. Barnett. "The Recovery of Masada: A Study in Collective Memory." *Sociological Quarterly* 27 (1986): 147–64.

Watson, Rubie S. ed. *Memory, History, and Opposition under State Socialism.* Santa Fe, N.M.: School of American Research, 1994.

Zelizer, Barbie. *Covering the Body: The Kennedy Assassination, the Media, and the Shaping of Collective Memory.* Chicago: University of Chicago Press, 1992.

CONTRIBUTORS

Roger D. Abrahams is Hum Rosen Professor of Folklore and Folklife at the University of Pennsylvania. He is the author of numerous books in African American studies and on oral culture, most recently, *Singing the Master: The Emergence of African American Culture in the Plantation South* (1992).

Houston Baker, Jr. is Albert M. Greenfield Professor of Human Relations at the University of Pennsylvania and Director of the university's Center for the Study of Black Literature and Culture. Among his many books are *Workings of the Spirit: The Poetics of Afro-American Women's Writing* (1991) and *Black Studies, Rap, and the Academy* (1993). Along with Manthia Diawara and Ruth H. Lindeborg, he edited the reader *Black British Cultural Studies* (1996).

Dan Ben-Amos is Professor of Folklore and Folklife at the University of Pennsylvania. He is the editor of *Folklore Genres* (1975) and several studies of oral narrative. His edition of Micha Joseph Bin Gorion's *Mimekor Yisrael: Classical Jewish Folktales* was published in 1990.

Tamar Katriel is Professor of Communication at the University of Haifa. She is the author of *Talking Straight: Dugri Speech in Israeli Sabra Culture* (1986), *Communal Webs: Communication and Culture in Contemporary Israel* (1991), and *Performing the Past: A Study of Israeli Settlement Museums* (1997).

Dorothy Noyes is Assistant Professor of English at Ohio State University. She is the author of *Uses of Tradition: Arts of Italian Americans in Philadelphia* (1989). A specialist in Catalan language and culture, she is currently working on a book provisionally titled *The Mule and the Giants: Contest and Incorporation in the Patum of Berga.*

313

Roberta Pearson is Senior Lecturer in the School of Journalism, Media, and Cultural Studies at Cardiff University of Wales, where she is also Deputy Director of the Tom Hopkinson Centre for Media Research. She is the author of *Eloquent Gestures: The Transformation of Performance Style in the Griffith Biograph Films* (1992) and, with William Uricchio, of *Reframing Culture: The Case of the Vitagraph Quality Films* (1993). She is also coeditor (with Edward Buscombe) of the forthcoming anthology *Back in the Saddle Again: New Writings on the Western.*

Robert Blair St. George is Associate Professor of Folklore and Folklife at the University of Pennsylvania. His work is primarily concerned with concepts of space and material culture. St. George published the anthology *Material Life in America, 1600–1860* in 1988. He is the author of *Conversing by Signs: Poetics of Implication in Colonial New England Culture* (1998), and editor of the forthcoming collection *Possible Pasts: Becoming Colonial in Early America.*

Peter Stallybrass is Professor of English at the University of Pennsylvania. A specialist in early modern literature and material culture, Stallybrass is also the director of a seminar on the History of the Book. He coauthored, with Allon White, *The Politics and Poetics of Transgression* (1986), and he is the editor, with David S. Kastan, of *Staging the Renaissance: Reinterpretation of Elizabethan and Jacobean Drama* (1991) and, with Margreta DeGrazia and Maureen Quilligan, of *Subject and Object in Renaissance Culture* (1996). He is currently completing a book with Ann Rosalind Jones on clothing and textual production in Renaissance culture.

Daniel Traister is Curator for Research Services in the Department of Special Collections, Van Pelt-Dietrich Library, at the University of Pennsylvania. He has written on English Renaissance poetry and on several aspects of rare book librarianship, and is currently engaged in a study about the ways in which books drop out of use.

Liliane Weissberg is Professor of German and Comparative Literature and holds the Joseph B. Glossberg Term Chair in the Humanities at the University of Pennsylvania. She is Chair

314

of the Program in Comparative Literature and Literary Theory. She has published in the fields of literary theory, eighteenth-century German literature, and German-Jewish studies. Her most recent book is the critical edition of Hannah Arendt's *Rahel Varnhagen: The Life of a Jewess* (1997).

Barbie Zelizer is Associate Professor of Communication at the Annenberg School of Communication at the University of Pennsylvania. In 1992, she published *Covering the Body: The Kennedy Assassination, the Media, and the Shaping of Collective Memory*, and she is the author of *Remembering to Forget: Holocaust Memory through the Camera's Eye* (1998).

INDEX